ADDITIONAL PRAISE FOR *FIGHTING BACK THE RIGHT*

"*Fighting Back the Right* offers a clear look at the missteps that have allowed fear, religious policies, and greed to overwhelm critical thinking, evidence-based policies, and logic at every level of government. David Niose provides a plan to escape the morass we are in—do we have the will to try?"

—*Amanda Knief, author of* The Citizen Lobbyist

"In his direct, clear-eyed analysis, David Niose ably diagnoses America's problem as the demise of human-centered public policy. He then zeroes in on its cause as a toxic combination of anti-intellectualism, religious fundamentalism, corporatism, and ineffectual democracy. But he doesn't leave us dangling. Niose provides a way forward and a toolkit for social repair that includes a more vocal and public secular community. This is a must-read for anyone who thinks America has taken leave of its senses and wants to know what to do about it."

—*Robyn Blumner, Executive Director, Richard Dawkins*
Foundation for Reason and Science

"With clarity and passion, David Niose makes a powerful case for why politics needs secularism—and why secularism needs politics."

—*Greta Christina, author of* Coming Out Atheist:
How to Do It, How to Help Each Other, and Why
and Why Are You Atheists So Angry?
99 Things That Piss Off the Godless

"Why shouldn't public policy that affects all Americans be open to question and criticism, without giving religious ideas extra respect? Dave Niose presents a reasoned argument that the Congressional Prayer Caucus on Capitol Hill warrants the creation of an Atheist-Humanist Caucus that will provide good secular arguments to counter private religious beliefs."

—*Herb Silverman, author of* Candidate Without a Prayer: An
Autobiography of a Jewish Atheist in the Bible Belt

"This book is a powerful call for government of, by, and for the people in the twenty-first century—not gods and not private corporations, whether religious or secular. Stirring!"

—*Jamie Raskin, Professor of Law, American University*
Washington College of Law, and Maryland State Senator

Follow David Niose on Twitter: @ahadave

FIGHTING BACK THE RIGHT

Reclaiming America from the Attack on Reason

DAVID NIOSE

palgrave
macmillan

FIGHTING BACK THE RIGHT
Copyright © David Niose, 2014.
All rights reserved.

First published in 2014 by PALGRAVE MACMILLAN® TRADE in the United
States—a division of St. Martin's Press LLC, 175 Fifth Avenue, New York, NY
10010.

Palgrave® and Macmillan® are registered trademarks in the United States, the
United Kingdom, Europe and other countries.

ISBN 978-1-137-27924-8

Library of Congress Cataloging-in-Publication Data

Niose, David.
    Fighting back the right : reclaiming America from the attack on reason / David
Niose.
        pages   cm
    ISBN 978-1-137-27924-8 (hardback)
    1. Liberalism—United States. 2. Progressivism (United States politics)
3. Political culture—United States. 4. Right and left (Political science)—United
States. 5. United States—Politics and government—21st century. I. Title.
JC574.2.U6N56   2014
320.51'30973—dc23

                                                                    2014018726

Some names have been changed to protect individual privacy.

Design by Letra Libre, Inc.

First edition: December 2014

10 9 8 7 6 5 4 3 2 1

Printed in the United States of America.

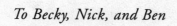

To Becky, Nick, and Ben

CONTENTS

THE POLITICS OF ANTIREASON

AFTER MY BOOK *NONBELIEVER NATION: THE RISE OF SECULAR Americans* was released in the summer of 2012, I had an opportunity to tour much of the country to speak about the culture wars, with visits to many college campuses. In chatting with an undergraduate student at a stop at Ohio State University, I mentioned the fact that many Americans think negatively of atheism because they associate it with communism. Although I considered this statement to be common knowledge, not a point that would be contested, the undergrad looked very puzzled. After a few seconds she smiled, shook her head, and replied: "That's *so* twentieth century!"

What an eye-opening response! And she was right. Those of us who grew up during the Cold War still carry the cosmic ideological clashes of that era with us, whereas younger people have an entirely different view. Most college students today weren't even alive when the Soviet Union fell in 1991, and they certainly don't go about their lives with a Cold War mentality. Unburdened by outdated prejudices, they are more likely to realize that any attempt to vilify atheists as presumptive communist sympathizers—a baseless allegation even back then—would be ludicrous.

In fact, her casual statement exposes issues much broader than the public's view of nonbelievers. In the realm of politics and public policy, even on the liberal/progressive side of the spectrum (where many consider themselves forward-looking), much of the predominant thinking is *so twentieth century,* grounded on turf that allows little consideration of a truly progressive agenda. Just as many Americans—liberal, moderate, and conservative—carry around outdated stereotypes about atheists, too often prevailing American views on politics, the economy, the role of government, education, the environment, and foreign policy are also rooted in paradigms that should have faded long ago.

Because of this, conservative assumptions rule the day, and we live with the results: Wall Street thrives while Main Street boards up its buildings; multinational corporate interests control the system, enjoying immense wealth and enormous public subsidies while simultaneously complaining about "big government" and regulation; public education is in crisis; ordinary citizens are powerless, as the middle class shrinks and the gap between rich and poor grows; huge percentages of the population are incarcerated, many for nonviolent crimes; and the richest nation on the planet struggles to provide universal health care and affordable higher education to its citizens. All of this happens in a climate of anti-intellectualism, where men and women frequently are elected to high offices on platforms that openly and proudly reject science and embrace fundamentalist theology.

A central premise of this book is that we owe the dismal state of affairs in America to the failure of rational, human-centered public policy to gain traction—and that this failure is a direct result of a multipronged attack on reason. The promotion of antireason, which comes in a variety of forms, is often encouraged and guided by the large institutional interests that benefit most from it—corporations and industries as well as certain governmental and religious interests—but it would not be possible without a broad base of popular acceptance. That is, while the "reason deficit" primarily serves nonhuman, institutional interests, the system that allows it is dependent on a passive, obedient public.

Consider comments such as those of Representative Paul Broun, a Georgia Republican, who told an audience in 2012 that the big bang and the theory of evolution are "lies straight from the pit of hell."[1] Understandably, many rational Americans simply brushed off this statement as the ranting of yet another fundamentalist legislator from the Deep South; but as we will see, it's a symptom of a problem far more serious and pervasive than many would like to admit. There is a direct causal link between this level of anti-intellectualism and the demise of human-centered, progressive policy, and by examining the assault on reason in American public life, both historically and currently—including the question of why, in a democracy, the voting public has been largely unsuccessful in repelling it—we'll see what might be possible if sensible Americans rethink their strategies.

I use the term "the Right" in this book in its usual context, to mean the conservative end of the political spectrum.[2] In American politics, of course, Republicans are generally to the right of Democrats on both economic and social issues, but most observers would agree that today's Democrats are far from what the rest of the world would call "the Left." Thus, the title "Fighting Back the Right" shouldn't be interpreted merely as opposing the GOP agenda—although that's part of it—but rather as fighting back against the pervasive conservative presumptions that dominate the entire American political system today.

As we'll see, those presumptions affect all kinds of policy—social, economic, even foreign policy—and are often rooted in an outright rejection of reason that arises from several sources: conservative religion, apprehension about modernity, overzealous patriotism, the distortion of science, fear of both internal minorities and external enemies, and an obsession with short-term corporate profit and growth. These forces, though they may often appear unrelated, have individually and collectively fueled what we today call "the Right." With such a foundation, it's little wonder that our current environment is anti-egalitarian, anti-intellectual, and more responsive to institutional interests than those of real humans.

Since I will often use the term "conservatives" interchangeably with "the Right," I should mention that conservatism has not always been synonymous with antireason. In its more benign form, conservatism can refer simply to a belief that change should come slowly or, alternatively, to a preference for limited government; but in modern usage, especially in America, conservatism has a distinct ideological definition that is antigovernment (often rabidly so), militaristic, moralistic, pro-corporate, and sympathetic to the entanglement of religion in government. This is the conservatism of today's Right, and it is an ideology that is shared by disparate groups—religious fundamentalists, foreign policy hawks, economic libertarians, multinational corporate interests—whose unifying thread is a willingness to set aside reason for political and financial gain.

Opposition to the Right frequently implies an advocacy for a progressive vision—and I accept that framing here—but my aim is not to portray traditional liberalism (again using the modern American definition of the term) as always being enlightened. Keeping in mind the need to avoid thinking that is "so twentieth century," this book is not an exaltation of failed liberal/progressive strategies and solutions. Instead, in a nonideological manner, we will examine and critique those strategies and solutions to see why they failed; and, most important, we will see why there is hope for a pragmatic *twenty-first-century* approach to progressivism that balances the important values of egalitarianism, individual rights and liberties, critical thinking, and a willingness to question institutional authority.

Those who mourn the demise of American liberalism often point to particular factors as being key to that decline. The weakening of labor unions, for example, is cited by many.[3] Others see the GOP's exploitation of white social conservatives, starting with Nixon's southern strategy and then reaching full stride with the rise of the Religious Right in the 1980s, as being critical.[4] Still others explain the conservative tide as a reaction to the turbulence of the 1960s and 1970s, particularly America's disastrous escapade in Vietnam, and the collective national desire to move past those experiences.[5] And of course, especially within the modern GOP, there is no shortage of those who attribute the success of conservatism primarily to the sheer personal dynamism of Ronald Reagan, who almost single-handedly turned "liberal" into a dirty word.[6]

None of these explanations, however, quite gets to the heart of why American public policy, with just a few significant exceptions (such as the success of the gay rights movement), has lurched rightward over the last three-plus decades. For example, although the collapse of American labor has no doubt contributed to the decline of liberal public policy, one could argue that it's as much a *result* of that decline as a cause. And while socially conservative white voters have been mobilized by Nixon, Reagan, and every GOP presidential candidate since, often with hot-button, culture war issues playing a prominent role, that doesn't explain *why* such mobilization is possible.

As we will see, when fairly considered, these phenomena and others reveal a puzzling common denominator: *an aversion to reason.* That is, no matter how we dissect the success of modern American conservatism to find its causal roots and ongoing motivating forces, we discover some combination of fear-based thinking, anti-intellectualism, racism and sexism, emotional appeals to religion and patriotism, an unquestioned acceptance of corporate power, and incessant psychological manipulation of the public—with resulting policy that caters to institutional interests over those of real humans.

Since progressive policy should be synonymous with human-centered policy, the fight against the Right can accurately be described as an effort by real people to take back the system from institutional, nonhuman interests; and since the Right consistently relies on antireason (in its various forms) for staying power, any strategy to reverse course must actively *promote* reason. Of course, the common subcategories and issues within progressivism— women's rights, social justice, environmentalism, labor, militarism and peace, the regulation of commerce, secular government, LGBT (lesbian, gay, bisexual, transgender) rights, and others—remain important, but for too long progressives engaging in these issues have failed to address them with collective cohesion, and this has surely empowered the opposition. As we'll see, since the conservative position in all of these areas relies in one way or another on antireason, rational Americans stand to gain by promoting their full agenda from a broader, integrated standpoint that recognizes the assault on reason, exposes it, and forcibly rebuffs it.

On an encouraging note, once we look beyond the formidable interests promoting antireason, we find a general public that is otherwise eager for progressive, human-centered policy. In fact, if we accept the common description of the crisis in American politics and culture as a clash between the Right (loosely defined as an alliance of religious conservatives, corporate interests, and antigovernment populists) and the Left (loosely defined as those advocating secular government, worker and consumer rights, and egalitarian social and economic policy), there is little doubt that the public, nationally and in most geographic regions, is on our side. As we'll see, polling indicates that the policy flowing from Washington is well to the right of public sentiments.

In fact, the Obama campaigns of 2008 and 2012 were won with rhetoric and imagery—hope, change, and a fair shake for average working people—that was ardently progressive. Interestingly, however, despite Obama's riding to election on a wave of popular enthusiasm for egalitarian change, most would agree that the actual policy delivered by his administration has fallen far short of such trailblazing. Therefore, we need to consider the disparity between the progressivism that people want and the underwhelming policy that their leaders consistently deliver.

We'll find that the successful progressive coalitions that have elected Obama and others need not be content with policy that is so unprogressive—*so twentieth century.* By strategizing better, rational Americans can reject policy making that is presumptively confined by an outdated conservative framework. Almost all other developed countries, for example, take for granted universal health care, affordable higher education, relatively modest military spending, and strong social safety nets—progressive concepts that are generally accepted by even their *conservative* political parties—because there is consensus in these societies that ordinary citizens expect such policies and will resist large institutional interests that attempt to dismantle them.

Those same countries look at the United States, meanwhile, and they see a nation with rates of incarceration, violent crime, teen pregnancy, and other social ills that are at or near the worst in the developed world. For all our national pride—and we have much to be proud about—we are perceived with some accuracy as anti-intellectual, violent, ultra-patriotic, hyperreligious, and hostile to human-centered public policy. Europeans and others from around the world see America routinely electing politicians who deny evolution, proudly proclaim themselves to be biblical literalists, and even question the wisdom of affordable birth control—baffling characteristics for a nation that claims economic and military leadership in the world.

Many of these embarrassing facts are attributable, directly or indirectly, to conservative political domination and the diminished role of reason in policy making that has accompanied it. To reverse the damage, we'll consider why the American public dialogue has become so irrational, who is responsible for obstructing human-centered policy, and what strategies are needed for real change.

Make no mistake: Any lasting turnaround will require not just single-issue advocacy but a more macro view that recognizes and addresses the widespread antireason upon which the conservative movement has relied. By affirming the higher American values of sensible egalitarianism, pragmatism, individual autonomy, and reason and critical thinking, while simultaneously defusing the opposition's simplistic appeals to fear and ideology, ordinary Americans can reclaim their country.

ONE

CORRUPT BLESSINGS

PRESIDENTS GIVE MANY SPEECHES, BUT THIS ONE WAS MORE IMPOR-
tant than most. Critical domestic events were unfolding, and the president
needed to connect with the American people, so this address would be delivered on live national television. Trying to convey a sense of optimism, he
sat before the camera in the Oval Office and discussed in detail the drama
that the nation was facing. Toward the end, he asked his fellow citizens for
their prayers, and then he concluded his remarks with the following words:
God bless America. And God bless each and every one of you.

The year was 1973, and the president was Richard Nixon. The subject
of the speech was the resignation of three administration officials, including
the attorney general, in the midst of the Watergate scandal, which of course
would claim the president himself the following year.

Ironically, this speech—delivered by the president whose name has become most synonymous with corruption, addressing the most notorious
White House scandal in history—was the first known instance of any president concluding a speech with the words "God bless America."[1] To those
of us who have grown up since that time, when it seems that every major
presidential address necessarily ends with those three words, it may come as
a surprise that the idea of incorporating God into virtually every political
speech is very much a modern phenomenon.

"God bless America" is just one of the numerous religious-patriotic references that many Americans mistakenly assume has roots going back to the nation's founding, or close to it. In fact, even the song "God Bless America," which first injected the phrase into popular culture, dates back less than a century. Written by Irving Berlin, a Jewish immigrant, the song wasn't popularized until it became the signature hit of Kate Smith, who first sang it in 1938.[2] The quintessentially patriotic image of the song has grown in recent years, as it has become a staple of professional baseball games and other sporting events in the post-9/11 era. This affirmation of public religiosity, with no basis in history, is consistent with other relatively recent efforts to combine religion and patriotism—such as the national motto of "In God We Trust" (adopted only in 1956), the insertion of "under God" into the Pledge of Allegiance (by legislation passed in 1954), and the creation of an annual National Day of Prayer endorsed by the federal government (by legislation in 1952).

All citizens, religious and nonreligious, would be wise to remember the Nixonian origins of "God bless America" in speech making, for the combination of religion, patriotism, and politics should be viewed with utmost skepticism. Elected officials are hired by the people to craft and implement rational public policy—to pass budgets, administer government, and much more—and there is no end to the important work to be done. Inevitably, there will be disagreements over how to solve the problems facing the country, but those disagreements only highlight the need to utilize time wisely, intelligently analyzing facts and considering viable options.

Thus, one must wonder what lawmakers in Pennsylvania were thinking, for example, when in 2012 they broke from earnest legislative tasks to instead debate and pass a bill to declare that year the "Year of the Bible," or what motivated Louisiana legislators to push a bill in 2014 to make the Bible the official state book. When politicians opt to digress like this from serious policy discussion to make references to religion and deities, constituents should immediately ask themselves an important question: With all the complex issues that need to be addressed, why are these public servants distracting us with religious pandering? The presumptive answer, absent compelling evidence to the contrary, should be that the politicians lack constructive, intelligent ideas for addressing the social and economic issues facing their constituents.

THE AMERICAN WAY

Today, it's natural to assume that every president since Washington has concluded every major speech with "God bless America." If that's all you've ever heard, why would you think otherwise? Even liberal politicians, who supposedly are less prone to wearing religion on their sleeves, proclaim "God bless America" all the time, so there would be no reason to suspect that it's a relatively recent innovation.

In fact, however, these kinds of common misunderstandings help explain the tragic state of public policy today. Although the brief history of "God bless America" may seem trivial, it is just one example of the widespread misperceptions Americans have about their country, its history, and its core principles, and the sum total of these misperceptions has had calamitous consequences. What we now unquestioningly accept as "the American way"—politically, economically, and socially—is often a relatively new invention, far less deeply ingrained than we realize, yet these flawed assumptions greatly impact contemporary society.

Indeed, for those frustrated by the less admirable aspects of American culture—the plethora of social problems, for example, from high incarceration rates to rampant anti-intellectualism—it helps to realize that our current trajectory was not inevitable, that the seeds of democracy planted by the framers were not necessarily destined to create the conditions that now define the culture. As we shall see, there were many directions that the nation could have taken after the founding era and many junctures thereafter. The current state of affairs was not a preordained destination but the result of developments—institutions, technologies, systems, and paradigms—that were unimaginable to the framers, just as today's realities would be unrecognizable to them.

As the ink dried on the Constitution in 1787, for example, it would have been unfathomable to the drafters that in 2008 a candidate such as Sarah Palin would have been a leading contender for the vice presidency of the nation they had created. In some ways this reflects positive social and political developments (not only have women won the right to vote, but they now can stand as viable candidates for high office), but in other ways the developments are less admirable. The framers, after all, were intellectuals who would be dismayed to learn that over two centuries later—after generations of stunning scientific discoveries and advancements in human knowledge—the nation almost elected a person, man or woman, who embraced fundamentalist religion and was sympathetic to biblical literalism, a candidate who was ignorant of basic facts of geography, history, and science.[3]

There can be no dispute that American economic and military powers have grown mighty since the nation's humble beginnings, but it is just as indisputable that this success has not always translated into positive social and economic outcomes for the general population, and that many of the realities facing average citizens and families—the disappearing middle class, the exportation of jobs overseas, rates of violent crime and other social ills that are among the worst in the developed world, the spiraling costs of health care and higher education—reflect a serious political dysfunction. Indeed, these negatives are especially puzzling in light of the image of economic and military greatness that the nation promotes for itself on the global stage, and they indicate that certain institutions—governmental and corporate— are more often the real beneficiaries of the nation's might, whereas ordinary citizens are not.

These kitchen-table realities result from the failure of rational, progressive Americans to effectively advocate for human-centered, fact-based public policy. Reminders of this failure are constantly present in the political arena, where the nation's elected lawmakers regularly provide us with embarrassing fodder. The "lies straight from the pit of hell" statement of U.S. Representative Paul Broun, mentioned in the introduction, is just one example, but it's especially pertinent since it came not from an obscure backwoods state legislator, and not even just an ordinary U.S. congressman, but a member of the House Science and Technology Committee! Broun, sitting on a key panel responsible for shaping national science policy, claims the earth is "about nine thousand years old" and "was created in six days as we know them."[4] God bless America, indeed.

Antireason has become too strong a force in the United States—to the detriment of rational, progressive policy—in part because even progressives have been too quick to define "the American way" using incorrect conservative assumptions about history, the economy, patriotism, and religion. For example, as Americans unquestioningly accept that God blesses their nation, they also accept the simplistic statement, often repeated by liberals as well as conservatives, that America is (and always has been) a very religious country. As we'll see, this is not only wrong but inherently hostile to the progressive agenda (even though, of course, many progressives are religious). By exaggerating the real role of religion, historically and currently, in the lives of most Americans, such a definition lends legitimacy to religious fundamentalists and their agenda, thereby ushering the nation down a path that is anti-intellectual, fear-based, and hostile to the interests of ordinary people. Moreover, it downplays or ignores the important role that reason, science, and religious skepticism have played in the American saga.

Such misperceptions have redefined the nation, shaping present reality to conform to a mythical narrative. They go far beyond questions of religion, affecting beliefs and attitudes toward corporations, the role of government, war and peace, and a myriad of other issues. These misperceptions have too often allowed the politics of fear and anti-intellectualism to succeed, thereby serving interests that conflict with those of average working people. By understanding these misperceptions, rational progressives can strategize more effectively to give fact-based, human-centered policy a better chance of success.

From a progressive standpoint, the intermingling of religion and politics would be less troublesome if the theology promoted by America's activist Christians were some variation of the social gospel—urging the use of public resources for feeding the poor, healing the sick, and promoting peace. Sadly, that's not the case. The most politically outspoken fundamentalist Christians nowadays tend to see their theology as justifying—if not requiring—a harsh brand of conservative policy that would make Jesus look like a radical hippie.

Consider Tennessee congressman Stephen Fincher, an excellent example (and there are many) of this breed of Christian conservative. Fincher, citing his religious values, not only supports cutting aid to the poor but quotes the Bible to justify doing so. In 2013 he argued that $4.1 billion in food stamp funding should be slashed from the federal budget, quoting 2 Thessalonians 3:10: "For even when we were with you, we gave you this command: Anyone unwilling to work should not eat."[5] Of course, many Christians, perhaps most, are appalled by such rhetoric, which would seem to contradict the commonly understood Christian message of charity and compassion. But as we will see later, despite their opposition, moderate and liberal Christians have failed to advance more progressive policy, in part because they've actually contributed to the promotion of antireason by accepting conservative narratives like the notion that America is a "very religious country."

Even most of these more rational Christians would acknowledge that, from a standpoint of political visibility and outspokenness, fundamentalist and conservative Christians often dominate the media spotlight. It's not that moderate and liberal Christians are inactive in politics, but they are less likely to emphasize their religion as a political selling point or as a basis for policy positions. Conservatives, in contrast, routinely ramp up the religious rhetoric, with direct references to Christianity and talk of "morals" and "values" at seemingly every opportunity, while simultaneously exhorting antigovernment positions that would decimate social safety nets.

CONVERGING FORCES

Fincher's statement is a good example of how two seemingly unrelated forces—*conservative religion* and *anti-egalitarianism*—have converged in modern America to create a potent conservative formula that has had terrible consequences for the nation. The utter failure of progressive, rational, people-oriented public policy in America—a failure that coincides with the nation's lurch to the right in recent decades—stems from this convergence. Politically, the institutional interests backing conservative religion and anti-egalitarianism have developed a symbiotic relationship that has suffocated the progressive agenda, ensuring that almost all real-world policy making takes place on the conservative end of the spectrum.

Most Americans are well aware of the Religious Right's influence on social policy and issues such as reproductive rights and church-state separation, but its role in advancing the entire anti-egalitarian conservative agenda—including the attack on social services and regulatory agencies and much more—often goes unnoticed. Because of the convergence of religious and anti-egalitarian interests, the advocates of the harshest conservative economics often become the darlings of the Religious Right.

For example, Wisconsin representative Paul Ryan, whose "Ryan budget" has been the centerpiece of Republican efforts to dismantle the federal government, is seen by the Religious Right as a great hope for the future. When Mitt Romney chose Ryan as his vice presidential running mate in 2012, leaders of the Religious Right lauded not only Ryan's pro-life and other socially conservative stances but also his fiscal positions. Tony Perkins of the Family Research Council, a fundamentalist Christian advocacy group, said the selection showed that Romney "is serious about getting America's fiscal house in order," adding that Ryan "believes that social, fiscal and national security conservatism is indivisible."[6] Ralph Reed of the Faith and Freedom Coalition called Ryan "an inspired, outstanding selection" and specifically noted that Ryan was known for "sound budgets."[7] And even the Catholic Association praised not just Ryan's extreme pro-life position (like the Catholic Church, Ryan opposes abortion even in cases of rape and incest) and opposition to same-sex marriage, but even implied that it approved of his anti-poor budgetary priorities, saying Ryan "has been thoughtful and articulate in applying Catholic principles" beyond those of abortion and marriage.[8]

Unfortunately, these conservative religious voices and the anti-egalitarian politicians they support are empowered by the misperception that America is a very religious country where the intermingling of religion and politics is generally welcomed. Even liberals have come to expect, and too often accept, an atmosphere of visible public piety, even though it is historically invalid and unquestionably obstructs egalitarian policy. The entire American political landscape has swung violently to the right since the rise of the Religious Right, yet those who oppose the conservative agenda seem blind to the correlation, or at least unwilling to seriously address it.

As conservative religion and anti-egalitarianism have come together to empower the Right in modern America, it's important to understand their histories. Each arises from an underlying conflict that has been ongoing since the early days of the Republic: the former from the struggle of *religious versus secular* worldviews and the latter from the struggle of *egalitarian versus anti-egalitarian* worldviews. In the religious versus secular conflict, we see continuous debate over the proper role, if any, of religion in American politics and government. In the egalitarian versus anti-egalitarian debate, we see constant disagreements over how the high-minded ideals of liberty and equality should be applied, both socially and economically.

The ongoing and still-unresolved dialectical tensions of religion versus secular and egalitarian versus anti-egalitarian, when considered in appropriate context with other factors (such as, for example, the advancement of technology), shed light on our current political landscape. In both of these conflicts, the two sides have historically traded victories and defeats, but the strong conservative trend of recent decades can be understood as the simultaneous predominance of the *religious* side in the former struggle and the *anti-egalitarian* side in the latter. Moreover, by discovering the power of working together for political ends, these religious and anti-egalitarian interests have redefined the American political landscape.

Interestingly, each side in both of these conflicts claims to carry on the "true" vision of the country's founders, and each cites historical quotes, documents, and legislation to support its position. Religious conservatives, for example, point to any favorable statements the founders made about religion and pounce on any historical act that suggested the slightest tolerance for church-state intermingling. Advocates for church-state separation, meanwhile, can point to strong evidence that most of the founders were quite wary of religion in government.

Similarly, today's anti-egalitarians claim direct descent from the framers on both economic and social issues. In economic debates, they insist that the "true" American tradition is one of laissez-faire, as if the framers considered few things more repugnant than government intervention in the economy. Modern egalitarians, meanwhile, argue that promotion of the "general welfare" through government was commonplace in the founding era. On social issues, today's anti-egalitarians claim "heritage" and "traditional values" in resisting efforts to promote equality for women, gays, and racial and ethnic minorities, whereas their egalitarian opponents insist that modern standards of equality are the natural extension of the ideals enunciated by the framers.

Of course, all of this debate about the intent of the founders only reflects the impossibility of applying the mind-set of eighteenth-century wealthy white men to today's society. Frankly, given the enormous technological advances and other factors that would make modern American society unrecognizable to the framers, it seems presumptuous that anyone could claim to know what they would think of most contemporary issues. A more sensible approach would be to discern the fundamental principles of the founding era that might be relevant and desirable to any given situation today, then consider them as one factor in an overall analysis that doesn't pretend to know how Jefferson or Madison would view today's world.

Regardless of what the framers would think, it's pretty clear who's been winning politically in recent decades. With a few exceptions, the *religious* camp has dominated over the *secular,* and the *anti-egalitarian* over the *egalitarian.* (More accurately, *economic* egalitarianism has fared particularly poorly, whereas *social* egalitarianism—in terms of gay rights and slowly declining rates of prejudice in other areas—has made some strides.)[9] Moreover, in stark contrast to the powerful, coordinated political activism exhibited by the converging religious/anti-egalitarian interests, the secular and egalitarian forces have failed to unify behind anything resembling a broad, coherent agenda.

As we'll see, this explains the baffling state of affairs today and the staggering preponderance of antireason: large sectors of the population willing to vote against their economic interests, numerous politicians proclaiming that evolution and climate change are liberal hoaxes, and much more. It also highlights the dire need for a coordinated movement advocating a human-centered, reason-based, progressive agenda.

THE FREETHINKING PROGRESSIVE

Although it is rarely framed this way, the progressive position in modern America is in many ways consistent with the nation's long tradition of freethought.[10] Moreover, just as progressivism has struggled since the rise of the conservative movement in the late 1970s, so too has the concept of freethinking often been abandoned as conservative religion and anti-egalitarianism have gained influence. If progressive public policy is urgently needed, it would not be hyperbole to say that its success hinges on a successful renewal of American freethinking.

Progressives sometimes use the term "wing-nut" to refer to the extreme anti-intellectuals who have become so vocal and visible in the Republican Party—people like the aforementioned Paul Broun, for example, and others such as Sarah Palin, Rick Perry, and Michele Bachmann, who proudly allow fundamentalist religion to dictate their political views, even if it means rejecting science. The conservative political trend of recent decades, which has given rise to this cast of characters, has been possible only because the principles of freethought have been expunged from American public discourse, leaving fertile ground for brazenly anti-intellectual candidates. These modern GOP firebrands have delighted religious conservatives and multinational corporate interests alike, but have decimated virtually every area of public policy—the economy, the environment, education, social policy, and much more—and left average citizens, small businesses, and communities struggling to make ends meet.

Even for deeply religious progressives, an understanding of the marvelous consistency between freethinking and progressivism can help clarify what has happened in America over the last three-plus decades. Specifically, the relationship between freethinking and progressivism can help explain the success of the antireason agenda, particularly the failure of the mass population to demand more rational policy. As such, a few words about freethought and freethinkers are in order.

Having been immersed in culture war activism for the last decade, I've found that almost everyone, if asked, would call themselves freethinkers. One woman I met, a devout Catholic who looks to the Vatican for moral instruction yet simultaneously believes in reincarnation and reads her horoscope daily, was quite sincere when she smiled and declared to me, "I'm a freethinker!" After chatting with her for a bit, I learned that she defined "freethinker" as being more or less synonymous with "open-minded." Thus, her willingness to consider all notions regardless of degree of flimsiness—the healing power of crystals, telling fortunes by Tarot cards, conversing with the dead—allowed her, at least in her own mind, to proudly proclaim herself a freethinker.

The word "freethought," however, is not defined as giving license to believe any idea that is suggested but instead refers to a philosophical view that is more disciplined, holding that opinions should be based on reason, logic, and evidence. Most important, the "free" in "freethought" refers not to a freedom to believe any preposterous idea that is put forward, but instead means that the adherent is free *from* dogma, superstition, and other irrational authority. Having come into use in the seventeenth century, during the historical period known as the Enlightenment, the term indicates that one is free from the shackles of illegitimate authority.

Freethinkers think for themselves and therefore are at times perceived as somewhat subversive, defiant of existing power structures. They are not influenced by church doctrine, claimed revelation, nationalistic rhetoric, or any traditions that reflect beliefs and biases that cannot be objectively validated—by science if the claim is one of truth; by the sensible application of nondogmatic, enlightened, contemporary standards if the claim is one of morality. As such, freethinkers sometimes have a reputation as being nonconformists, independent personalities who reject a herd mentality. And although freethought might influence one's views on all areas of life, it most often is seen as directly threatening traditional religion, since few areas rely more on authority that is so obviously questionable. Freethinkers will have strong opinions on other ideas and institutions as well, but few of these areas are as steeped in irrationality as traditional religion, where the exaltation of faith over reason is often the central point.

For this reason the term "secular," which simply means "worldly" or "temporal" or "not religious," often has become interchangeable with "freethought" in recent times. The modern secular movement, which promotes church-state separation and the rights of America's nontheistic and nonreligious populations, is sometimes even called the freethought movement. Secular groups frequently use the term "freethought" (the Freedom from Religion Foundation's monthly publication is called *Freethought Today*, for example, and many secular groups, such as the Triangle Freethought Society in North Carolina and the Tufts Freethought Society in Massachusetts, have adopted the term as well) because it affirms their values and, quite frankly, is often received more warmly by the general public than other secular terms, such as "atheist."

The term "freethought," however, is not completely synonymous with the word "secular" and in fact refers to a more general worldview and tradition that goes beyond questions of religion. Because the term "secular" is defined so sharply by religious questions, when a person says, "I'm secular," she is presumably referring either to her personal view on religion (she is not religious or perhaps not theistic) or to her belief in church-state separation (i.e., secular government). But when a person says, "I'm a freethinker," she is saying something different, making a broader declaration about her way of thinking, though usually there is some element of religious skepticism implied. To be a freethinker is to carry a certain disposition, the central aspects of which are a refusal to accept unsupported claims of authority and a belief that reason and empiricism are the best means of attaining truth.

Today, although the forces opposing freethought remain extremely powerful, we see the freethought tradition reflected among the millions of Americans who, while often averse to identifying as atheist or agnostic, are quite willing to dismiss the legitimacy of religious institutions as sources of ultimate truth or moral authority. About half the American population does not attend regular religious services, for example, and one in five Americans claims no religious affiliation, a number that has more than doubled in the last two decades.[11] Still, even though they reject dogma and church authority, these individuals often are otherwise ambivalent about religion; they may see little reason to believe in any kind of divinity and no evidence of any kind to suggest that another world awaits after we depart this one, but for various reasons most of them refrain from identifying as atheist or even agnostic.

In fact, even many Americans who retain traditional religious identity manage to compartmentalize their thinking, moving forward in life at most times with a freethinking view that expects a rational approach to important issues, despite their traditional religious affiliation. The variations on this theme are numerous. There are many who participate in traditional religious practice from time to time only because it is part of their cultural tradition. They'll attend services on Christmas and Easter, perhaps even call themselves Catholic or Protestant if asked, but they don't believe much, if any, of the theology. At almost all times, their beliefs and actions are no different from those of people who identify as atheist or agnostic. Most important, even though they retain traditional religious identity, they understand that their churches (or synagogues or mosques) have no legitimate role to play in politics.

Others may be more regular in their religious practice but will approach almost all matters of politics and public policy through a standard of reason, seeing no role for religion. These individuals, though perhaps only part-time freethinkers, are likely to find the style and substance of the Religious Right—vocally proclaiming righteousness, promoting religion through the government, rejecting science when it conflicts with scripture, imposing their claimed moral standards on all of society—not only distasteful but dangerous. We need not psychoanalyze those who seem theistic on Sunday morning only to comport themselves as freethinkers the rest of the week; rather, from a political standpoint, we should recognize them as an important part of the political alliance that can drive rational public policy.

Note that the thread that unites almost all progressives, but that has been too long ignored, is the belief that public policy, regardless of one's religious views, must be human-centered and based on reason and evidence. This is what makes the terms "progressive" and "freethinker" so closely related and why the two labels often refer to the same constituency. That said, "progressive" is the term that is more common in a political context, whereas "freethinker" is more of a philosophical term that would describe those who question authority, embrace reason and critical thinking, and reject religious and anti-intellectual arguments. In the pages ahead I will generally use the terms in these contexts—"progressive" when referring to the political, "freethinker" when referring to general philosophy—but the line between the two often is blurred.

Such subtle distinctions are less important than the common values that unite—or at least *should* unite—those opposed to the disastrous agenda of the Right. As conservative religious and anti-egalitarian interests have galvanized around antireason methods and goals, opponents have failed to find a corresponding unity. It's time to change that.

What is also noteworthy, however, is that the conservative interests promoting antireason are backed by institutions that have almost unlimited resources to pull levers of political power, dominate the media, manipulate public opinion, utilize the courts, influence the economy, and do all the other things that money and power can do. It may seem hopeless at times to the average humble voter, but real people still can win the power struggle if they finally unite around the common values that support human-centered policy. Progressives have been outspent and outmaneuvered by the Right for decades, but by rallying behind a vision of pragmatic, egalitarian policy—rejecting ideology, questioning concentrated power, respecting science and empiricism, celebrating pluralism, and valuing rational arguments over fear and psychological manipulation—we can reverse the onslaught of antireason that has overtaken the country.

TWO

REAL-WORLD CHANGE

A GENERATION AGO, IT WAS UNIMAGINABLE THAT A SERIOUS MAJOR-party candidate would launch a presidential campaign with a huge Christian prayer rally. Even in the more conservative Republican Party, the idea of candidates wrapping themselves in such fervent religious fundamentalism would have been considered politically suicidal.

But what a difference a few years make. In August 2011, Texas governor Rick Perry hosted just such an event—a revival that filled Houston's Reliant Stadium with 30,000 enthusiastic believers and was simulcast at churches around the country, billed as a day of prayer and fasting to reverse America's decline. Sounding more like a preacher than a statesman, Perry read from the books of Isaiah, Joel, and Ephesians and tied his patriotism closely to his Christianity. "Like all of you," he told the crowd, "I love this country deeply. . . . Indeed, the only thing that you love more is the living Christ."[1]

Not long ago even Republicans would have been aghast at such behavior from a presidential aspirant, but such impassioned displays of fundamentalist Christianity can be a smart strategy in today's GOP. Indeed, commentators noted that Perry's prayer and fasting rally served the purpose of solidifying the conservative religious electorate behind him. Writing in the *Guardian,* Ewen MacAskill noted that the event "virtually guaranteed him [Perry] the support of the Christian evangelical movement, with its network of volunteers and finance, plus a large bloc of votes in Republican caucuses and primaries."[2] (MacAskill also observed that "prayer" was more noticeable than "fasting" at the Houston rally, judging by the long lines for vendors selling hamburgers, nachos, hot dogs, and other fast food.)

Rational Americans may take solace in the fact that Perry's campaign was ultimately unsuccessful, but make no mistake: his downfall in the GOP race had little to do with his overt religiosity. In fact, when Perry announced his candidacy shortly after the prayer rally, polls showed him leading the field. His demise as a candidate is attributable not to his relationship with Jesus but to his unimpressive performance as a candidate. In one debate, for example, Perry insisted that, if elected, he would eliminate three government agencies but then was able to name only two, resulting in a prolonged, awkward silence as he struggled to recall the third.[3] By the time actual voting started in Iowa and New Hampshire in January 2012, it was clear that Perry was simply not ready for prime time despite having ridden high after the prayer rally. As such, the remaining contenders scrambled to attract the fundamentalist Christian base he left behind, with frequent references to God and conservative stances on social issues.

MORE THAN JUST RELIGION

Few would deny that Perry's rally is a reflection of the increased influence of conservative religion in modern American politics. But less obvious is how the event reflects the convergence of conservative religion and anti-egalitarianism mentioned in chapter 1. As Perry and others cite scripture and praise Jesus, they also sprinkle rhetoric that validates their harsh, anti-egalitarian political and economic views. "Father, our heart breaks for America," Perry proclaimed at the rally. "We see discord at home. We see fear in the marketplace. We see anger in the halls of government, and as a nation we have forgotten who made us, who protects us, who blesses us, and for that we cry out for your forgiveness."[4]

Tellingly, as Perry surveys all the problems confronting America, he notes "fear in the marketplace"—not poverty, not health, not the environment, not even jobs—as being worthy of a call-out for divine intervention. Financial markets, not real human problems, need God's attention, as if the divinity is some sort of stockbroker in chief. Of course, the performance of securities and commodities markets ultimately can have a ripple effect that reaches the lives of ordinary people, but it is revealing that Perry and many others like him would place these markets so near the center of their world-view and their public prayers. This alarming combination of fundamentalist religion and conservative economics has driven America away from human-centered policy.

To understand this, just imagine if conservative religion had become a trendy social phenomenon in America without also becoming a powerful political force. After all, people can be deeply religious without also engaging politically; in fact, some (if not most) major religious movements are completely apolitical. If, for example, rather than launching the highly politicized Moral Majority in the late 1970s, Jerry Falwell had instead called for a purely *religious* uprising of fundamentalist believers, it is doubtful that American public policy would have been much affected. We might still have a large portion of the population with biblical literalist beliefs, but few of those adherents would have infiltrated local, regional, and national party machines; instead, they likely would have focused their energies on pure evangelism and worship. While such a trend might have had some negative social impact (because widespread biblical literalism is unlikely to lead to a highly enlightened population), its repercussions would be relatively mild compared to what we have seen with the rise of the *politically* mobilized Religious Right.

The path of intense political engagement has allowed conservative religion to have a devastating anti-egalitarian impact in America. In modern times, a voter's religiosity is among the most accurate predictors of behavior at the polls, with regular churchgoers and self-described born-again Christians showing a devotion to conservative candidates that is unmatched by other demographic categories.[5] By giving reliable numbers to anti-egalitarian interests, religious conservatives allow those interests to claim mass support that otherwise would not exist.

This is true both in the area of *social* anti-egalitarianism, where religious fundamentalists frequently back policies that obstruct equality for women, gays, racial minorities, and religious minorities, as well as in *economic* anti-egalitarianism, where the support of religious conservatives enables policies favoring corporate interests and the wealthy and disfavoring the poor and middle class. The resulting irony is millions of devout Christians, often of modest economic means, actively supporting candidates who pander to their socially conservative views on abortion, gay rights, creationism, and other culture war issues, even as those same candidates push economic policies—such as tax cuts for upper income brackets and deregulation of industries—that cater to the rich and to large corporate interests.

OPPOSING ANTI-INTELLECTUALISM

Though Rick Perry provides an easy example of what progressives don't want in a candidate, he also highlights one of the vulnerabilities of the progressive position. If we criticize Perry as a religious fanatic and a sort of simpleton, conservatives fire back that we are intellectual snobs. This accusation is a potent weapon in the conservative political arsenal, one that immediately puts progressives on the defensive. After all, at a glance it seems to make sense. If the country's rightward tilt has been achieved through the manipulation of ordinary citizens, often by exploiting fundamentalist religious views and other anti-intellectual tendencies, one might assume that those on the other side are the highly educated intellectuals.

But this is not necessarily the case. More accurately, the typical progressive is not so much an intellectual but simply *not anti-intellectual.* This distinction often gets lost, since conservatives are astonishingly effective at painting their opponents as "elites," academics, or otherwise out of touch with the problems of average people. In reality, of course, human-centered public policy is beneficial to—and sought by—ordinary people, most of whom have no advanced degrees or other intellectual credentials. Those opposed to anti-intellectualism in politics are not necessarily fluent in complex scientific ideas or sophisticated art and culture, but they do recognize the value of critical thinking. Put another way, while an aversion to anti-intellectualism is a common denominator among progressives and freethinkers, it would be just as accurate to say that the *embrace* of anti-intellectualism is a defining characteristic of their *opponents.*

Consider, for example, the baffling belief—held by many Americans—that Barack Obama was not born in the United States, even though irrefutable evidence has been produced showing that he was born in Hawaii in 1961. Even years after Obama was elected, one in four Americans surveyed—and almost half of Republicans and Tea Party supporters—stated that they believed he was foreign born.[6] This is the kind of senseless thinking that can proliferate only in a society that has not learned to ex-trapolate facts, that doesn't value honest analysis of widely accessible data. A slightly lower number of Americans (17 percent) believed Obama was a Muslim, according to a Pew survey conducted almost four years into his presidency, another absurd belief given the available facts.[7] Obama was raised a freethinker by a secular humanist mother and was nonreligious well into adulthood; when he finally joined a church, it was a Protestant con-gregation in Chicago. Whether one supports Obama or not, there is simply no factual basis for a belief that he is a Muslim. Yet the conviction persists.

When more rational Americans criticize or ridicule blatant public ig-norance, they run the risk of being called elitist, which is a right-wing code word for those opposed to anti-intellectualism. This is another example of the contrast between the anti-intellectualism of conservatives and the free-thinking of progressives. The typical progressive is not an elitist but merely one whose habits of thought are sufficiently independent. Of course, all hu-mans are susceptible to lazy thinking, groupthink, and emotional appeals, but the freethinker is at least mindful of such tendencies and, therefore, more likely to be on guard against them. No individual is always rational, and few would want a world without emotional impulses and spontaneity, but an appreciation of rational and critical thinking, especially on the sub-ject of politics and public policy, is hardly in itself elitist. In fact, accusations of such are surely a sign of affirmative anti-intellectualism.

Rational debate becomes impossible when anti-intellectualism has taken root, because the anti-intellectual position is usually based on fear, unsupported prejudices, or some other irrational impulse, making it im-mune to the influence of facts and data. One could try to reason with the enraged citizen who screams, "Keep your government hands off my Medicare!"—but it probably won't work.[8] Even if one gently points out that Medicare is itself a government program, the mind-set of the angry citizen rarely changes. Similarly, the panic-stricken belief that Obama's Affordable Care Act, better known as Obamacare, will eventually result in some kind of quasi-Stalinist "death panels"—an idea that gained currency as the bill was being debated—is usually unmoved by pesky facts.

To be sure, there are many sensible arguments in opposition to the Af-fordable Care Act: that it forces individuals to purchase health insurance, to the great benefit of profit-driven corporate entities; that it's a cash cow for the pharmaceutical industry and other medical businesses; and certainly that universal, single-payer health care could deliver quality health care more efficiently and affordably. But these objections get less airtime than positions that stoke irrational fear. Even after the law was implemented, Representative Michele Bachmann (R-MN) warned that "it will be very unpleasant if the death panels go into effect," describing them, baselessly, as "the greatest fear that Americans have."[9]

Now, factual inaccuracies, stupid arguments, and fear-based manipulation are nothing new in politics, nor are they uniquely American, but the heights of idiocy reached in the modern American dialogue are downright embarrassing. Anti-intellectualism is not just a reality but a point of pride for many officeholders and candidates. Examples of this are abundant, but the poster boy for American anti-intellectualism is, of course, George W. Bush, who scorned analytical thinking and instead made decisions from his "gut," regularly mispronounced common words, and relied on fundamentalist religious leaders for policy advice. Such traits would be less troublesome if we were discussing the leader of an obscure backwater republic, but Bush of course was commander in chief of the world's most powerful military, a fact that became clear as he defied world opinion and stormed into Iraq in 2003, with horrific consequences.

Under Bush, America and the rest of the world saw the disastrous results of the rise of the Religious Right. Bush did not just pander to religious conservatives, he was one of them; and despite his rhetoric of "compassionate conservatism," his hard-right policies made clear that he saw egalitarianism—in either its social or economic form—as anathema. And not surprisingly, after eight years of his presidency, the country was absolutely devastated, in complete financial collapse at home and grossly overextended overseas.

REAL CHANGE YOU CAN BELIEVE IN

Coming out of the Bush years, many saw the need for change—thus giving Barack Obama his campaign theme in 2008: "Change we can believe in"—and the country did move to the left in electing Obama and a Democratic majority in Congress. Yet any "change" has been incremental at best. Underlying assumptions that obstruct egalitarian policy too often go unchallenged, meaning that all feasible policy options, even those coming from liberals, tend to reinforce a system that serves institutional interests rather than those of ordinary citizens.

To see what I mean, let's take a cursory look at the Obama administration. Despite all the alarmist rhetoric about Obama being a liberal extremist, his administration immediately bowed to almighty Wall Street in a manner not all that distinguishable from a GOP administration. As the economy was collapsing in 2008 and 2009 due to a financial crisis triggered by irresponsible practices of major investment banks, the incoming Obama turned to Wall Street insiders to lead his economic policymaking team. "The omnipresence of Goldman Sachs does make one wonder about the insularity of this world," wrote *Newsweek* economics correspondent Michael Hirsh. "Is there no one else to fix the crisis but specialists from the company that created it?" Referring to the "Wall Street–Treasury complex," a term coined by economist Jagdish Bhahwati, Hirsh went on to ask: "If Wall Street elites continue to make government policy, will the new regulatory controls we hear so much about—the ones that are supposed to prevent this from happening again—ever really be adopted?"[10]

Given the economic mess the country was in, one could perhaps defend Obama's enlistment of Wall Street insiders for advice and assistance as necessary crisis management, but the facts show that a cozy relationship between Democrats and major investment banks and other corporate interests is the norm, not the exception. Obama's 2008 campaign received $42 million from "Wall Street bankers and financial insiders," according to a report verified by factcheck.org—more than any other candidate in history, even adjusted for inflation.[11] And Obama is no anomaly among Democrats in cozying up to Wall Street. Bill Clinton's treasury secretary, Robert Rubin, spent 26 years with Goldman Sachs before joining the Clinton administration. Larry Summers, who also served as treasury secretary under Clinton, is famously reported to have asked in more than one White House meeting, "What would Goldman think?"[12] And the marriage of the Clintons and Goldman Sachs became quite literal in 2010, when Chelsea Clinton wed Marc Mezvinsky, a veteran of the investment firm.

Progressives who criticize the role of Wall Street insiders in policy making often risk being called unrealistic—after all, who could be more qualified to run the economy than the brightest minds from America's top financial institutions? This argument, however, reflects a basic misunderstanding of the progressive view, because few progressives would deny that America's economic policy makers should have the financial experience needed to navigate the complex issues inherent in the job. No one would argue that the economy should simply be turned over to academic theorists who lack real-world experience.

But it's beyond troubling that both sides fail to acknowledge that the interests of large corporations often run directly contrary to those of ordinary citizens. Democratic leaders may pay a bit more lip service to the need for regulation of those interests, but in the end they almost always yield to them. If we examine the issue critically, staying firmly grounded in reality but also willing to question fundamental assumptions, we find deep systemic flaws that cannot be easily reversed but must be.

When one speaks of systemic problems and the need for major change, the question inevitably arises as to whether the sought-after change is realistic. There is surely a time and place for grandiose theorizing, and no doubt some of humanity's biggest breakthroughs would never have happened without it. Outside-the-box thinking often comes from the minds of those who can be described as freethinkers—from Albert Einstein to Steven Hawking—but an abstract mind-set can become a handicap in the world of practical politics, and this book is less about theory and more about the practical and the possible. Therefore, for example, while excessive corporate power is a big part of the problem in America today, serious progressives don't suggest abolishing corporations as a solution. Similarly, while excessive governmental power is also problematic, the dismantling of government is not a real option.

The American system needs major change, even radical change, but the modern progressive movement must operate within the framework of the real world, not theory. The country has veered away from some of its founding principles, but the remedy should not require complete upheaval. With workable changes aimed at underlying problems—a recognition of the need to intelligently control all forms of institutional power; a true appreciation of diversity, equality, and individual rights; a stronger commitment to reason and critical thinking—we can get to a better place.

FREETHINKERS AND LIBERTARIANISM

This preference for the practical over the theoretical is part of the reason why most freethinkers do not see libertarianism, or at least economic libertarianism, as the answer to America's problems. At first glance, libertarianism, with its minimalist approach to government, seems consistent with the freethinking inclination to question authority. (After all, few institutions are more synonymous with authority than government!) For this reason I often say, only half-jokingly, that every intelligent young person should go through a libertarian stage. When young people ponder their individual autonomy in relation to the power of the state, it's only natural that libertarian ideas would have an allure. But as we'll see, it seems just as predictable that most rational minds eventually will realize that the virtual elimination of government is hardly the best solution.

In fact, libertarianism applied to social issues—under a guiding principle that government shouldn't regulate personal behavior that harms no third party—poses few core philosophical problems for most progressives and freethinkers. Reasonable minds may of course have different opinions on issues such as legalizing recreational drugs or prostitution, for example, but many progressives and freethinkers are sympathetic to the general libertarian view that private behavior should not be dictated by the government. To many, this sympathy still won't translate to support for a Wild West legalization and deregulation of such activities, but it will at least indicate a general open-mindedness. And importantly, it will also repudiate the fear-based "tough on crime" and "war on drugs" appeals that so commonly emanate from conservatives, underlining that most social issues have numerous levels of complexity that require more serious consideration.

The good-and-evil rhetoric of the Right on social issues tends to drive away progressives and social libertarians alike, and it's noteworthy that the simplistic nature of the moralistic appeals reflects the anti-intellectualism upon which the modern conservative movement so often relies. Note also that such rhetoric plays both to the conservative religious base (by portraying many issues as the righteous against the evildoers and advocating harsh punishment for the bad guys) and to anti-egalitarian sensibilities (by inevitably targeting the poor and minorities as the most likely to receive the government's "tough on crime" wrath).

Economic libertarianism, meanwhile, is another matter altogether. Here we have an ideology that, especially in the form advocated by major think tanks and other high-profile proponents, would dismantle government while empowering corporate interests at the expense of ordinary people. Under this banner and the "free markets" rhetoric that accompanies it, major institutional interests—that is, *corporate* interests—have cynically seized control of the American system in recent decades, enriching themselves while making a mockery of both the democratic process and the small-government philosophy that they claim to espouse.

So while economic libertarianism has never been, and will never be, actually applied in the real world, the theory itself provides invaluable legitimacy to anti-egalitarian interests. Corporations seeking to avoid regulation use libertarian theory to support their position, as do politicians demanding tax cuts for the rich and opposing social safety nets, whether it be food stamps, unemployment insurance, or Social Security. So it's no surprise that major donations flow from the corporate sector to libertarian think tanks such as the Cato Institute (with a budget of over $22 million) and the American Enterprise Institute ($38 million) to promote ideas and policies that validate stripping government of its regulatory powers over major corporations.[13]

It is predictable, though nonetheless troubling, that vocal libertarian sympathizers tend to be rich white men. "I don't believe in safety nets," declared John Elway, the retired NFL quarterback who now runs football operations for the Denver Broncos. "I believe we're given the opportunity to succeed or not succeed. . . . My philosophy is when given the opportunity to go take advantage of that."[14] Of course, not everyone is "given the opportunity"— genetically or otherwise—of earning millions of dollars for playing professional sports, but this doesn't seem to concern Elway. Such a statement, coming from a strong, rich, exceptionally talented white guy—a man who enjoys much more privilege than most people could ever imagine—reeks of audacity, but to that we also can add a smidge of hypocrisy: Elway voiced no objections when taxpayers doled out $300 million to build his football team a new stadium. That's quite a safety net.

In fact, there's a good deal of hypocrisy in the reliance of American conservatives on libertarian arguments to justify tax cuts and business deregulation. Economic libertarianism, after all, is supposed to be much more than just low taxes and deregulation; its raison d'être is the downsizing of government. This, however, would interfere with the enormous government contracts that so many corporations enjoy, so it's not a serious goal that conservatives actually seek. Libertarian advocates in Washington, funded by large corporate interests, are quite effective at promoting lower taxes and the deregulation of corporate activity, but meanwhile the overall size of government continues to swell. Even under supposedly "conservative" administrations, the money flowing into and out of government—almost always to major corporations, especially in the defense establishment—is staggering, as we will see.

Not surprisingly, the antigovernment rhetoric that naturally accompanies libertarian philosophy resonates when it is directed at populist issues such as lowering taxes. In recent years the top marginal federal income tax rate has been around 35 percent, and conservative lawmakers go ballistic at the suggestion of even modest increases. Historically, however, such rates are extremely low, and in fact top tax brackets were around 50 percent during the Reagan years, even higher (70 percent to 90 percent) throughout America's prosperous decades following the Second World War.[15] Nevertheless, despite historically low rates, great political pressure forces many contemporary politicians to sign a "taxpayer protection pledge" promising to oppose *any* tax increases for individuals or business. Grover Norquist, the leader of Americans for Tax Reform, explained the political leverage in a CNN interview: "The American taxpayers are a powerful force. They don't want their taxes raised. Obama and the Democrats have a fight with the American people, not with me."[16]

What Norquist doesn't adequately explain, and can't, is why ordinary Americans would vehemently oppose raising taxes on only the richest percentage of the nation, thereby starving government of necessary revenue.

In contemporary America, somewhat paradoxically, high-profile politicians claiming libertarian credentials tend to surface in the Republican Party, which of course is hostile to the idea that government should stay out of the personal lives of its citizens. This results in supposedly libertarian-leaning politicians, such as Kentucky senator Rand Paul and Wisconsin representative Paul Ryan, advocating for anti-libertarian positions on social issues consistent with the positions of religious conservatives within their party. Neither supports a woman's right to choose, for example, neither supports marriage equality, and neither supports the legalization of drugs or prostitution. Thus, while conservative politicians paint themselves as defenders of personal liberty, and while libertarian think tanks enjoy lucrative funding and high-profile stature in today's Washington, true libertarians remain as frustrated as ever, as no candidates really support their agenda, the size of government grows, and the extent of government meddling in the private lives of its citizens increases.

Interestingly, while most progressives and freethinkers are not economic libertarians, they share some of the broader frustrations of libertarians. Whereas libertarians tend to see big government as the problem, the critically thinking progressive sees a more nuanced situation. Aspects of government are indeed worthy of harsh appraisal—it is too big, too wasteful and inefficient, reflects the wrong priorities, and so on—but that is largely due to special interests, particularly corporate interests, that have undue influence. In the next chapter we take a closer look at those interests, and we see how they've obstructed the progressive agenda.

THREE

OF PEOPLE AND HUMANS

WHEN LIBERTARIAN SENTIMENTS TAKE A POPULIST FORM, IT LOOKS like this: a mix of anger, fear, anti-intellectualism, and fierce antigovernment hostility. Welcome to the Tea Party movement.

"Government is not the answer to the problem, government *is* the problem," declared Senator Rand Paul, quoting Ronald Reagan, in the official Tea Party response to the president's State of the Union address in 2013. The Kentucky Republican was so keen on that quote that he used it again in his 2014 State of the Union response, going on to decry "burdensome, job-killing regulations" and sing the praise of lower taxes and small government. Striking all the right rhetorical chords, his 2014 speech told the story of a drug-abusing welfare mother who took advantage of the system, profiting from government-run daycare centers, free medical vouchers, and food stamps—then turned her life around by rejecting those state handouts. Paul's message was clear: Government programs "suffocate our resolve to better ourselves and our country," whereas "hard work and sweat invigorate the spirit."[1]

First materializing in the early days of the Obama administration in 2009, the Tea Party phenomenon illustrates how anti-egalitarian policy, which benefits an elite few at the expense of the many, can be sold effectively to a mass audience. Moreover, although its core themes of lower taxes and smaller government have nothing to do with religion, the Tea Party also demonstrates how religious fundamentalism is never far from conservative political activism in modern American politics. (Rand's anecdotal welfare mother, for example, attributed her newfound prosperity not only to rejecting government aid but to "trusting God.")[2] This only further demonstrates why progressives can and should utilize reason as a potent antidote to such populist conservatism.

A high point for the Tea Party movement came in September 2009, when a massive crowd of protesters (estimates vary, but most agree that at least 75,000 were on hand) rallied outside the Capitol in Washington to take a stand against what they saw as big government. "Terrorists won't destroy America, Congress will!" declared one sign. "The American dream R.I.P.," said another. "You want socialism?" cried one protester. "Go to Russia!"[3] With intense animus directed toward the Democratic president and his plan to provide health care for all, the demonstrators seemed oblivious to the unprecedented expansion of federal government that had occurred under the recently departed Bush administration—the creation of a Department of Homeland Security, the widening of Medicare to cover prescription drugs, the funneling billions of dollars to religious groups through a new Office of Faith-Based Initiatives, the new police powers created by the Patriot Act. Along with the accusations of socialism were expressions of love for freedom, and many of the demonstrators seemed to claim great expertise in constitutional law, insisting that Obama's efforts to expand health care were unconstitutional. Although the Supreme Court itself would disagree three years later, one protester held a sign, typical of many, deriding Obama's "blatant disregard for the Constitution," telling a reporter that he reached his opinions by watching Fox News host Glenn Beck "all the time."[4]

While a reliable segment of the American population has always had sympathy for small government and low taxes, the orchestration of this modern grassroots antigovernment movement would have been impossible without a solid foundation of religious conservatives. Distrust of government (with the glaring exception of the military), hatred of socialism, and a willingness to declare themselves the true patriots (and their opponents un-American) have always been core themes of the Religious Right, and the Tea Party provided the perfect outlet for such sentiments. It's not surprising that a Bloomberg survey found that Tea Party members were not only older and whiter than the population as a whole but also more likely to describe themselves as "born again."[5]

Because of this conservative religious influence, the Tea Party agenda, as it evolved, expanded far beyond the need to downsize government, eventually echoing the God-and-country righteousness of the Religious Right's messaging machine. Thus, although the Tea Party is sometimes described as a libertarian movement, that applies only to certain economic issues, not social issues. The Tea Party Caucus in Congress was founded and led by Representative Michele Bachmann, a stalwart of the Religious Right, and all of its fifty-plus members are Republicans, most of whom are social conservatives.[6] Polling by Pew confirms the socially conservative slant of Tea Party supporters, showing that they are much more likely than the population at large to oppose reproductive rights for women, same-sex marriage, and open borders for immigration. Tea Partiers were also much more likely to say that religion was the top influence in shaping their opinion on social issues. Of all religious groups, white evangelicals were most likely (44 percent) to say they agree with the Tea Party. The figure was only 12 percent among atheists/agnostics and only 7 percent among black Protestants—the two smallest categories.[7]

I experienced the Tea Party's interest in noneconomic issues firsthand when I argued a case challenging the "under God" language of the Pledge of Allegiance before the Massachusetts Supreme Judicial Court in 2013. Though the case had no inherent connection to the issues of small government or low taxes, I nevertheless saw sharp attacks from Tea Partiers. On a Web site called the Tea Party Command Center, under a headline declaring that the pledge challenge was an "Attack on America's Soul," an article connected the "under God" issue to core Tea Party themes by insisting that such challenges are part of an effort "to create a socialist nation" and undermine "basic biblical principles of character and heartland values."[8] (I put such articles, along with angry correspondences I received, in a folder labeled "Love Letters.")

Now, with a decade of culture war activism under my belt, it would take more than the ranting of a few Tea Partiers to hurt my feelings. I can't help but chuckle, for example, at the call for "biblical principles of character." If we followed such instructions, we would have a society in which men refuse to accept women as teachers or authority figures of any kind (1

Timothy 2:12); slavery is acceptable (1 Peter 2:18 and others); and death is the punishment for adultery (Leviticus 20:10–12), lying about virginity (Deuteronomy 22:20–21), prostitution (Leviticus 21:9), being the victim of rape and not being sufficiently vocal in screaming for help (Deuteronomy 22:23–27), and engaging in homosexual sex (Leviticus 18:22), among others. Even the morality of Jesus is sometimes questionable, such as when he instructs followers in Luke 14:26 that they must "hate" their families if they wish to be his disciples. Of course, some will insist that all of these horrible moral standards can be explained—that they are taken out of context (which leaves me wondering what context would allow the killing of a girl for lying about her virginity); that they are misunderstood; or that they no longer apply but that other, more admirable, biblical maxims (such as the Golden Rule) are still valid—but such rationalizing seems to be little more than cherry-picking.

The Tea Party and the sentiments that drive it, however, are no laughing matter, as angry conservative populism has elected a slew of severely conservative politicians across the country. Governor Scott Walker of Wisconsin is a good example; he is a young conservative who has attacked unions, public education, and Medicaid funding with a zeal that old-time conservatives rarely showed. Elected in 2011, Walker so enraged citizens that they petitioned for a recall election in 2012. He was supported by the Tea Party in that election, however, and survived the challenge.[9] Fitting the mold of a Tea Party darling, Walker is not only hostile to collective bargaining rights and other liberal economic linchpins, he is also an evangelical Christian who opposes abortion in all cases, even rape and incest.[10] He signed a bill in 2013 requiring women seeking an abortion to undergo an ultrasound and establishing unnecessary, obstructive qualifications for doctors performing abortions.[11]

To say that progressives are usually opposed to Tea Party policy positions would be putting it mildly, but we should nevertheless acknowledge that a few morsels of legitimacy can be found in some Tea Party rhetoric. The general concern over expanding government power, for example, is not so absurd. Rather than dismissively rejecting Tea Party supporters, progressives would be wise to point the public dialogue in a constructive direction: *Yes, Mr. and Ms. Tea Party, government power must indeed be kept in check, but we also need to pay attention to other forms of concentrated power that work against the interests of ordinary citizens like you and me—and there are many!* In doing this, we shouldn't expect to convert the Tea Party crowd en masse to progressive politics, but we might be able to extinguish some of the populist antigovernment anger and redirect some of the grassroots energy toward a more productive agenda.

NONHUMAN PEOPLE

"Power to the people!" was once a rallying cry for those who sought direct political action. Popularized by John Lennon through a song by the same name, it was a call for real participatory democracy, a declaration that the will of the people cannot be crushed by any governmental institution.

Unfortunately, however, it's an inadequate prescription for our current ills, because "people" are already in control. The problem is that those "people" are not human—they're corporations. That is, in today's America, *corporations are people.* And thanks to the success of the conservative movement, unrestrained corporate interests maintain a tight control over the American system, at the expense of actual human beings and real democracy. Thus, as odd as it sounds, progressives and others interested in human-centered public policy must determine how to seize control of the system from *corporate* people and effectively give it to *real* people, or *humans.*

The issue of corporate personhood vaulted to the front pages in 2010, when the Supreme Court ruled on *Citizens United v. Federal Election Commission,* holding that certain political spending restrictions aimed at corporations violated First Amendment free speech protections. In fact, however, the problem of corporate personhood goes back to the nineteenth century, when the nature of corporations began to change radically, evolving from extremely rare and highly regulated legal entities to a common and largely unregulated business model. The *Citizens United* decision is just the latest chapter in the long saga of these large institutional interests overtaking the interests of flesh-and-blood Americans. This historical context helps us understand not only how corporations came to be so excessively powerful in America, but why they should be restrained.

Before embarking on that discussion, however, it must be noted that the issue of corporatism alone should refute any argument for economic libertarianism. Corporations, of course, do not exist in a state of nature, as they can be created and maintained only via government action. Statutes, passed by the government, allow for the creation of corporations, and anyone wishing to form one must fill out the necessary government paperwork and utilize the apparatus of the state in numerous ways. Thus, the corporate entity is by definition a government-created obstruction to the free marketplace, so the entire concept should be appalling to libertarians, who loathe any government activity beyond the bare-bones necessities. A true libertarian would instead advocate for enterprise via traditional common-law means, mainly proprietorships and partnerships, but you don't see Rand Paul or his brethren touting this path. Instead, they wield their claimed ideology to unleash corporate power in a fully deregulated environment.

Contrary to popular understanding, the notion of a corporation being a person is in fact inherent in the corporate concept. The word "corporation" derives etymologically from the same roots as the word "corpse" (meaning "body"), and the corporate entity has always been understood legally as a fictitious body, or person. In eighteenth-century England and its American colonies—and also in the early decades of the United States— corporations were extremely rare, because special permission from the crown or the legislature was needed to create one. (One could not, as one can today, choose to set up a corporation by simply filing paperwork with a government office.)

Corporate legal status provides exceptional benefits for shareholders, protections that do not exist with ordinary noncorporate business entities such as sole proprietorships or partnerships, and therefore corporate status was a rare privilege reserved for those few instances where the crown or the legislature felt it was *in the public interest* to allow it. Permission to incorporate was granted only for exceptional situations, often connected with high-risk ventures involving shipping on the high seas (such as the British East India Company, which played an important role in asserting British influence around the globe), because such circumstances justified giving investors the special protections that corporate status conveys.

Conservatives today like to talk about free markets, where corporations can operate without regulation, but in the early days of capitalism, corporate activity was itself seen as *unnatural* and *contrary* to market freedom.

Unlike other business models, the corporation not only allowed individuals to pool large amounts of money for a venture, it also allowed them to do so without the risk of any personal loss beyond the amount of their investment (as it still does today). Thus, if you own shares of a corporation and it acts negligently or breaches a contract, resulting in a huge court judgment against it, there is no chance, absent exceptional circumstances, that you will face personal exposure for that liability. This model, which naturally encouraged larger business ventures, also tended to separate ownership from management, creating a new class of characters in the general scheme of commerce: investors and professional managers.

Because corporations were a departure from the norm, attractive to investors for obvious reasons but an affront to classical free markets, governments were hesitant to allow them, doing so only when there seemed to be no alternative, and then only under strictly regulated terms. Corporations were required to act only within the narrow confines of expressly defined activity and could be dissolved by the government if they were seen as acting against the public interest. This was all considered sensible, because corporate activity was correctly understood as potentially dangerous. Left unchecked, the well-financed corporation could wreak havoc on both private markets and the public sector, asserting undue influence on both.

Free market advocates today like to claim to be the rightful heirs to Adam Smith, whose 1776 treatise *The Wealth of Nations* is frequently cited to explain the fundamental principles of capitalism. "What America needs is not Robin Hood but Adam Smith" is one of Rand Paul's favorite sayings.[12] In fact, however, such claims of free market purity badly misconstrue Smith and his doctrines, as the eighteenth-century Scotsman actually opposed the notion of corporate power. Smith, writing before the rise of the modern corporation, presents a vision of efficient capitalism through local ownership and small scale, not corporations. He even criticized the idea of any business model that would separate ownership from management, because in such situations the managers would be overseeing "other people's money." Such a quaint view of economics is so far removed from today's world, where immensely powerful multinational corporations exert staggering power across the globe, that it almost seems irrelevant. This is no criticism of Smith but of those who would dishonestly enlist him as the patron saint of today's predatory corporatism.

Though writing on the other side of the Atlantic, Smith was a contemporary of America's founders, and of course their economic views likewise predate the rise of corporate power as we know it. Like Smith, they would have understood incorporation as an exceptional and privileged status arising only from a special grant by the sovereign. The framers' understanding of the corporation is described well by Scott Horton, a legal scholar from Columbia University. Lecturing on the subject of corporate power, Horton cites James Madison's opposition to Alexander Hamilton's proposal to charter a Bank of the United States for context: "Madison began by stressing that corporations, unlike natural persons, had only the exact measure of rights that was conferred upon them by the state in express terms," Horton explains. "[I]n other words, they did not have 'inalienable rights' which arose under natural law, like the 'people of the United States' invoked at the outset of the Constitution."[13]

Thus, even though corporations can be seen correctly as creating a sort of fictional person, the idea that such nonhuman people would enjoy "inalienable rights" would be anathema to the man primarily responsible for writing the Constitution. Corporations in the late eighteenth and early nineteenth centuries were so different from those of today—many were chartered for nonprofit educational or religious purposes, for example, while the few for-profit corporations that were chartered usually were created for a very specific and finite purpose, such as building a canal or a bridge—that today's corporate environment would have been *unimaginable* to the framers. Madison called the ability of religious corporations in his day to accumulate property and hold it forever, beyond the mortal lives of founders and shareholders (a privilege that all corporations today enjoy), an "evil which ought to be guarded against."[14]

Such skepticism of corporate power is absent from today's libertarian and conservative movements, which in fact are fueled by corporate interests. Searching the term "abolish" on the Cato Institute's Web site, for example, will result in a long list of articles calling for the abolition of the minimum wage, abolition of various governmental agencies, abolition of the income tax, abolition of jobs programs, and abolition of other governmental activities, but the notion of abolishing *government-created corporations* is nowhere to be found. In fact, Cato and other leading libertarian think tanks act as stern apologists for corporate power, having blind faith that the corporate-dominated marketplace can regulate itself efficiently. This is delusional, unsupported by empirical evidence.

Those seeking rational public policy view all concentrated power—not just governmental but corporate as well—with suspicion, understanding the need for pragmatic regulation of corporate activity. As we'll see, unrestrained corporate power virtually guarantees anti-egalitarian outcomes, as corporate entities and their owners—which also usually are not humans but other corporations—enrich themselves at the expense of everyone else.

Imagine what Smith, Madison, or anyone else who was alive over two centuries ago would think of modern society, where the entire economic engine is driven by corporate activity, virtually all daily activity involves the use of corporate products, and corporate interests exercise immense influence on the political process—where, in short, corporate interests are the dominant institutions in society. If corporations were benevolent, working for the greater good of humanity, this might not be so problematic. But as we'll see, such is not the case.

WHAT KIND OF PEOPLE?

If corporations are people, they're not the kind of people you'd want to take home to meet your parents. Imagine a person who is totally self-absorbed, greedy, phony, amoral at best, and downright immoral at worst. And if that's not bad enough, corporate "people" are also rich, immune from physical injury, and, for all practical purposes, immortal.

Knowing this, it's a bit bizarre that the Right immediately decries any attempt to rein in corporate power as "socialist." This is where anti-egalitarian interests, which are synonymous with the interests of corporations and the richest individuals, get a payoff from their marriage with religious conservatives. Most religious fundamentalists are not personally wealthy, and their interests certainly don't align with those of major corporations and the richest individuals. Yet they vigorously support pro-corporate public policy. They do so partly because the politicians advocating it also support fundamentalist positions on social issues, but there is another, more ominous reason: With anti-intellectualism so widespread and corporate messaging power so vast, socially conservative voters often are duped into believing that the pro-corporate position is actually in their best interests. Thus, they support anti-egalitarian economic policies not as a compromise in order to advance their social agenda, but because they sincerely believe the corporatist propaganda.

Most of us understand that corporations often act against the interests of the general public, but few understand why. Corporate wrongdoing, whether criminal or just immoral, usually is not an accident of judgment by corporate officers or agents but is necessitated by the very nature of corporate management and governance. "The corporation's legally defined mandate is to pursue, relentlessly and without exception, its own self-interest, regardless of the often harmful consequences it might cause to others," writes Joel Bakan in his masterful 2004 book, *The Corporation: The Pathological Pursuit of Profit and Power*, which was also made into a documentary.[15]

Pathological is indeed the right word, for no real "person" with the psychological profile of a corporation would be considered stable or healthy. Those managing a corporation are duty-bound to shareholders to earn maximum profit, and this fiduciary responsibility cannot be hindered by pesky concerns such as the health or safety of employees or the general public—unless the law requires it. If there were not laws protecting workers or consumers from corporate wrongdoing, you can rest assured that corporations would run roughshod over them, except to the extent that sales and profits were affected. In fact, this was the reality of nineteenth-century capitalism before the rise of progressive reforms.

To truly digest the awesome repercussions for a society wherein these artificial people—corporations—wield such enormous power, we need a little distance. Living in modern society, constantly seeing corporate symbols and products all around us and absorbing nonstop advertising and publicity from the corporate sector, is bound to dull our judgment a bit. We also know that undeveloped countries lacking a visible corporate culture (and the consumer products that accompany it) seem, at least to the spoiled Westerner, to be "behind" the rest of the world. And those of us old enough to remember the Cold War can recall that even the developed nations of the Soviet bloc seemed somehow stark, lacking the commercial vibrancy and comforts of the First World. (Of course, the political repression behind the Iron Curtain contributed to this stark image as well.) Thus, for most of us, corporate images and brands are ingrained aspects of life, often more a positive than a negative. Only by truly understanding the complexity of corporatism's impact on society—that it's not simply a matter of black and white or good and bad—can we appreciate its insidious nature and the need for critical dissection and reassessment.

Technology has raced forward over the last two centuries, and the corporation often has been the main vehicle that delivers these advancements to the general population. That doesn't change the fact that corporations will harm you, or even kill you, if it is profitable to do so and they can get away with it. And the bigger the corporation—the more removed its ownership and management is from knowing you personally—the more dangerous it is.

If the previous paragraph sounds like hyperbole, be assured it is not. One might argue that while corporations have no innate moral compass, the people who run them do, but the nature of corporate structure minimizes any such nagging human moral hesitations. Because a corporation's officers are *required* to maximize growth and *must* answer to investors (which often are institutions themselves), their moral preferences become irrelevant. As we go down the ladder the moral landscape gets no better. Middle-level and lower-level employees must answer to their superiors, so again the only universal goal is to increase sales and maximize profits.

Moreover, the nature of corporate action, where bureaucracy dictates that most of the actors are far removed from the actual harm that might occur as a result of their decisions, increases the likelihood of egregious conduct. This explains why a tobacco executive, who might admonish his own teenager for smoking, would nevertheless be part of a decision-making process that would aggressively market his company's product to other children if the law allowed. Recall the infamous case of the Ford Pinto: in the 1970s the automaker did a cost-benefit analysis and decided not to remedy a defective gas tank design because doing so would be more expensive than simply allowing the inevitable deaths and injuries to occur and then paying the anticipated settlements.[16]

Tobacco companies and exploding Pintos are obvious examples, but they share two common denominators with countless other lesser-known instances of corporate malfeasance: They all result from the systemic pursuit of profit, and they all require government intervention or regulation to remedy. Corporate behavior against the public interest is inevitable, not just a result of bad decision making, because the growth-centered structure of the corporation requires it; and the only counterbalance to that inclination is a strong legal and regulatory apparatus. If corporations have no moral compass—and they don't—then morality must be *imposed* on them through the law. The alternative would be to allow these immensely powerful, psychopathic "people" to operate unchecked, throwing their weight around in society in a way that ordinary people can't. This may be the libertarian dream, but for most of us it would be a nightmare.

WHEN NONHUMANS OWN NONHUMANS

It's important to note that not all corporations are the same and that smaller, locally owned, closed corporations (corporations whose shares are not publicly traded on the stock market) are much more likely to be responsive to their communities, their consumers, and society at large. The owners of such corporations have reason to be concerned with their image and reputation in the community, and they are not under intense pressure from institutional investors to meet quarterly profit-growth expectations. Publicly traded corporations, however, which increasingly comprise the bulk of America's economic engine, are an entirely different animal; their officers are almost always far removed from the communities their products and services affect. Those officers have no worries about their personal reputations on Main Street, but they spend enormous time and energy attending to the concerns of Wall Street, where analysts and institutional investors await quarterly earnings reports with great anticipation. (These earnings reports are what make not just profit but *short-term* profit so critical to the American system. If quarterly earnings are off by even a few cents per share from analyst expectations, the stock price will surely drop—the worst of all possible disasters for the publicly traded corporation.)

The growth and consolidation of publicly traded corporations has increased rapidly in recent years, so much so that now it would be an oversimplification to suggest that major corporations generally are owned by rich shareholders. The corporate system has become so massive and complex that most corporations are not even owned by humans anymore; instead, they are owned by *other corporations*.

Just as an example, and not a unique one by any means, consider the ownership of General Electric, in which the largest institutional investors hold over 400 million shares each, and even the twentieth-largest institutional investor holds over 70 million shares.[17] No real human shareholder comes close to these figures (the largest individual shareholder held just over one million shares).[18] GE's corporate shareholders, meanwhile, are themselves owned by other corporations. State Street Corporation, a top GE shareholder, is itself owned almost entirely (91 percent) by institutional investors, and many of those institutions are corporations in which State Street owns shares.[19] The closer we look, the more we see that real humans (and human interests) are far removed from the system. And this is the norm on Wall Street.

The fact that real-life human ownership is so far removed from the typical corporate "person" in America has profound implications, yet the issue is totally absent in the bombast of American politics. Even if the Tea Party and its sympathizers are correct in their general criticism of federal government power, their solution—to allow profit-obsessed and growth-obsessed corporate interests to rule the land—is staggeringly myopic and contrary to reason.

In considering all of this, we must bear in mind the truly narcissistic personality of these corporate "persons." Everything they do—even charity—is motivated by their own self-promotion. In an article bluntly titled "The Social Responsibility of Business Is to Increase Profits," economist Milton Friedman (1912–2006), an icon of American libertarianism, pointed out that officers who direct corporate assets toward charity are breaching their fiduciary duty unless they can show that doing so somehow adds to the corporate bottom line.[20] In essence, charitable actions must be justified as having *public relations* value, improving the corporation's image in the public eye, or some other institutional value. This should not be surprising, since the corporation itself, not being human, cannot possibly have compassion or empathy for real humans, and corporate officers are forbidden by their fiduciary duty from wasting corporate resources.

Nor should the public image motive surprise us when we consider the immense resources that corporations spend on shaping our opinions and even our desires. Annual advertising industry revenues worldwide today are estimated at well over half a trillion dollars, almost all arising from corporate "persons" promoting themselves and their products.[21] Imagine a real person spending that much money on sophisticated media efforts to get you to like, feel good about, and have a certain image of him. (The only thing that comes close, of course, would be political candidate advertising.) We all accept corporate self-promotion as part of our social landscape, and we can even concede that it serves a practical purpose, but from the standpoint of corporate personhood the narcissistic nature of such promotion is undeniable.

When we know the true nature of the corporate person, we see even the most seemingly benevolent corporate actions through new eyes. When CVS, the second largest pharmacy chain in America, announced in 2014 that it would stop selling tobacco products, most politicians and media reacted as if the move could be understood only as a corporation acting with no motive but to promote public health. The chain would lose $2 billion in annual revenue, reports said, and its willingness to sacrifice that cash flow is a clear indication that it cares about the greater good. Even the White House joined in the praise of CVS, saying it was a "powerful example" that would "reduce tobacco-related deaths, cancer, and heart disease, as well as bring down health care costs."[22]

Perhaps this is true, but it ignores how far the world of corporate balance sheets is from that of ordinary citizens. Tobacco sales, at $2 billion, still account for only about 1.6 percent of the chain's revenues, so the sacrifice can hardly be called crippling—more akin to a typical household losing about $1,000 of its annual income. And most important, this loss of revenue is part of a savvy branding and growth strategy for CVS, for the move paid enormous benefits to the chain immediately. The decision to remove tobacco received extensive media coverage, publicity that was worth millions, and it allowed CVS to position itself as the leading, forward-looking brand in the competitive world of retail pharmacies. Its competitor, Walgreens, was immediately put on the defensive, forced to say that it was "evaluating this product category" in light of the CVS move.[23] As the industry moves into the future, with large chains gobbling up smaller pharmacies, the move by CVS can be seen not so much as corporate compassion but as a brilliant business decision that will benefit its public image and brand appeal for many years to come. Given that the CVS corporation is itself owned almost entirely by institutional investors and mutual fund companies, such as Vanguard, State Street, and Fidelity—entities that demand a return on investment and closely scrutinize the financials of the companies they own—there is no reason to believe that CVS management allowed benevolence to trump the interests of shareholders.[24]

Again, none of this criticism means the corporate model must be thrown out with the rubbish, but surely common sense requires that we keep an eye on these powerful beasts. At the very least, let's put to rest any notion that libertarianism—the dismantling of government regulation—would be the solution to the problems facing modern society.

THE NEED FOR INSTITUTIONS

As each of us wakes up each morning in our warm home, turns on the lights, makes a stop at the indoor bathroom, goes to the kitchen to get a cup of imported coffee, and unplugs our smartphone from the charger to check for messages, we have already enjoyed numerous benefits of modern, advanced civilization—technologies that would not have been available even to royalty in previous generations. In those first five minutes of the waking day, we have already interacted, directly or indirectly, with more outside institutional entities than most of our ancestors would have in a lifetime. The chains of supply that bring us all of the comforts and conveniences of modern living are incredible: providers of electricity, heating, and water and sewer; the manufacturers of the furniture, phones, and countless other products that we utilize, along with the wholesalers, transporters, and retailers of those products; the phone service company and various communications firms providing messaging and social media; and the various companies involved in importing the coffee from overseas and producing and delivering the other foodstuffs that we consume.

As we go about our day, we constantly interact with the complex web of modern technological society, and we tend to take much of it for granted. If we give it even a passing thought, however, it becomes obvious that such a society would be impossible without institutions to deliver the technology. Most of us don't even change the oil in our cars anymore, as our busy lives require us to block out twenty minutes at a local quick lube (probably a corporate-owned chain) to do that. For better or worse, we all are dependent on an immensely sophisticated infrastructure just to trudge through our daily routine. And there's no way around it: This infrastructure requires institutions. Except for the most determined recluses, the days of the lone wolf, of old-fashioned rugged individualism, are over.

If modern living necessitates institutions, the suggestion that a healthy public sector is not needed to regulate the immensely powerful corporate sector—to suggest that such governmental activity amounts to "socialism," as some conservatives would argue—is either stunningly ignorant or diabolically deceptive. The existence of such alarmist cries only points to the need for sober thinkers—who are wise enough to question concentrated power in all forms, not just governmental—to engage politically. Simplistic answers, such as the broad-brushed claim from the Right that "big government" is the source of society's ills, need rational rebuttal. The only sector benefiting from such rhetoric is the one that has been raking in profits for decades while ordinary Americans have struggled: the anti-egalitarian interests of the corporate elite.

Corporate dominance, or at least the degree of corporate dominance that we see in America today, has been made possible politically by the rise of the Religious Right, which has paved the way for anti-egalitarian policy to proliferate. Knowing that, we can see why the emergence of an organized, focused secular-progressive movement would stand as such a formidable opponent to both the Religious Right and the anti-egalitarian interests that have grown so powerful. Rational thinking, independent thinking, and an attitude of questioning *all* authority is precisely what has been lacking in America and precisely what freethinkers and progressives can deliver. As we'll see in the next chapter, the last three-plus decades are an example of what can happen in a modern society when freethinkers and progressives are suppressed.

FOUR

THE BOOMER BUST

IT WAS A BIG MOMENT FOR TED KENNEDY. HIS OCTOBER 3, 1983, VISIT to Liberty Baptist College (now Liberty University), the Lynchburg, Virginia, school founded by the Reverend Jerry Falwell, was a momentous day for both the Massachusetts senator and the fundamentalist preacher who hosted him. Falwell had stormed onto the national scene in 1980, after the new group that he led, the Moral Majority, had mobilized conservative Christians into a formidable political force (which had come to be called the Religious Right—a common term in political vernacular today but then a new phenomenon), helping to elect Ronald Reagan to the presidency.

Kennedy, an astute politician whose name was synonymous with the liberalism that both Reagan and Falwell so vocally criticized, knew he was venturing onto enemy turf. As an iconic liberal from an iconic political dynasty—having already served over two decades in the U.S. Senate—Kennedy was seen as a key figure in opposing the powerful new right-wing religious coalition, and this no doubt would be an important speech. As a liberal Democrat, Kennedy symbolized everything the Religious Right opposed, so his words would in many ways define the liberal response to the Falwell agenda. Thus, one might have hoped that Kennedy would come out with a full-frontal attack on the Christian Right's mix of religion and politics, that he would tell Falwell and his followers that professed religious faith is absolutely no indicator of "morals" or "values"—two words that religious conservatives liked to claim as uniquely theirs—and that outspoken religiosity has no place in the politics of the pluralistic society that America had become.

But if anyone had such hopes, they were quickly dashed. Instead, Kennedy pointed out that Falwell and his followers had no monopoly on religion, that liberals could also play the religion card: "I'm an American and a Catholic," the senator proudly proclaimed. "I love my country and treasure my faith!"[1]

Hence Kennedy, a high-profile leader of the opposition to the Religious Right, engaging in serious oratory on the subject of religion in politics with all eyes on him, was asserting his faith publicly as well. We liberals are religious too, he was telling Falwell and the country. *We treasure our faith!*

To be sure, Kennedy's overall message would never be mistaken for a Falwell sermon. He urged his audience to respect the separation of church and state, and he warned against the idea that any one religious group should impose its view of morality on all of society: "The real transgression occurs when religion wants government to tell citizens how to live uniquely personal parts of their lives," he said, pushing back against the righteousness that defined the Moral Majority (and continues to define its successors). But he also emphasized his own religiosity and the unquestioned importance of faith generally in America. "I hope for an America where the power of faith will always burn brightly," he said, "but where no modern Inquisition of any kind will ever light the fires of fear, coercion, or angry division." Note that the first half of that sentence could have just as easily been excerpted from a Falwell speech.

Kennedy wasn't alone among Democratic leaders embracing religion in response to the challenge of the Religious Right. Few politicians speak as easily about their faith as Bill Clinton, who always made a point of not being outdone by Republicans in enlisting Jesus. "Politics and political involvement dictated by faith is not the exclusive province of the right wing," he told an audience at Riverside Church in the summer of 2004. Delivered just before the Republican convention, the speech was laced with references to the Bible and Jesus, and it was surely intended to remind America that GOP does not stand for God's Own Party. "Religious values can include commitment to the common good, concern for the poor and vulnerable, and middle-class families, the preservation of our God-given environment, unity over division, and for truth in campaign advertising. . . . So, we have values too, those of us who respectfully disagree. And we believe God redeemed us too."[2]

Of course, there's nothing wrong with politicians occasionally discussing their religious views, but unexpected consequences can result when the highest-profile politicians *opposing* the Religious Right are publicly reassuring voters that they too look to faith to guide them, with language suggesting devout religiosity is universal among Americans. After all, millions upon millions of good, decent Americans find the idea of being "redeemed" by a divinity to be a rather puzzling and unfounded belief, yet this demographic seems invisible to politicians. Rather than elevate the dialogue beyond God-talk, Kennedy, Clinton, and others helped cultivate a political arena that oozed piety, creating an environment that insulates much of the conservative agenda from criticism. Individual liberal politicians may find electoral success by playing the religion card, but acquiescing to these rules of the game plays directly into the hand of the Religious Right.

Perhaps most important, an atmosphere of piety naturally marginalizes America's nonbelievers and religiously unaffiliated—over one-fifth of the population and growing—and gives credence to the lie that their worldview is out of the mainstream. The result is a political landscape that is far more religious—and more conservative—than society as a whole. Virtually all politicians must now pay some sort of lip service to religion. Few dare to be openly nonreligious, and nonreligious constituents are basically invisible to both politicians and the media. Everyone involved has accepted the Religious Right's game, and the center of political gravity therefore shifts rightward.

Moreover, the practice of religious politics, whether liberal or conservative, necessarily reinforces conservative elements that work against progressivism. After all, traditional religion is by definition a conservative institution, even though it sometimes contains liberal messages such as the Sermon on the Mount. Any emphasis on traditional religion through politics, therefore, is a double-edged sword at best. A message such as Clinton's, for example, can utilize traditional religion to advocate for liberal public policy, but by doing so it also indirectly validates in the public psyche the concept of religious values driving political engagement. This in turn validates all the conservative associations that might flow from linking traditional religion to politics: God-and-country patriotism, righteous militarism, the belief that America is a Christian nation, and the marginalization of religious minorities and nonbelievers.

RECIPE FOR DISASTER

After the rise of the Christian Right, some of its most vocal liberal opposition came not from politicians at all but from advocacy groups. As a direct response to the sudden emergence of the Moral Majority as a powerful force in the 1980 election, television producer Norman Lear founded the advocacy group People for the American Way (PFAW) in an effort to rebut the notion that conservative Christians were in a position to dictate morals, values, and public policy to the rest of society. As such, Lear became a prime target of scorn for fundamentalist Christian leaders. "Norman Lear is an atheist and he doesn't believe in any religious values in our life," fundamentalist leader Pat Robertson declared in 1986, adding that PFAW was promoting "radical feminism," "abortion on demand," and "casual sex."[3]

Most interestingly, however, according to a report from the *Chicago Tribune*, a PFAW spokesperson responding to Robertson's outburst "flatly denied that Lear, who is Jewish, holds to an atheist philosophy."[4] Regardless of whether Lear was an atheist—and most reports indicate that he is not, that he falls into the vague category of "spiritual but not religious"[5]—the immediate, sharp denial of the accusation reveals much about the approach of PFAW and other high-profile advocacy groups opposing the Religious Right in the early years: God forbid they associate themselves with the vilified nonbelievers!

PFAW's strategy of associating with religion—and keeping a distance from open secularity—can be seen in an early television advertisement for the group. In the ad, a blue-collar worker, complete with hard hat, beer belly, and bad grammar, leans on his forklift, looks directly into the camera, and addresses the television audience:

> I'm religious. We're a religious family, but that don't mean we see things the same way politically. Now here come certain preachers on radio, on TV, and in the mail, telling us that there's just one Christian position and implying if we don't agree we're not good Christians. So, my son is a bad Christian on two

issues. My wife is a good Christian on those issues, but a bad Christian on two others. Lucky me, I'm one hundred percent Christian because I agree with the preacher on all of them. The problem is, I know my son's as good a Christian as me. My wife? She's better! So maybe there's something wrong with people, even preachers, who suggest that other people are good Christians or bad Christians depending on their political views.[6]

The ad then concludes with information on how to contact and support PFAW.

It's not hard to understand PFAW's strategy here of pointing out that liberals can be religious too, that religious leaders shouldn't be exerting themselves in politics as Christian Right leaders were doing; but few stopped to consider at the time how this approach would completely isolate America's secular demographic, the segment of society that was probably most capable of rebutting the Religious Right's claims that religiosity was synonymous with morals and values.

Thus, the approach of the Religious Right's high-profile opposition was to concede that Americans are religious, so that the important issue to resolve was *how* America's deep religiosity should affect politics and public policy. Note that all individuals mentioned by Lear's regular-guy construction worker—his son, his wife, and himself—were described as religious. In hindsight, this ad might have had more punch if the construction worker, after describing his wife and his son as religious, had said, "And me? I'm not even religious, but who are those preachers to suggest I don't know right from wrong?"

This kind of messaging—emphasizing that we don't even need religion to be a good person and decent citizen—would have struck at the heart of the Religious Right: its claim that somehow religiosity equals morality and values. Instead, the ad's main message reinforced the importance of religion, quibbling with the Religious Right only by arguing that religious individuals can sometimes disagree on political issues. Seeing how the Religious Right's influence only expanded in subsequent years, we know now that this was a recipe for disaster.

PFAW was by no means unique in embracing religion and generally downplaying or avoiding secularity. The American Civil Liberties Union,

Americans United for Separation of Church and State (AU), and other advocacy groups played the religion card in similar ways, often by placing religious figures in leadership positions. AU is recognized as one of the country's key church-state watchdog groups, yet its executive director for over two decades has been the Reverend Barry Lynn, a graduate of Boston University's School of Theology and an ordained minister in the United Church of Christ. The clerical credentials no doubt give Lynn some clout when he takes to the airwaves to argue with religious conservatives on church-state issues. Other nonprofits were equally eager to put clerics on their boards, and in the 1990s liberal religious activists attempted to push back against fundamentalist politics by founding a new national group called the Interfaith Alliance. Headquartered in Washington and led by a Baptist minister, the Reverend Welton Gaddy, the Interfaith Alliance advocates for church-state separation, marriage equality, and other positions discordant with those of the Religious Right.

All of this, while well intended and sometimes effective, helped solidify the conventional wisdom that religion is very important in American society and must be a major factor in politics and policy making. It was in this atmosphere that Congress in 1993 overwhelmingly passed the so-called Religious Freedom Restoration Act (RFRA), which has been used to greatly expand the definition of religious freedom, often giving those with religious objections an exemption from otherwise applicable laws. RFRA passed with enthusiastic support from liberals, who have since come to see the invidiousness of religious privileging under the guise of religious freedom. With religious freedom now deserving exceptional legal status, we are seeing pharmacists use it to refuse birth control to customers, and there is considerable support, especially in traditionally conservative areas, for allowing businesses to discriminate against gays and lesbians on similar grounds.[7]

In 2014 the Supreme Court expanded the limits of religious privileging even further, interpreting RFRA to allow for-profit corporations to claim religious freedom. In *Burwell v. Hobby Lobby*, a 5–4 majority (consisting of the court's five conservative Catholic justices) ruled that religious freedom claims could be used to allow corporate employers the right to deny employees contraception coverage that otherwise would be required under federal law.[8] This troubling ruling expanded the concepts of both corporate personhood and religious privileging, while downplaying concerns about reproductive rights. We could correctly complain that such an outcome is just another example of the real-world impact of the Religious Right, but it's important to remember that RFRA—and for that matter the general environment that allowed for the exaltation of religion in American society—could not have happened without the assistance of liberals.

THE BOOMER FACTOR

The post-1980 strategy of opposing the Religious Right by calling attention to liberal religiosity is especially puzzling if we consider the mood and the demographic landscape of the times. Liberalism had been alive and well—surviving, if not thriving—up to 1980, and the baby boom generation was entering adulthood at that time (ranging in age from late teens to early 30s when Reagan was elected), so it's not totally clear why politicians and the media would have felt that religion needed to be vitally important in politics. In fact, since we're often told that baby boomers carried more modern, enlightened attitudes than previous generations, their coming of age presumably should have delivered a much more effective resistance to the Jerry Falwells of the world. To understand why this didn't happen, we must dispel some common misperceptions about the baby boom generation.

Born between 1946 and 1964, the years immediately following the Second World War, baby boomers have always been an important demographic, partly because of their sheer numbers (the Depression and war had caused many to delay childbearing, resulting in the postwar boom) and partly because of their importance in shaping American popular culture in the prosperous postwar years. Unlike their parents, boomers grew up with television, rock and roll, relative abundance, and an understanding of their nation as a global superpower—but against the incongruous backdrop of the Cold War and the possibility of nuclear annihilation. Their maturation process was, in retrospect, fairly predictable: In their childhood, they generally enjoyed much more material comfort than their parents had known; as they grew up, they went through a rebellious period, questioning many of society's norms and assumptions; and then as they grew older, they settled down and generally conformed to the system that had produced them.

To listen to the baby boomers, however, one might think that their generation launched a liberal revolution—when in fact the exact opposite is true. Never has a generation been so overrated in its contribution to liberal progress, so self-congratulatory in light of facts that are undeserving. Boomers wax nostalgic about their younger days of marching for civil rights and protesting against the war in Southeast Asia, and they'll get sentimental about Dylan concerts and the Summer of Love, but their wistful narrative usually ends just before they lurched to the right in adulthood and led the nation toward decades of conservative—and anti-egalitarian—dominance. "If you can remember Woodstock, you probably weren't there," wrote humorist Jim Shea in a column about his generation, paraphrasing 1960s icon Wavy Gravy. "Yeah, we were cool."[9]

The operative word here is "were."

Although they think of themselves as the generation that brought the language of peace and love to the American dialogue, boomers have spent most of their lives serving institutions and values that find such ideals quaint, if not repugnant. Having enjoyed college without incurring insurmountable debt and graduated to an economy that provided good jobs and affordable housing, boomers subsequently grew up to make the term "born again" part of the American vernacular, help elect Ronald Reagan to the presidency, give a harshly antigovernment GOP control of the House of Representatives in 1994 (for the first time in four decades), and then, in their crowning achievement, put George W. Bush (one of their own) in the White House to start the twenty-first century.

Boomers were in their prime when the Soviet Union fell in 1991, ending the Cold War, and thus could have pushed for demilitarization, rational public policy, and economic fairness, but instead they allowed Wall Street and anti-egalitarian interests to dictate policy under the guise of "globalization" and "free markets," thereby decimating the middle class. As corporate profits have continuously reached new heights, the gap between rich and poor has expanded, and real income has declined for average Americans. Driving SUVs to large expensive homes in the suburbs or exurbs, where they can now watch on their oversize televisions as their pop culture icons raise money for struggling public broadcasters, boomers have for many years been a generation in denial. An understanding of this fact allows one to more fully appreciate the impressive steps that today's younger generation (boomers' children and grandchildren) have taken toward freethinking.

In hindsight, the boomers' drift away from liberalism and their eventual conservative embrace of the Establishment that had produced them makes sense. Their formative childhood years were defined by Eisenhower-era values—corporatism, consumption, material acquisition, militarism, and American exceptionalism—that became deeply ingrained in their collective psyche, imposing a cultural hegemony that would ultimately define them. Former defense secretary Charles Erwin Wilson, once president of General Motors, was criticized when he quipped that what's good for GM is good for the country, but most Americans understood that Wilson's only mistake was his honesty. The American system was entirely reliant on the health of major corporations such as GM, but such unpleasantries were best left unspoken. It shouldn't be surprising that the boomers, entering young adulthood, would rebel against this system, especially in light of the unjust war in Southeast Asia that was occurring at the time, but neither is it surprising that this rebellious attitude would wane as the years progressed. In the end, many boomers actually moved to the right of their parents and became even more accepting of unrestrained corporate power.

Despite the fact that boomers obtained college degrees at a higher rate than any previous generation, they were still prone to anti-intellectualism and superstition, for various reasons. Having initially rejected the religion of their upbringing, many in the middle and late 1970s returned to the fold or adopted other means of unscientific thinking. The era can be defined in many ways, but it was far from an age of rationalism. Even in academia, the dominant school of thought at the time was postmodernism, which often portrays central concepts of freethought—reason, science, the Enlightenment—as little more than constructs of Western imperialist culture. The postmodernist idea that there is no absolute truth often meant that empiricism itself was seen as passé, which allowed for the emergence of mainstream cultural fads such as New Age, astrology, biorhythms, and pyramid power.

More important, many boomers eventually returned to traditional Christianity. This trend emerged around the time that Jimmy Carter, in 1976, became the first high-profile presidential candidate (and then president) to call himself born again. This struck many people as strange but not necessarily dangerous, and in fact Carter's wholesome, ethical image was something of a relief after the corruption-ridden Nixon administration. Boomers would help propel the Democrat Carter to the presidency, and many of them would join in the born-again evangelical trend he popularized, finding Jesus as the answer in a difficult and confusing world. In fact, the phrase "born again" had been injected into popular culture a few years earlier via the lyrics of John Denver's hit "Rocky Mountain High," giving it a young and cool patina far removed from conservative politics. By the late 1970s even Bob Dylan, who came from a Jewish background, was going through a Christian stage.

The rise of fundamentalism—not just American Christian fundamentalism but also Muslim, Hindu, and Jewish fundamentalism around the world—sometimes is explained as a reaction to modernity, and we see this dynamic at work in the late 1970s among the baby boomers and their drift toward religion. The world was rapidly changing, not just technologically but socially, and many found comfort and stability in religion, with its certainty and unchanging values. The born-again concept also differed from the mainstream Protestantism or Catholicism most boomers grew up with, thereby giving them a sense that they were not just accepting the religious framework of their parents. By offering a way of bucking the system while still leading a life of relative conformity, evangelical religion fit the needs of a generation ready to leave the turbulence of the 1960s and early 1970s behind. Many boomers, now out of college, were facing adult concerns, such as careers and raising young families of their own, and found that religion complemented those ends. If boomers had marched for peace or civil rights (and bear in mind that many didn't—the stereotype of the baby boomer protesting on a college campus is an overgeneralization), those days of saving the world were over—now they would save themselves.

When Carter used his religion to get elected in 1976, few realized that he was starting a trend that would set America on a course toward hard-right, anti-egalitarian public policy for decades to come. Carter himself was a moderate Democrat, so there was little reason at that time to associate born-again, evangelical religion with extreme conservative politics as we reflexively do today. Carter used his religion mainly to contrast himself with the political establishment, not to promote a particular agenda. A popular poster during the campaign depicted the smiling Carter as a Christ-like figure in a robe with long hair, the caption reading: "J.C. can save America!"

The Christianity of today's Religious Right is extremely judgmental, quick to condemn gays, anyone who engages in sex outside marriage, and even sometimes those who use birth control, but in the late 1970s this was not the popular image of Jesus, especially among young people. This was the era of theatrical productions such as *Jesus Christ Superstar* and *Godspell*, not fire and brimstone, so boomers were more likely to see Jesus as cool, a kind of early hippie, than as an intolerant, vengeful deity. And Carter's moderate politics and ethical message conveyed evangelical Christianity to the general public in a benign way, with no indication of the forthcoming lurch to the right.

But the connection between evangelical Christianity and conservative politics became clear before the end of Carter's term with the formation of Jerry Falwell's Moral Majority. Ironically, the born-again president would become Falwell's first major political casualty.

THE TURN TO THE RIGHT

The Religious Right certainly enabled the conservative movement of the late twentieth century, but the main beneficiary of the movement has always been the corporate establishment. In fact, it's important to understand that corporate interests do not necessarily coincide with the interests of conservative religion but can be made sufficiently compatible only through a process of compromise, manipulation, and opportunism. Since corporations and their products—from satellites to birth control to computer applications—are the vehicles that often drive modernity, the materialistic lifestyle accompanying these products would, in theory, seem to conflict with the more spiritual message of most traditional theology. Hence, only with some effort could conservative religion and corporate interests be made politically complementary. But when it happened, they made powerful bedfellows.

Fortunately for corporate interests, fundamentalist Christians by and large have little trouble reconciling their theology with a modern, materialistic lifestyle. Those who claim to be the most devout followers of Jesus, who loathed material acquisition and said it would be easier for a camel to get through the eye of a needle than for a rich person to enter heaven, rationalize their way to acceptance of modern consumption-enthralled society with seemingly little difficulty.[10] Of course, occasionally they object to specific aspects of corporatism—for example, "immoral" adult programming (which is usually defined as depicting nudity, not violence) or the sale of contraception—but the basic notion of mass consumption is well accepted.

In fact, conservative Christians not only tolerate living in materialistic capitalist society, they often embrace it and celebrate it as ideally suited for Christian living. Some promote the so-called prosperity Gospel, which claims that your earthly wealth is a reflection of your righteousness. Others simply believe that America itself—a land of freedom and unquestioningly a force for good in the world, a nation that is "under God" and claims in its national motto to trust in God—necessarily reflects what a strong Christian society looks like. We are the good guys in the world, the theory goes, and much of the rest of the world hates us for our freedom, so our system, even if imperfect, must be compatible with Christian living.

Thus, although the relationship between religion and capitalism hasn't always been cordial, in the modern American conservative movement the two have found ways to become not just compatible but symbiotic. As boomers were finding religion, corporate interests were doing their part not only by shaping America into a society of materialistic consumers, which would be expected, but also by promoting anti-intellectualism and political passivity. This laid the groundwork for the eventual convergence with conservative religion. The rise of the Christian Right in 1980 was a tipping point of sorts, creating a political machinery that would allow both corporate interests and social conservatives to dominate politically for the rest of the century and beyond.

The election of Ronald Reagan in 1980, the first presidential election in which the modern Religious Right was a visible factor, was a turning point for American politics, the start of a conservative era—or, more accurately, an anti-egalitarian era—that still has not ended. During the liberal heydays of the 1960s and 1970s, even Republicans often had to swallow many liberal concepts if they wished to be elected. Richard Nixon created the Environmental Protection Agency by executive order in 1970, hardly an antigovernment gesture, and it was Nixon who enacted wage and price controls in an effort to combat inflation, an interventionist move that would have him crucified by his own party today. Indeed, before the election of Reagan, conservative ideology was considered politically toxic on the national level, partially due to Senator Barry Goldwater's disastrous 1964 presidential campaign. Goldwater, the GOP nominee that year, was known as the face of conservatism in his time, and he spoke from the heart when he famously declared in his acceptance speech that "extremism in defense of liberty is no vice." This indelicate, if sincere, statement of his principles didn't endear him to voters, and he went on to lose the election in a landslide to Lyndon B. Johnson, whose Great Society program epitomized a liberal vision of America.

The liberal era, however, would come to a screeching halt with the election of Reagan, who campaigned in 1980 not only against the vulnerable Democratic incumbent Carter but against liberalism itself. Suddenly "big government" and "taxing and spending" were the problems, and "liberal" was a label most Democratic candidates tried to avoid.

This abrupt turnaround was made possible in large part by white evangelical voters, who accounted for two-thirds of Reagan's margin of victory, according to analysts (a statistic made even more puzzling by the fact that his opponent Carter was a vocal born-again Christian, whereas Reagan was a divorced Hollywood actor).[11] These religious conservatives had no interest in funding government programs to feed the poor, but they were energized by social issues, especially abortion, which had gradually become more controversial after the 1973 Supreme Court decision in *Roe v. Wade*. Oddly, most American Protestants didn't take a strong position on abortion before *Roe*—the Catholic Church had staunchly opposed abortion historically, but Protestants had more often been indifferent—but by the late 1970s, many fundamentalist leaders discovered that the issue could mobilize followers. The Moral Majority utilized abortion as a key wedge issue while also taking strong stands against women's equality (the Equal Rights Amendment in particular), homosexuality, and "antifamily" media.

Despite the Religious Right's public focus on abortion and other "family" and "moral" issues, however, the record shows that the fundamentalist leaders who mobilized America's conservative Christians in the 1970s were motivated not by abortion but by racism and, more specifically, segregation. The Religious Right formed in the late 1970s not as a response to *Roe v. Wade,* but mainly as a response to the federal government challenging the tax-exempt status of schools that refused to desegregate. When the IRS in 1976 stripped the tax-exempt status of Bob Jones University, a fundamentalist school in South Carolina that refused to desegregate, war was declared, as outraged conservative Christians responded with zealous political action. Jerry Falwell and Paul Weyrich, leaders at the center of the Christian mobilization effort at the time, were savvy enough to know that pro-segregation positions would be politically ineffective, so they instead learned to use abortion and other morality issues to mobilize the mass audience. Together with the anti-feminist messaging of Phyllis Schlafly, whose "Stop ERA" campaign had already been resonating with conservative Christian voters, Falwell, Weyrich, and company would soon make their vision of a powerful voting bloc of religious conservatives a reality.[12]

In fact, some commentators see racism as the underlying catalyst not just for the Christian Right, but for the modern conservative movement itself. Paul Krugman, the Nobel laureate economist, points out that whites in the South were a key factor in blocking passage of universal health care at least as far back as the 1940s, when the Truman administration attempted to create a national system similar to Medicare. Southern whites at the time feared that such a system might lead to—God forbid—integrated hospitals, and therefore they adamantly opposed it.[13] "[T]he ability of conservatives to win in spite of antipopulist policies has mainly rested on the exploitation of racial division," Krugman explains.[14]

Krugman is no doubt correct that racism is at the roots of what he calls the "movement conservatism" that has driven public policy rightward in America, but it's noteworthy that racism itself is not completely removed from the more general problem of anti-intellectualism, for in the modern world the absence of reason and critical thinking would seem to be a necessary condition for allowing racist attitudes to influence policy making. Thus, though he doesn't say it, Krugman is actually pointing to the problem of antireason when he suggests that the issue of race has driven modern conservatism. Moreover, given the resources of the corporate institutions that dominate American society, it seems doubtful that racist whites, in the South or elsewhere, would ultimately exert much political power if their views in any way obstructed the goals of corporate interests.

Race and religion were major factors in the success of the conservative movement in the late twentieth century, but they weren't the only ones. To better understand the success of the right-wing agenda—and conversely the failure of progressive policy efforts—we must examine some of the more subtle efforts that have suppressed freethought and progressive elements. After doing so, we'll consider the strategies that can effectively reverse the damage.

FIVE

NO CORPORATIONS IN FOXHOLES

IF YOUR GOAL WAS TO CRUSH FREETHOUGHT—TO MARGINALIZE THOSE individuals who dare to challenge the system, think for themselves, and inspire others to do the same—there are plenty of ways to do it. You could try to dismantle the educational system, for example, or you might try to pacify the masses through mindless entertainment and distractions. But there is one foolproof measure, more efficient by far than the rest. If you really want to eliminate independent thinkers, simply crank up the patriotism.

With roots in a primal tribalism, often accompanied by an us-against-them mentality that encourages collective action against outsiders, the patriotic impulse can be lethal. When national pride and unity reach such a fever pitch that dissent—even rational and thoughtful dissent—is met with hostility, most people will quickly conform to the perceived consensus of the herd. Such an environment is anathema to freethought, which is precisely why we often see institutions and leaders utilize patriotism as a means of silencing opposition and consolidating power. Indeed, as Samuel Johnson implied when he called patriotism "the last refuge of a scoundrel," those in power need not resort to brute force if they can rally the public to demonize dissenters.

And of course, nothing triggers the patriotic impulse like a good war. Militarism and patriotism go hand in hand, so much so that for many, there is nothing more synonymous with patriotism than the military; and this is especially so at a time of war, when men and women are risking their lives on behalf of the homeland.

As such, the military presents a political minefield of sorts for freethinkers and progressives, because it is an area that requires thoughtful discussion but certainly does not invite it. The nuance and candor required to discuss militarism intelligently in the public forum are too often in short supply, since anything short of enthusiastic, unqualified support risks being perceived as unpatriotic. Especially in a society in which the general public is easily persuaded to begin with, the democratic process will naturally invite references to patriotism and military strength in politics, and discourse can quickly descend into appeals to fear, national greatness, looming enemies, and imminent danger.

TWO LACKING CHARACTERISTICS

To offset the natural tendency toward militarism, a democracy must exhibit two characteristics. First, the institutional interests that favor militarism must be controlled; and second, the population must be thinking critically, so that it can process information accurately and not be vulnerable to pandering. Unfortunately, modern America possesses neither of these characteristics. Corporate and other institutional interests have undue control over government, resulting in outrageous military spending that cannot be justified by any rational standard; and the population is so uninformed and passive that it eagerly endorses—or at least fails to challenge—outlandish military spending and hawkish foreign policy. This is what happens when freethought is abandoned.

To say that the American military budget is out of control would be a gross understatement. Most years, in fact, American military spending comes close to or exceeds that of the rest of the world combined. The Stockholm International Peace Research Institute lists the top four nations for 2012 military spending as the United States ($682 billion), China ($166 billion), Russia ($90 billion), and the United Kingdom ($60 billion). Thus, in that year, American spending was more than four times that of the second-highest nation and more than seven times that of the third. And this enormous number does not even include items such as nuclear weapons research and maintenance, homeland security, counterterrorism, and veterans' pensions, all of which fall outside the American military budget. This massive military machine dwarfs any other the world has ever seen.

Without a healthy and vibrant freethinking element in society, emotional appeals to patriotism and national greatness are much more likely to gain traction, as are fear-based claims of imminent threats. Never mind that the Cold War ended decades ago and that there is no likelihood of any foreign army landing on our shores; in the rhetoric of ambitious politicians, evil lurks all around, so we must be prepared. The unquestioning, receptive public agrees, supportive of military action even though most citizens are unable to find the enemy country on a map. In this atmosphere the government is responsive not to real humans, because true participatory democracy with an informed and engaged citizenry is nonexistent. Instead, it caters to corporate interests that stake a claim to the billions of dollars spent each year. These corporations, which spend millions upon millions on lobbying and influence peddling, are Washington's true constituents.

Politically, the results are both pathetic and tragic. Politicians will rant about the need to balance budgets and control spending yet insist on increasing defense spending every year. Mitt Romney chose this posture in the presidential election of 2012, hammering away at traditional "conservative" themes such as cutting taxes, reducing spending, and downsizing government, but then expressly exempting military spending from the budget ax. Since military spending is by far the largest part of the federal budget, accounting for more than half of all discretionary expenditures, the inconsistency is glaring. Nevertheless, Romney charged forward with simultaneous claims of downsizing government and upsizing the military: "Rather than complete nine ships a year, I would complete fifteen," he told an interviewer, criticizing Obama's military spending as being too modest. "I would add more F-22s and add more than 100,000 active duty personnel to our military team."[1]

The audacity of this proposal is staggering, especially coming from a candidate who lectures the nation about fiscal responsibility. "Getting our fiscal house in order has become more than an economic issue," Romney insisted, calling the task "a moral imperative."[2] Yet no one seemed to notice when he simultaneously called for adding $2 trillion to the defense budget over ten years, a move that would seem to be the height of irresponsibility and hypocrisy. The fact remains that such disjointed national defense arguments are seen as safe and reliable in American politics.

GUNS, GOD, AND SUPPRESSION

Not surprisingly, Romney repeatedly invoked God as he criticized Obama for being soft on military issues, combining theology and militarism in the same stump speech by simultaneously assuring audiences that he would ramp up military spending and keep "under God" in the Pledge of Allegiance and "In God We Trust" as the national motto (even though nobody had seriously challenged the pledge or the motto in the campaign).[3] Such emotion-driven appeals, imbuing patriotic militarism with divine references, are typical of anti-freethought politics. Critically thinking voters would find such pandering to be not just unpersuasive but insulting, yet large segments of the American public find it compelling.

Indeed, even for candidates who are less inclined to God-and-country rhetoric, land mines abound when there is a general sense that the public expects flattering gestures of national greatness. Thus, in modern times politicians are expected to wear flag lapel pins (another tradition that started with Nixon), lest they be perceived as insufficiently loyal, as Barack Obama discovered when controversy erupted because he briefly chose not to wear one during the 2008 campaign.[4] Those who do not stroke the collective ego risk being called weak, unpatriotic, or even dangerous.

In times of war, individuals are under even greater pressure to submit to governmental authority, as society circles its wagons to fight off a perceived enemy. Freethinking and dissent are rarely tolerated, let alone encouraged, in such situations. This tribal reflex, demanding unquestioning loyalty, is found throughout human history and is prominent in the American narrative. Despite all our rhetoric about cherishing freedom, dissenters have not always been treated warmly. Even in the era of the founders, when possible war with France loomed in 1798, the nation passed the Alien and Sedition Acts, severely restricting free speech and resulting in the imprisonment of newspaper editors and others who criticized the government.

As is commonly the case in most human societies, not just America, this quashing of dissent would become a recurring pattern in times of war. Thus, during the Civil War the writ of habeas corpus was suspended, allowing the government to imprison citizens without charges. Some particularly oppressive measures were seen during the First World War, when legislation targeted those who spoke out with "disloyal, profane, scurrilous, or abusive language" against the government, the flag, or the military, essentially making dissent illegal. These laws were not just theoretical affronts to civil liberties but were actively enforced to silence those whom the government saw as rabble-rousers. Eugene Debs, an outspoken labor advocate who had garnered almost a million votes as a presidential candidate in 1912, was sentenced to ten years in prison under the legislation merely for speaking out against the draft in 1918. During the same period, hundreds of foreign citizens were deported for no reason other than their left-leaning political views in the infamous Palmer Raids, named for Woodrow Wilson's notorious attorney general, A. Mitchell Palmer. The Second World War and its aftermath were no more accommodating of perceived dissenters, as is evident from the internment of innocent Japanese American citizens during the war as well as the intense anticommunism and blacklisting that followed during the Cold War.

THROWING THE SPITTER

Such suppression is predictable during times of war, but we can learn even more about the phenomenon when we consider those instances when, despite an ongoing war, dissent is not silenced. In those rare circumstances when militarism becomes so unpopular that substantial portions of the citizenry speak out against it, those dissenters still face deeply entrenched social and institutional forces that obstruct efforts to inject critical thought into the public dialogue.

One major reason Ronald Reagan was successful in the presidential election of 1980 is that he managed to associate his Democratic opponent, Jimmy Carter, with foreign policy weakness and failure. Reagan was helped by the fact that several dozen American hostages were held in Iran for an entire year preceding the election, a crisis that clouded Carter's presidency. The hostage taking came in the midst of the Iranian revolution, when the American-supported shah was overthrown by a popular uprising that installed an Islamic regime (which in hindsight we can now see was an early manifestation of the modern surge of Islamic fundamentalism). Nightly newscasts counted the days of the hostage crisis as a constant reminder of Carter's helplessness, and Americans wondered why their nation was so vulnerable against what appeared to be a bunch of unruly religious fanatics. Exacerbating the problem for Carter was that the crisis came at a time when the nation's collective ego was already deflated by recent memories of the disastrous war in Vietnam, which was understood by many as the first war that the United States had ever lost. Reagan, emphasizing military strength, confidence, and national pride, encouraged voters to associate the liberalism of Carter and the Democrats with weakness, and he rode to an easy victory.

Within the Reagan presidency, and indeed throughout American culture in the 1980s, we can see the masterful work of anti-egalitarian and anti-freethought forces. Emotion, image, patriotism, corporatism, and militarism—none of which is conducive to freethought—were emphasized, and critical thinking was deemphasized. This was reflected not just in the policies of Reagan and his administration but, as we'll see, in other segments of the culture as well, as history was rewritten and conventional wisdom was redefined to push freethinking and progressive politics to the margins.

This was perhaps most apparent as the country tried to come to terms with the mistake of Vietnam. If one refuses to question authority but instead obediently accepts that all American military adventures are righteous, then the only question to ask with regard to Vietnam would be: *Why did we lose?* A less hypernationalistic approach, however, would suggest a more basic, objective question: *Was the war necessary?* And indeed, this latter question spawned one of the largest antiwar movements the country has ever seen, as the war raged and baby boomers faced the draft.

By the early 1980s, however, the Vietnam experience had been largely whitewashed in the collective consciousness. The semantics of "unjust war" faded, replaced by a different sense of regret that disregarded the wrongfulness of the war and instead focused on the military failure and the mistreatment of the returning troops. This was reflected in popular culture, such as in the popular 1982 Rambo movie, *First Blood,* when the macho protagonist, a Vietnam veteran played by Sylvester Stallone, recalls being spat upon by antiwar demonstrators. "Protesting me. Spitting. Calling me baby killer," says Rambo. "Who are they to protest me?"[5] This view was typical of popular culture in the early 1980s, when Americans were still recovering from difficult years of Vietnam, Watergate, and the Iran hostage crisis.

National pride had taken a beating, and a healthy dose of Reagan-Rambo was just what the doctor ordered.

There's one big problem, however, with Stallone's portrayal of the returning veteran Rambo being spat upon by unruly antiwar protesters. While there's no question that the war in Southeast Asia was unpopular, the representation of the internal American conflict as being between antiwar protesters and the actual soldiers (many of whom were drafted) is grossly fallacious, as the real clash was between those opposing the war and the institutional power brokers (governmental and corporate) who were waging it. Of course, filmmakers aren't concerned about historical accuracy— they're just telling a story and making money—but it's remarkable how the film, unwittingly or not, catered to the patriotic impulse of those who would promote militarism.

In fact, the war in Southeast Asia was widely unpopular among the GIs fighting it; and by inaccurately casting the image of antiwar protesters as being rabid, irrational haters of everyone in uniform, *First Blood* (and popular culture in the Reagan era in general) was certainly fiction. But conservatives didn't care. By adopting this narrative, using GIs as a sort of straw man when in fact the wrath of the antiwar movement had been directed at the politicians and institutions that were driving the war machine, conservatives could rewrite history. By striking a patriotic nerve in a public that lacked a long-term memory, they successfully portrayed demonstrators as little more than immature students and fringe radicals.

Though it still enflames emotions on both sides, a sober look at the Vietnam experience is especially instructive. The spat-upon returning veteran, for example, is widely accepted today as fact but was never documented in any news accounts from the time. Not one piece of video footage or even one contemporaneous news story from the Vietnam era includes an antiwar protester spitting on a GI, yet popular culture continues to propagate the anecdote. Jerry Lembcke, himself a Vietnam veteran, tried to debunk the myth of the spat-upon veteran in his 2000 book, *The Spitting Image: Myth, Memory, and the Legacy of Vietnam,* but the story won't go away, as even major media outlets continue to promote it. (In a profile of John McCain in 2007, for example, *Newsweek* magazine stated matter-of-factly that vets were "spat upon in airports.")[6] Not surprisingly, Lembcke and other writers have faced severe backlash from some veterans who will today insist that they were spat upon, or at least that they witnessed such behavior. Of course, it's entirely possible that some of these accounts are true, but the fact that there are no reliable news accounts of such actions certainly contrasts with the perception that they were widespread.

Regardless, the key point that gets overlooked in the controversy is that certain institutional interests have successfully manipulated public opinion so that the antiwar protesters are viewed as unpatriotic. Given the size of the antiwar movement, it wouldn't be at all surprising that some antiwar demonstrators were venomously (and wrongly) hostile to individual GIs; but even if that's true, surely it is unfair to suggest that the antiwar movement was primarily geared toward such an agenda. In real life, GIs themselves were an important part of the antiwar movement. Over 58,000 Americans would die in Vietnam—a tragic toll, to be sure—and even that figure is only a small fraction of the overall devastation of the war. Conservative tallies suggest that well over a million Vietnamese military were killed in the conflict, as were hundreds of thousands of civilians. Many more were wounded, of course, and these numbers don't even include the casualties resulting from the extensive American bombings of neighboring Cambodia and Laos.

Even facing such facts, most rational Americans still would agree that opposition to such military action should not vilify the individual soldiers involved. This is why the dominant narrative, which convinces the public and the media that "antiwar" is synonymous with "anti-soldier," is so effective at silencing dissent. Instantly, it removes the focus from the real issue—unnecessary militarism—and puts antiwar advocates on the defensive, raising questions about their national loyalty and whether they "support the troops." There is little room in such a discussion for freethinking, which depends largely on questioning authority.

Note that it's not only the general public that is being manipulated here, but also the veterans themselves. Fighting in a war is miserable and dangerous under the best of circumstances, but an unpopular war of questionable justification (and a war that, unlike some others, is killing an untold number of civilians, including children) is even more difficult. Those serving in the military in the midst of such a conflict are in a most unenviable position, for they are risking their lives in a campaign that doesn't even have popular support. Death and destruction are the expected by-products of war, of course, and soldiers engaged in a war effort are, by definition, both putting their lives at risk and participating at least indirectly in systematic killing. Nevertheless, even in an unpopular and unjust war, few military personnel themselves would be inclined to protest, since the price of doing so in a military environment can be extreme.

Opposition might not be possible for those in uniform, but it is for the rest of us. In fact, many would argue that those in a position to speak out have a moral obligation to do so. In a society that values freedom and freethinking, all wars should be questioned and unjust wars should be criticized. Moreover, although debate over such criticism is to be expected, pro-war factions should be called out when they cast those who criticize war as being unpatriotic and rewrite history to use GIs as pawns in their strategy.

CALLING A MISTAKE A MISTAKE

This is where the tragedy of Vietnam becomes so obvious, as does the danger of abandoning critical thinking. Vietnam had been an independent society for many centuries before it was occupied by France in the nineteenth century—one of many lands around the globe that fell under control of colonizing European powers in that era. French occupation of Indochina was typical of European colonization elsewhere, with economic exploitation and frequent rebellions by the indigenous population, and it continued even into the Second World War. When France quickly fell to Germany in 1940, most of French Indochina remained nominally under the sovereignty of conquered France's pro-German Vichy government, with much actual control exerted by Germany's ally, nearby Japan.

A key figure in the resistance against both French and Japanese occupation was a Vietnamese communist named Ho Chi Minh, who was widely recognized, even by American intelligence, as leading Vietnamese political and military efforts during the Second World War. The American Office of Strategic Services aided Ho Chi Minh during Japanese occupation, and after the war there was no question that he was seen as leading the opposition to French reoccupation. "Postwar" would be the wrong term to use for Vietnam in the years following the Second World War, because the nation remained a bloody battleground for three decades, and any objective assessment would conclude that the main problem was simply a refusal of Western powers—first France and then the United States—to accept Vietnamese autonomy.

Had elections been held in Vietnam after the Second World War, there is no question that Ho Chi Minh would have won in a landslide, a fact acknowledged even by President Eisenhower, who wrote in 1954: "I have never talked to or corresponded with a person knowledgeable in Indochinese affairs who did not agree that had elections been held as of the time of the fighting, possibly eighty percent of the population would have voted for the Communist Ho Chi Minh as their leader."[7] In fact, under the 1954 Geneva Accord establishing a cease-fire between the French and Ho Chi Minh's group, the Viet Minh, the country was geographically divided, and both sides agreed that elections would take place in 1956 to unify the country once again. But by 1956 the United States had entered the picture in a more prominent way and refused to allow the elections, as it knew that Ho Chi Minh would be the clear winner.[8]

Apologists for American military action argue that the Cold War required fighting communism on every frontier, even in a small, remote country in Southeast Asia, but even they must acknowledge the antidemocratic, imperialistic nature of such action. The "domino theory," suggesting that one small communist victory (even a democratic one) will inevitably lead to others, was the primary public justification for the action, but that argument usually assumed the "spread" of communism was occurring only against the will of the people of any given society. This was not the case in Vietnam, as eventually became apparent, when we lost the war because the political and military will of the Vietnamese people was with Ho Chi Minh and his successors, not America or its puppets.

Our collective amnesia with regard to the Vietnamese experience—not just among the general population but even among our leaders—confirms the predominance of anti-intellectualism in modern America. George W. Bush was asked in 2006, in the midst of the war in Iraq, whether he saw any lessons from Vietnam that could be relevant in Iraq. Yes, he said, "one lesson is that we tend to want there to be instant success in the world, and the task in Iraq is going to take a while."[9] Thus, shockingly, the "lesson" Bush took from the Vietnamese experience—which saw decades of warfare and millions of casualties, and resulted in American withdrawal and communist victory—was not to be wary of intervening unnecessarily in foreign lands but to be *persistent* when doing so. Commentator Keith Olbermann, a dogged critic of Bush, didn't let the error go unnoticed, saying "It is pathetic to listen to a man talk unrealistically about Vietnam" and that "his avoidance of reality is going to wind up killing more Americans."[10]

NOT DIABOLICAL, BUT SYSTEMIC

It's ironic that it was Dwight D. Eisenhower—the general credited with leading the military force that defeated Germany in the Second World War—who warned Americans of the growing "military-industrial complex." Given his credentials, few men could better have known the immense power of the governmental and corporate institutions that were behind the awesome American war machine, and few would have been expected to be more supportive of it. Instead, Ike's tone was foreboding as he cautioned the nation: "[W]e must guard against the acquisition of unwarranted influence, whether sought or unsought, by the military-industrial complex. The potential for disastrous rise of misplaced power exists, and will persist."

That 1961 speech, though considered one of Eisenhower's most important, still doesn't get the attention it deserves. Speaking to the nation just three days before the new young president, John F. Kennedy, would take office, the older, experienced Eisenhower would use his farewell address as a platform to issue a wake-up call to the nation. Having served in the military since 1911, when American armed forces were tiny and almost irrelevant on the world stage, Ike had seen the military transform into the world's greatest, with nuclear weapons and destructive capabilities that were previously unimaginable; and he had also witnessed the vast expansion of a massive defense establishment—a corporate-governmental syndicate that generated immeasurable wealth and affected the lives, directly or indirectly, of virtually everyone on the planet.

Importantly, although Eisenhower's speech would warn against the power of the military-industrial complex, he did not oppose the sector outright. Rather, given the atmosphere of the Cold War, he seemed to accept the need for a robust defense sector, but he pleaded for rational Americans to recognize the necessity of tightly regulating it:

[A]n immense military establishment and large arms industry is new in the American experience. The total influence—economic, political, and even spiritual—is felt in every city, every State house, every office in the Federal government. We recognize the imperative need for this development. Yet we must not fail to comprehend its grave implications. . . . We must never let the weight of this combination endanger our liberties or democratic processes. We should take nothing for granted. Only an alert and knowledgeable citizenry can compel the proper meshing of the huge industrial and military machinery of defense with our peaceful methods and goals so that security and liberty may prosper together.[11]

Over half a century later, we unfortunately must conclude that, for the most part, Eisenhower's warning went unheeded. It would be easy to point to the massive American military budget as evidence of this point, but the argument is made even more compelling when we look at the specific words that Eisenhower used. The "military establishment and large arms industry," as Ike warned, has undue influence—"economic, political, and even spiritual." Such "misplaced power" and "unwarranted influence" have "grave implications," for they "endanger our liberties [and] democratic processes." With most impressive foresight, Eisenhower even understood the prescription that would be needed to address the problem: "an alert and knowledgeable citizenry." In other words, Ike warned that a new syndicate had emerged in American society, a combination of corporate interests with parasitic reliance on government military spending that had never been seen before, and this sector undoubtedly would exert great influence in politics and government, so American citizens must be alert and vigilant in checking its power. Otherwise, politicians would be under the control not of the people but of these powerful interests, and government therefore would cater to those interests instead of to the interests of citizens. Ike was spot on.

This all sounds rather diabolical, but that's not how Eisenhower meant it. Although certainly there is corruption and malfeasance to be found, corporate dominance of American government is explained more accurately as a natural progression of unchecked institutions working for their own interests within a system that allows them to do so. The problem arises from systemic flaws, not any evil genius with a grand plan. As explained in chapter 3, corporations are singularly focused on one goal—profit—and the existence of an almost endless stream of revenue through government spending—military spending—is an incentive that they cannot ignore. It is only natural that entire industries would arise around such spending and that the corporations within these industries would work very hard to ensure that the cash cow of government spending not only continues but increases.

Immense sums can be spent by these corporations and their industry groups—sums far exceeding anything that would be spent by ordinary citizens—on politics and lobbying. Almost all of the lobbyists in Washington—and there are many of them!—work for corporate and industry interests. Aside from a few relatively small nonprofits, almost all of the money and energy expended in Washington to influence policy making—whether under Democratic or Republican leadership—is spent on behalf of corporate and industry interests, not ordinary people. On defense issues, that means lobbying to increase spending, secure contracts, and conduct foreign policy that will ensure continued spending and open new business opportunities.

The money involved here is so massive that it quickly becomes impossible even to pretend that the business being conducted in Washington has anything to do with ordinary voters, as we can see by observing just one small microcosm as an example: military profiteering in America's relationship with Egypt. One might question whether the United States really needs to convey up to a billion dollars or more annually in military aid to Egypt, but you can rest assured that major American corporate interests, such as Lockheed Martin, Boeing, and Raytheon, will not be among those objecting to such aid packages. Those three companies benefit nicely from the spending—to the sum of over $300 million just from contracts between 2009 and 2011, for example—and there are many others whose revenue streams are enhanced by just this one foreign policy relationship.[12] We should bear in mind that these are just three of numerous corporations, that the revenues mentioned are from just one short time period, and that there are many countries besides Egypt getting military aid. If this is government "for the people," it's for *corporate* people.

THE CORPORATE PATRIOT

Corporate spokespersons will respond by pointing out that those revenues eventually flow back into the American economy. Egypt may be buying jets and missiles from Lockheed, Boeing, and Raytheon, but that means jobs for American workers, not just profits for major corporations. Indeed, the American economy rides on the backs of such corporations, which not only employ many thousands of citizens but also funnel money into the economy through contractors and vendors of all types. One of the ironies about this statement is that it supports the notion of Keynesian economics—that government spending can help drive the economy and should not be seen as an obstacle to economic health. The views of John Maynard Keynes (1883–1946), the British scholar generally considered the most influential economist of the twentieth century, whose views shaped liberal capitalism in his era and beyond, came under great attack as so-called conservative economics became trendy toward the end of the twentieth century. Ronald Reagan and others in the 1980s promoted the notion of supply-side (sometimes called trickle-down) economics, which urged lower taxes and less government spending as the better means of attaining growth. (Reagan did indeed cut taxes, but his increased military budgets resulted in an increase in overall government spending.) But as for the point that military spending creates jobs, we can see that this is an argument not for *military* spending, but simply for spending. Since in practice all sides agree that government spending invigorates the economy, the more important issue is whether a rational, thoughtful society would direct its job-creating spending toward investments in militarism. In the next chapter, we'll look at the payoff on such investments.

There is one more important irony to bear in mind, however, when considering the corporate connection to military adventurism and patriotism. As we all know from seeing television ads that use flags and other nationalistic imagery to sell us everything from automobiles to mutual funds, corporations know how to play the patriotism card. What we shouldn't overlook, however, is that the corporate "person" has no innate patriotism and in fact will quickly abandon national loyalty if doing so is in its interest. This is not an accusatory statement but a matter of plain fact that is undeniable from the nature of the corporate entity. The standard foundational documents of corporations—the articles of incorporation and bylaws—do not include any pledge of national loyalty but instead make clear that the entity exists for one purpose only: to succeed as a business enterprise, which is measured by profits and shareholder value.

Before he retired in 2006, ExxonMobil chairman Lee Raymond made this point eerily clear when he was asked at an industry meeting whether his company would consider building more oil refineries inside the United States.

"Why would I want to do that?" Raymond asked.

"Because the United States needs it . . . for security," the questioner responded.

"I'm not a U.S. company and I don't make decisions based on what's good for the U.S.," the ExxonMobil chairman replied.[13]

In describing this exchange, author Steve Coll noted that Raymond regards himself as "as a very patriotic American and a political conservative, but he was also fully prepared to state publicly that he had fiduciary responsibilities" to corporate shareholders. In a different context, those same duties compelled ExxonMobil not only to deny the causal link between fossil fuel use and global warming but to lobby internationally to derail American diplomatic efforts on climate change.[14] Nevertheless, both Exxon and Mobil are seen as solid American brands, and it's no coincidence that both use red, white, and blue for their signs and other marketing.

Of course, touting national loyalty often helps the bottom line, so corporations will use patriotic messaging in their advertising and public communications, but that messaging should not be misconstrued as real national loyalty. If they can get away with it, those same corporations will send jobs overseas to boost profits, sell weapons to potential enemies, place assets overseas to evade taxes, and conduct all sorts of other activities that would hardly seem patriotic. And unlike atheists, who are real humans who have fought to defend this country, there are no corporations in foxholes.

SIX

"OUR SON OF A BITCH"

ALTHOUGH EISENHOWER CONCEDED THAT HO CHI MINH WOULD HAVE easily won a fair election in Vietnam in 1954, many foreign policy hawks nevertheless contend that the United States had a moral obligation to stand firm against nations and leaders that did not uphold its values. (Of course, democracy is supposed to be one of its values, but other values took priority when the democratic process pointed to a communist victory.) This same principle, they would argue, justifies our intervening anywhere in the world to fight for important American values: liberty, justice, human rights, and, yes, even democracy.

The problem with this argument is that it is utter nonsense, and our leaders know it. To the extent such arguments carry any weight at all with the general public, it's because that public is failing to rationally assess facts. The record shows that the United States has happily supported tyrannical regimes that wholeheartedly reject purported American values. A comprehensive list would be virtually impossible because there are so many, but some of the more obvious examples would be the following:

AUGUSTO PINOCHET. The brutal right-wing general took power in Chile in 1973, overthrowing the democratically elected president, Salvador Allende, with support from the United States. Under Pinochet's reign of terror, tens of thousands were killed and tortured, political opponents and journalists disappeared, yet American support continued, mainly because Pinochet reversed most of the leftist economic policies of his predecessor in favor of "free market" reforms that favored American business interests.

The Somoza Regime. Making dictatorship a family affair, the Somoza dynasty controlled Nicaragua with brute force and corruption for much of the twentieth century, aided by support from the United States. "Somoza may be a son of a bitch, but at least he's our son of a bitch," said Franklin D. Roosevelt of the regime's founder, Anastasio Somoza.[1] Somoza-controlled governments exploited Nicaragua until driven from the country in 1979 by the left-wing Sandinista revolution.

Saddam Hussein. The former Iraqi leader is etched into the psyche of modern America as an archenemy, the evil dictator toppled by our military forces in the war launched in 2003. This depiction of Hussein is partially accurate, for he was indeed a ruthless tyrant who used poison gas on his own people and held little regard for recognized standards of human rights, but what is too often not mentioned is that this despot was once a key ally of the United States, even when his despicable tendencies were well known. After the Iranian revolution of 1979, the United States sided with Hussein when he attacked Iran and began a conflict that would be among the bloodiest of the twentieth century. In a widely circulated photograph from 1983, U.S. envoy Donald Rumsfeld, the former defense secretary who would return to that position in the second Bush administration, is seen shaking hands with Hussein while meeting to discuss "mutual interests," which included the mutual enemy Iran.[2] The United States provided aid to Iraq, including not just weapons but critical intelligence, even knowing that Hussein's military had a long track record of using chemical weapons in violation of international law. Retired Air Force Lieutenant Colonel Rick Francona, who was a military attaché in Iraq in 1988, reported that although Hussein's military never officially announced the use of chemical weapons, "They didn't have to. We already knew." According to *Foreign Policy* magazine, the declassified documents show "that senior U.S. officials were being regularly informed about the scale of the nerve gas attacks" in what is "tantamount to an official American admission of complicity in some of the most gruesome chemical weapons attacks ever launched."[3]

FULGENCIO BATISTA. The Cuban regime of this right-wing dictator was noteworthy for its brutality and corruption until it was overthrown by the revolution led by Fidel Castro in 1959. Though there is much about Castro worthy of criticism, Americans are largely unaware that the regime he overthrew was far from a Jeffersonian democracy. Batista profited immensely from his direct relationships with American mobsters, who used Havana for their gambling, drug, and prostitution operations, and ruthlessly suppressed opposition, all the while largely ignoring the plight of ordinary Cubans. Batista's willingness to assent to American ownership and exploitation of much of the island made him an ally of the United States, despite his horrendous record on human rights.

THE CONTRAS. Opposing the Sandinistas and other left-leaning popular movements in Central America in the 1980s were various right-wing militant groups, known collectively as the Contras, which relied heavily on the United States for support. According to Human Rights Watch, the Contras "were major and systematic violators of the most basic standards of the laws of armed conflict, including by launching indiscriminate attacks on civilians, selectively murdering non-combatants, and mistreating prisoners."[4] The Contras were guilty of "consistent and bloody abuse of human rights, of murder, torture, mutilation, rape, arson, destruction and kidnapping" of innocent civilians, left-leaning clergy, health care workers, and others, according to another human rights report.[5] Nevertheless, even knowing the atrocities committed by the Contras, Ronald Reagan called them "freedom fighters" and ambitiously supported them, to the point of illegally providing arms in what became known as the Iran-Contra scandal.[6]

GUATEMALAN DICTATORS. For most of the twentieth century, the nation of Guatemala was a colonial outpost for American corporate interests, ruled by repressive dictatorships that exploited the population for personal gain. Almost half the land in the country was owned by United Fruit, an American company that enjoyed a virtual monopoly on banana production and owned or controlled much of the country's communications and other industries. After a revolution in 1944 resulted in economic policies that threatened United Fruit's cushy situation, the Central Intelligence Agency helped orchestrate a coup that installed a new right-wing military regime, leading to decades of some of the most savage, inhumane practices of any government in the world. Death squads burned villages, murdered hundreds of thousands, and caused many thousands more to flee the country.[7]

THE SHAH OF IRAN. Viewed with historical amnesia, the Iranian revolution of 1979 and the hostage-taking of Americans that resulted from it would seem to be a puzzling display of anti-Americanism, but the episode is more understandable when considered in historical context. The revolution overthrew the shah, a corrupt autocrat who in 1953 had ousted, with American and British support, the democratically elected prime minister. The popular prime minister had nationalized the Iranian oil industry, thus threatening the huge profits of Western oil interests, a cardinal sin for any leader in the developing world. For this reason, not only can the outburst of anti-Americanism that accompanied the 1979 revolution be understood as resulting from America's own willingness to support a tyrant, but Islamic fundamentalism—a previously nonexistent force in international politics—became much more energized and relevant as well.

This list could go on, with names such as Ferdinand Marcos, the kleptocrat who ruled the Philippines for two decades with American support, then fled with his infamous wife, Imelda, in 1986 after plundering the Pacific nation's treasury, and numerous others. Even current, long-standing relationships, such as America's alliance with Saudi Arabia, with its well-documented mistreatment of women, hostility to religious minorities, use of torture, and barbaric criminal punishment, are highly suspect. Say what you will in defense of this record, but it hardly reflects a nation fully committed to human rights and other noble values.

And yet there are defenders. They contend that critics are naïve, eager to blame America without considering the thorny realities of geopolitics. The all-important "national interest," they insist, sometimes necessitates moral compromise, shady bedfellows, unprovoked warfare, or other distasteful actions. Dean Rusk, the U.S. secretary of state in the 1960s, repeatedly referred to "the vital national interest of the United States" in justifying the escalating war in Vietnam, and his successors have used similar rhetoric to defend everything from the war in Iraq to the use of armed drones against civilians.[8] The rationale even has a namesake think tank, the Center for the National Interest, which was founded by Richard Nixon and boasts his former secretary of state, Henry Kissinger—whose foreign policy, from supporting Pinochet in Chile to the carpet bombing of much of Southeast Asia, earned him a reputation for moral compromise—as longtime honorary chairman.[9]

Apologists for moral compromise might also invoke cultural relativism: that foreign societies have long-standing traditions and deep-rooted values that simply do not conform to Western standards, whether with regard to basic human rights, gender equality, the treatment of minorities, or a host of other issues. As such, they argue, the United States should not attempt to impose its standards on other cultures, for such "cross-cultural judgments" and chauvinism would be both ethnocentric and almost certainly doomed to failure.[10] Although this argument has an abstract legitimacy, it falls apart when rigorously scrutinized. What we find is that, yes, moral compromise is necessary from time to time and, yes, American standards of rights and liberties cannot be arbitrarily imposed on other societies without consideration of other factors; but these facts do not justify the active support of brutal tyranny and the disregard for human rights such as that wrought by the above-listed cast of characters.

NATIONAL INTEREST OR CORPORATE INTEREST?

Note that even apologists concede that America's foreign policy is not driven by a primary concern for human rights or democracy. The term "national interest" is not synonymous with either, but in practice it is indeed synonymous with American *corporate interests* (as opposed to those of ordinary

Americans and certainly those of the citizens of far-off lands who are often directly affected by our policies). In defense of nonhuman, corporate, institutional interests—but under the guise of "the national interest"—the lives and tax dollars of ordinary Americans frequently are invested in foreign policy that supports tyranny, opposes democracy and human rights, and obstructs the betterment of life for many.

The support of corporate interests through amoral or immoral foreign policy comes in several forms. America's backing of the despicable Pinochet in Chile, for example, can be traced to the corporate interests—such as ITT and various major mining interests—that benefited greatly from the downfall of the democratically elected Allende, who had nationalized many of Chile's industries while in office. The lesson is clear: Democracy is unimportant, so long as resources and markets remain open to American corporations. American military power all around the world, whether bases in foreign lands or huge naval fleets patrolling the seas, is in truth an extremely expensive security force for the protection of corporate interests, maintained and utilized with little regard for democracy.

And of course, as we saw in the last chapter, military spending itself provides an almost limitless trough at which corporate interests feed, enriching themselves at taxpayers' expense. Some will point out that these major corporations provide many jobs, that the economy would be in shambles without them, and this is partly true; but this argument ignores the obvious truth that government spending need not be devoted to military might. The economic stimulus gained through the production of weaponry and maintenance of military forces around the world could be attained just as well via an investment in science, health, education, infrastructure, and other constructive endeavors. (Indeed, it's also noteworthy that this emphasis on militarism has a defining effect on the culture as a whole. Consider, for example, that the educational subsidies accompanying military enlistment are increasingly the only way that many average young adults can afford college. Thus, the military path is increasingly the only gateway in American society to the social and economic benefits of higher education.)

Importantly, from the standpoint of anyone willing to question the carefully crafted messages of the military-industrial complex, amoral and sometimes immoral foreign policy is certain to have unintended consequences. The global rise of Islamic fundamentalism illustrates well the blowback from misguided policies that cater to nonhuman interests.[11] Although religious fundamentalism is a complex phenomenon with many causes, American foreign policy is far more responsible for its current metastasis than our leaders would like to admit. With so few functional democracies in Islamic countries today, it's easy to forget that secular democracy was probably within reach in various key places in the Muslim world in the twentieth century.

The Islamic theocracy that came to power in Iran in 1979, for example, almost certainly would not have materialized if the country had stayed on the democratic, autonomous path it held before the American-British coup of 1953, which installed the Shah Mohammad Reza Pahlavi as an authoritarian dictator. Only by allowing oil profits to dictate policy, by forgetting real human values of democracy and human rights and thereby destabilizing a government that was both popular and legitimate, did Western powers pave the way for Islamic revolution and theocracy a quarter century later. Similarly, America's eager embrace of Saudi Arabia—which has a horrid record on human rights and has long been a wellspring for radical Islamic activity (15 of the 19 hijackers on September 11 were Saudis, as was Osama bin Laden)—while maintaining lukewarm or even adversarial positions toward relatively democratic and secular governments, such as the Nasser and Sadat governments of Egypt from the late 1950s to the 1970s, reflects priorities that are at best questionable.

The strained justifications for America's support of dictators, immense military spending, and overseas military adventurism all lead back to something akin to "national interest" or its close cousin, "national security." In the latter half of the twentieth century, such interests justified the Cold War and the need to fight communism anywhere and everywhere, providing a trump card of sorts that allowed an array of morally offensive activity: the buildup of huge nuclear arsenals, the support of right-wing dictators all around the world, and the war that killed and wounded millions in Southeast Asia, to name just a few. Strangely, however, after the fall of the Iron Curtain and the disappearance of the communist threat in the late 1980s and early 1990s, America saw very little demilitarization other than a few base closings. Then, on September 11, 2001, with foreign enemies striking American soil, the country had a new justification for unprecedented levels of military funding and action.

FEAR AND FREETHOUGHT

The promotion of militarism is easy in a culture that has rejected freethinking, where fear is pervasive and patriotism is defined not just as love of country but unquestioned support of military adventurism. Understanding this, we can see why the buildup of the military-industrial complex has been irreversible since the Japanese attack on Pearl Harbor on December 7, 1941. After that, almost without exception, a serious and imminent threat of some kind has been constantly present in the American mind-set, thereby justifying—if not requiring—a massive military machine that just happens to subsidize a massive corporate war industry. Although America had a fairly prominent isolationist faction before Pearl Harbor, the attack ended any serious opposition to ramped-up militarism and overseas engagement. James Carroll documents this military expansion in his book *House of War,* showing how the Pentagon, a massive structure built during the Great Depression to house several government departments, quickly became home to the military alone. After the Second World War, fear of Japanese and Nazis would be replaced with fear of the communist menace, to be subsequently replaced by a fear of terrorism.

Of course, some of the public's fears were justified. There can be no question, for example, that Hitler and fascism were legitimate threats that offered few pacifist solutions.[12] Similarly, the Soviet Union posed a challenge to the United States in the years following the defeat of Germany and Japan. The fact that the postwar Soviet Union was ruled by Joseph Stalin—a paranoid maniac in the same league as Hitler—certainly made the task of selling fear to Americans easier. Stalin's ruthless purges of his opponents and perceived opponents, the lack of political freedoms behind the Iron Curtain, and the revolutionary intentions of international communism all contributed to a sense that America faced a real threat. On one side was the land of the free and home of the brave; on the other were gulags and totalitarianism. With the Cold War over, fundamentalist Islamic extremists can be depicted as posing a threat of some degree today, while China and Russia are portrayed as potential adversaries as well.

The question here is not so much whether these perceived threats were (and are) legitimate—surely there is some degree of legitimacy to them—but whether they have been assessed and responded to rationally. For the most part, since the end of the Second World War, the levels of militarism accompanying America's perceived threats typically have been disproportionate to the actual danger presented and in fact have sometimes exacerbated the danger. What we find is that institutional interests—corporate, governmental, and even sometimes conservative religious interests—have encouraged a militaristic culture through a mentality of exaggerated fear, blind obedience to authority, and a simplistic understanding of all international disputes, however legitimate, as battles between good and evil.

From the standpoint of America's nonhuman, corporate interests, the oppressive nature of Soviet government was never problematic; the real problem, in the corporate view, was the Soviet refusal to open markets. In contrast, there was much corporate interaction with Nazi Germany and little if any vocal opposition to Hitler from the corporate sector before war broke out. American corporate collaborations with the Nazis were numerous and are well documented, from Ford's manufacturing in Germany and Vichy France to Chase Manhattan's freezing of Jewish accounts at the request of Germany to numerous other dealings.[13]

The Nazis even turned to the technologies of IBM, the American company synonymous with business efficiency, for computational and organizational technologies that would assist in the systematic elimination of Jews. As reported by Edwin Black in his award-winning book, *IBM and the Holocaust: The Strategic Alliance Between Nazi Germany and America's Most Powerful Corporation,* IBM and its subsidiaries, almost certainly knowing the purposes for which the Nazis wanted automation technologies, nevertheless sold those systems to Germany, thereby facilitating the identification and roundup of millions of Jews. With over half a century having passed since the alleged wrongdoing, IBM's response to the accusations has been lackadaisical, questioning some of Black's research, claiming that many of its own records have been destroyed, but never directly contradicting the general thesis of the book. The fact that IBM technology was used is incontrovertible; the only question is how much its agents knew about the intended use.

More shocking than IBM's own defensive posturing is that of the procorporate media. In response to the claim that IBM's technicians must have consulted with the Nazis about how the technology would be used (in this case, sorting concentration camp prisoners and categorizing them by whether they were exterminated), Betsy Schiffman, writing for the business journal *Forbes,* doesn't see what all the fuss is about. "Does that really make IBM the bad guy?" she asks. "Who cares if the Nazis used IBM technology? The Nazis used pencils and pens, but should those manufacturers also be held responsible for their roles in the Holocaust?"[14] Thus, from the corporatist view, the sale of specialized, enabling technology is equivocated to the sale of a routine commodity such as a pencil. No big deal. Using Schiffman's logic, the sale of a hand grenade to a known terrorist would be no worse than selling that terrorist a pair of shoes.

If militaristic policies gain traction in a climate of fear, the opposite is true under the scrutiny of freethought. If the American population attempted to comprehend the root causes of Islamic fundamentalist violence, for example—which would require discussion of issues going all the way back at least to Western exploitation of the Middle East after the First World War—militarism would be on decidedly shakier ground. If we want to understand the terrorist mind-set, we would start by understanding that the map of the Middle East does not reflect the region's ethnic, national, or historical development but boundaries that were arbitrarily drawn by Winston Churchill in the 1920s, reflecting his efforts to establish pro-British monarchies in the lands taken from the defeated Ottoman Turks in the First World War. From there, we have generations of Western powers opposing secular democracy and supporting tyrants (and even, at times, religious fundamentalists). If democracy, freedom, and healthy economic development have eluded the Islamic world, a big part of the reason is Western colonialism and meddling.

The suggestion here is not the simplistic notion that America and its allies are the real "bad guys," but rather that we must get past "good versus evil" thinking, understand cause and effect in international relations, keep institutional interests from exerting undue influence on policy, and recognize the importance of facts, human values, and critical thinking. Unfortunately, that is not what's happening. We as a country are far more likely to conclude that God actually favors America, that the world is full of "bad guys" who "hate us for our freedom," and that global civilization would plummet into a pit of darkness without the constant assertion of American military muscle. In early 2003, over 50 percent of Americans were eager to launch an all-out war against Iraq in retaliation for the September 11 attacks, oblivious to (or, worse, in spite of) the well-documented fact that Iraq had no connection at all to the terrorist attacks. Corporate profiteers thrive on such ignorance and emotionally driven policy.

This is why many progressives and freethinkers, though supportive of the men and women who serve in the military, are dubious of efforts by governmental and corporate interests to glorify militarism. And such efforts have been increasing markedly since September 11, as the incorporation of patriotism and militarism into ordinary American life has been executed with seamless precision by the government-corporate establishment, aided by a population that has found much comfort and security in the notion of military strength. There is tragic irony in a yellow magnetic ribbon adorning an SUV in support of overseas American troops who would not be in harm's way if the nation (and some of its most powerful corporations) were not so dependent on fossil fuels originating from beneath the sands of combat. Of course, most freethinkers drive as well, but if nothing else they recognize that something is amiss, that the central problem facing America is not that too many people around the world hate us for our freedom, and that cranking up the militarism is certainly not the solution to our problems.

And if it isn't bad enough that American foreign policy caters to corporate interests, the corporations themselves are often so large that they conduct their own foreign policy. In fact, in some regions, American companies are often more involved in foreign affairs than the American government itself. ExxonMobil, for example, with a budget that dwarfs that of most nations, is deeply enmeshed in the affairs of countries all around the globe.[15] "In West Africa, ExxonMobil's managers continued to bring oil to market despite the coup plots, kidnapping raids, corruption, and factionalism menacing the corporation's host regimes in Nigeria, Chad, and Equatorial Guinea," writes Steve Coll in his 2012 book, *Private Empire: ExxonMobil and American Power*.[16] Meanwhile, on the other side of the world, ExxonMobil was being accused of responsibility for atrocities committed by Indonesian soldiers guarding the company's gas fields.[17] Clearly, as the title of Coll's book suggests, it's not unreasonable to compare major corporations to imperial nations with tentacles covering the planet.

MILITARISM, CORPORATISM, AND POP CULTURE

The injection of "God Bless America" into the seventh-inning stretch of professional baseball games is an example of how religious patriotism has redefined the national character. Nowadays we almost certainly will be confronted with high-profile references to "our men and women in uniform"—a constant reminder of the military might that has become a defining American characteristic—during every major sporting event, professional or college. In fact, these events hype not only militarism but also corporatism. Thanks to corporate sponsors and millions of dollars in ad revenue, even college games are far from casual amateur competitions; they are huge businesses. And of course by wrapping major sporting events in patriotism, corporate sponsors improve their own public image while adding grandeur to the events.

American news media have become formulaic in their presentation of the military. A standard television news story, seen at least once a week over most of the last decade in many markets, will show a soldier who surprises his or her spouse—or, even better, child—by returning from overseas duty unexpectedly. The Pentagon discovered the public relations value of this story line long ago, and its execution has been perfected in the highly militarized years since September 11, so that local news outlets will be ready to catch the surprised look of the unsuspecting spouse or child as Daddy, or sometimes Mommy, clad in military attire, suddenly appears. Shock and awe are apparent, loving embraces follow, and tears often are shed—a beautiful reunion, to be sure, a touching moment that makes for great television.

Of course, nobody would criticize the reunion of soldiers with their families (in fact, many progressives would question whether the separation was necessary at all), but it's also easy to find the exploitation of the reunion, for obvious propaganda purposes, distasteful. The Pentagon knows the strength of the emotional response generated by the scene and is betting, correctly, that few will dare to speak out against a child joyfully jumping into the arms of a long-absent parent.

Even mild dissent in the midst of official public patriotism is unwelcome, and if there's any doubt, just ask Brad Campeau-Laurion, who had the audacity in 2008 to leave his seat in Yankee Stadium in an attempt to use the bathroom during the singing of "God Bless America." Security personnel in the stadium had blocked off the aisles, effectively imposing compulsory participation in the patriotic experience, much to the chagrin of Campeau-Laurion, who felt nature calling. When he tried to pass by a police officer blocking the way to the rest room, a confrontation ensued that led to his being physically removed from the stadium. "I don't care about 'God Bless America,'" Campeau-Laurion said. "I don't believe that's grounds constitutionally for being dragged out of a baseball game." Of course, Campeau-Laurion is correct on the law, but he learned the hard way that official sentiment often pays it no mind. He eventually sued the City of New York over the fiasco, settling in 2009.[18]

Corporate interests, being persons on paper only, are incapable of loving America, but they find patriotism to be a very useful tool in their effort to ensure an environment that favors their interests nationally and internationally. Particularly when delivered in the cultural context of a major sporting event, patriotism helps corporations build a positive public image and brand appeal. And of course, it also nurtures militarism, which many corporations find immensely profitable.

INTERNATIONAL CORPORATISM

When an American schoolchild looks at a map of the world, she doesn't see a landscape of corporate emblems and brands; instead, she sees a globe divided into political units, the shapes and locations of which can be memorized by any diligent student. That long, skinny country down the west coast of South America is Chile; the large country to its east is Argentina; the landlocked nations to the north are Bolivia and Paraguay. Any ambitious student can learn about the cities, waterways, languages, and other details of such regions without even considering the notion of corporate power. But in the reality of human development on the planet, any such academic memorization of geography and political boundaries overlooks the real nature of global power. Although corporations are borderless and often invisible to the unwitting observer, they wield far more influence than most of the relatively weak nation-states that color the map.

Unlike nations, governments, armies, and human populations, multinational corporations do not seek glory, honor, land, food, or even respect. They seek only money. Of course, sometimes public self-promotion is necessary for such ends, and thus we see corporations spending billions of dollars to promote themselves and their products through advertising and public relations. This is why Coke, McDonald's, and other corporate brands are household names. But just as often, corporations can operate quite effectively without the need for such a high public profile, especially when they are influencing international politics and economies. John Perkins tells the chilling tale of global corporate malfeasance in his 2004 book, *Confessions of an Economic Hit Man,* an instant classic that revealed how corporate interests exploit developing countries through corruption and international finance.[19]

Economic hit men—or EHMs as they are called in practice—are enlisted by corporations to use any means necessary to ensure that the political leadership of developing countries remains subservient to the needs and wants of the international corporate elite. A key aspect of this system, Perkins explains, is the tactic of convincing small countries to accept enormous loans that will then make their economies beholden to American corporate interests. The loans enrich the countries' ruling elites but rarely the masses. Moreover, the indebtedness requires the country to open its borders to American corporate interests for exploitation of resources, meaning the revenues from that exploitation flow out of the country.

This activity is consistent with the general direction of global economics as prescribed by major economic institutions, such as the World Bank and International Monetary Fund, controlled in large part by American government and corporate interests. The so-called Washington Consensus, the widely used term for the standard prescription of policies expected of developing countries receiving aid, imposes requirements on those countries that allow multinational corporations access for exploitation that would be otherwise impossible. "Trade liberalization," for example, is one criterion, meaning recipient countries must lower tariffs and otherwise liberalize imports from multinationals. Privatization of state enterprises is another, an obvious perk for corporate interests and a loss for general populations. The "consensus," in fact, can be seen as an imposition of corporate values on the less developed world, a not-so-subtle form of conquest that would impress any imperialist from past generations.

Multinational corporations have untold millions at their disposal to spin the story in a way that reflects better on them, but the realities of global development show that corruption and exploitation are often rampant when American corporate interests become entangled in developing societies. Americans sometimes have an image of developing countries as being almost hopeless, havens of lawlessness and corruption. In truth, much corruption stems from the activities of multinational corporations themselves, and when rare leaders step forward to resist those interests, they are quickly vilified and often discarded quickly. Stories such as that of Allende in Chile—a democratically elected leader ousted with the blessing of America—are all too common. In 1981, for example, leaders Jaime Roldós in Ecuador and Omar Torrijos in Panama both died in suspicious plane crashes after pursuing policies that ran counter to American governmental and corporate interests.

We shouldn't be so naïve as to believe that multinational corporations care about the general populations of developing countries—as we've seen, by their very nature they cannot. Moreover, our blindness as individuals to their overseas malfeasance is not even uniquely American but a manifestation of humans' frequent inability to show interest or compassion at great geographic distances. This phenomenon was laid out well in philosopher Peter Singer's argument that the average person would surely ruin an expensive pair of shoes to save a drowning child but would not send that same amount of money to charity to feed a starving child overseas.[20] Thus, it shouldn't be surprising that populations in developed countries seem to show little concern that austerity measures imposed on developing societies—via institutions controlled directly or indirectly by corporate interests—lower the quality of life for distant populations. Not only are complex economic issues present, but the human suffering involved occurs far outside the circle of concern of Western populations. Clearly, if humans tend to have apathetic attitudes toward distant peoples, and this flaw can be exacerbated by unrestrained profit-seeking corporate power, we need to enact policies that compensate for both human and corporate shortcomings that lead to international exploitation.

The corporate desire for international resources and markets—combined with the indifference of the average voter to international issues—does much to explain American international policies. So-called free trade policies, for example, such as the North American Free Trade Agreement

(NAFTA) and similar treaties, cater entirely to corporate interests and would never be crafted by a government responsive to the desires of ordinary citizens. An estimated 700,000 American jobs were lost after NAFTA went into effect in 1994, as the agreement allowed corporations to produce goods outside American borders and sell them internally with no duties or tariffs. NAFTA and similar agreements are pitched to the public as the ultimate manifestation of global free enterprise, as if world economic progress is contingent on trade barriers being eliminated so multinational corporations can operate without restraint. This inaccurate view of economics brings few benefits to real people but enormous profits for corporations.

And with North America conquered via NAFTA, corporate interests soon turned to the rest of the world. We now have similar free trade compacts with most of Latin America, South Korea, Singapore, Australia, and several other countries, and these agreements are always touted as marvelously beneficial to all parties. The Central American Free Trade Act, for example, which opened most of that region for corporate activity, is described on the Web page of the Office of the United States Trade Representative as "creating new economic opportunities by eliminating tariffs, opening markets, reducing barriers to services, and promoting transparency."[21] What is not mentioned is that most of these "economic opportunities" are for corporations, not real humans.

The corporate drive for global domination is relentless, and it's instructive to contrast it with the drive of ordinary humans. Individual humans are multifaceted and have interests other than economic. Even the drive for comfort and security derives from more fundamental human needs, desires, and impulses. Corporations, however, in addition to holding resources far beyond those of mere humans, have a 24/7 focus on profit and nothing but profit.

Thus, we can see why Walmart and other retailers vehemently opposed improving safety conditions in factories in Bangladesh, even after a fire in 2013 killed over 1,100 workers at an unsafe garment factory there.[22] As human beings with a sense of ethics we can criticize Walmart, but as a matter of pure economics there is no reason for the corporation to favor improving the health and safety of Bangladeshi workers, unless of course the negative public relations fallout from such an inhumane position actually translates to a serious loss of revenue (which it rarely does). The cold financial position for the corporation would be to oppose any improvements for workers that might add to costs. This, in turn, is why *laws* and *regulations* are necessary to force corporations to consider factors other than profit.

Notice how the modern notion of "free trade" is defined by multinational corporations. It rarely translates to the globalization of workers' rights, instead allowing only the corporations themselves to operate freely in a borderless world. Those borders, however, are firmly in place if a worker in Mexico wishes to demand a minimum wage or other workers' rights that would be available in California. No labor unions unite the interests of workers across the globe, allowing them to collectively bargain internationally with major corporate powers—that would be unlawful! The one-sidedness of the "free trade" concept shows how the entire process is made by and for nonhumans.

Also worth noting in the saga of corporate meddling in the developing world is the active role played by religious groups in aiding the corporate agenda. Perkins, for example, notes that Ecuador's Roldós, before he was killed, ordered a religious group, the Summer Institute of Linguistics (SIL), out of the country, accusing the group of colluding with oil companies. Perkins reports a "disturbing pattern" of SIL activity, where the group would entice Amazonian communities to abandon lands that, coincidentally, had been found by seismologists to be likely oil rich.[23] The Dallas-based SIL, a nonprofit organization that reports contributions of about $35 million annually, says it is "motivated by the belief that all people are created in the image of God."[24] Thus again, at the intersection of religion and corporatism, we find something less than egalitarianism.

SEVEN

FAIR TO ALL

EVERY YEAR THE AMERICAN HUMANIST ASSOCIATION (AHA) HONORS, with its Humanist of the Year award, an exceptional individual who has made great contributions to the world, whether through science, education, literature, humanitarian work, or some other avenue. Recipients have included Carl Sagan, Kurt Vonnegut, Margaret Sanger, Gloria Steinem, John Kenneth Galbraith, Richard Dawkins, Betty Friedan, and Ted Turner, and the award ceremony is always the centerpiece of the AHA's annual conference, as the honoree gives a speech and mingles with the crowd for the evening.

In 1976 the Humanist of the Year was Dr. Jonas Salk, who discovered and developed the first polio vaccine, thereby solving one of the world's most devastating public health problems. Prior to Salk's breakthrough in the 1950s, polio killed thousands each year and crippled many thousands more; Americans cited the disease as one of their greatest fears, second only to the atomic bomb.[1] Announcement of the vaccine in 1955 made Salk an instant celebrity; he was hailed as a "benefactor of mankind" by President Eisenhower and showered with awards and honors. Asked who owned the patent on the vaccine, Salk magnanimously replied, "Well, the people, I would say. There is no patent. Could you patent the sun?"[2]

Salk's benevolence in not patenting the vaccine has become part of his mystique, but that legend, like many, is probably a bit exaggerated. In fact, lawyers for Salk's lab had researched the possibility of patenting the vaccine and concluded that, for technical reasons, it probably wasn't patentable, so they never applied.[3] Still, unlike modern pharmaceutical companies, profit clearly wasn't Salk's top priority—he was inspired by a love of science, with motives that were primarily humanitarian.

Most people would agree that individuals such as Salk, whose contributions are truly exceptional, would be justified in reaping huge financial gains. Americans see their country as a meritocracy, where hard work, talent, creativity, and enterprise are rewarded. Salk had labored long hours in his lab for years with the singular goal of eradicating polio, and through his persistence he improved the quality of life for countless individuals and families around the globe. Few Americans would have objected to Salk attaining multibillionaire status for his discovery, even though he never did. (If a patent for Salk's vaccine had been obtained, its estimated value would have been $7 billion.)[4]

THE DREAM OR THE MYTH?

This appreciation for hard work, creativity, and enterprise underlies the American dream—a deep-rooted belief that our system provides limitless opportunity to those with talent and ambition. This is the beauty of free enterprise, we are told, and why America produces so many great innovators, from Thomas Edison to the Wright brothers to Henry Ford. Our entire society—especially our marketplace—is geared to encourage a work ethic, so even those born on the lower economic rungs need only apply themselves to enjoy the upward mobility that America offers.

Closer scrutiny, however, reveals that much of this dream is no longer accurate. In fact, studies show that Americans today enjoy less economic mobility than the populations of most other Western countries.[5] Stories about upward mobility, from Horatio Alger's shoeshine boys to George Jefferson's "Movin' on Up," can be entertaining and inspiring, but in America they are increasingly limited to the realm of fiction. For example, whereas 42 percent of American men raised in the bottom fifth of income brackets remain there as adults, according to a 2012 report in the *New York Times,* only 25 percent do so in Denmark and 30 percent in Britain.[6] The same report cited at least five studies indicating lower mobility rates in the United States than in other developed countries.

What seems clear from the data is that one's status in America is contingent not so much on talent or hard work but on the family into which one is born. A study by the U.S. Department of Education revealed that students with high test scores but low-income parents were less likely to finish college than students with low test scores but affluent parents—or, as columnist Paul Krugman bluntly translated, "smart poor kids are less likely than dumb rich kids to get a degree."[7] One reason is surely the cost of college. Especially at top-tier universities, but increasingly at less prestigious schools as well, higher education has become so ridiculously expensive that more and more people no longer see it as an option.

One inescapable fact here is that the nations with greater economic mobility (i.e., just about all other developed nations) would be characterized by America's conservatives as "socialist." This description, like much conservative rhetoric, is exaggerated, since most other Western societies are not really socialist but have mixed economies that utilize both free enterprise and some public delivery of services, only with more emphasis than America on egalitarianism. If we dare to speak it, the logical conclusion is that egalitarian public policy creates a fair playing field that nurtures opportunity and true meritocracy.

Meanwhile, the experience of daily life is only getting harder for America's poor and certainly doesn't offer many opportunities for advancement. Jobs, to the extent they can be found, are unlikely to be secure and are increasingly obtained through temporary employment agencies, with wages, even for full-time work, at or near poverty levels, and with no benefits.[8] Few jobs are unionized anymore, as labor unions were long ago overpowered and outmaneuvered by corporate interests with far greater resources. Public schools are broke, especially in poor communities, and supplemental nutrition programs and other safety nets have been cut. These are all areas where anti-egalitarian interests have succeeded in implementing public policy that works against ordinary citizens, especially the poor—and against true meritocracy.

THE BUSINESS OF MAKING MONEY

Despite these unpleasant truths, we like to think that our flawed system reflects at least a general disposition toward hard work and enterprise. We may not be doing a good job of putting talented poor kids on a track toward economic success, but at least the individuals who do make it to the top are hardworking, creative contributors to society, right? Well, not exactly. The oft-repeated myth is that those in the upper economic strata are people like Thomas Edison or Steve Jobs—innovative geniuses whose contributions benefit everyone—but the reality is much different. Rather than great scientists, inventors, and innovators, the upper echelons of the American economic classes are more often populated by those who successfully exploit (or whose families have successfully exploited) the financial system, which is built upon the perceived value of corporate interests.

In America, the top one percent of income earners account for about 20 percent of total income, and relatively few of these individuals innovate like Edison or Jobs. Most are employed in the financial sector or senior corporate management, in careers that are primarily dependent on financial market valuations.[9] In essence, the American economy has evolved in a way that allows a lot of people to enjoy significant wealth via its financial system, reaping rewards not through any great social contribution, technological innovation, or advancement of knowledge, but by participating in an elaborate system constructed around the concept of corporate valuation. This financial sector has seen explosive growth in the last generation. Daily shares traded in New York in 1971 averaged about 15 million, whereas today that figure is around 4 *billion*.

The mutual fund industry handily illustrates this astonishing growth. Mutual funds, which allow ordinary investors to pool money so that professional fund managers can invest the funds in a variety of stocks and other investments, thereby allowing each investor to hold a more diverse portfolio just by owning shares of the fund, were almost nonexistent as a savings or retirement device in ordinary American households until the late twentieth century. In 1975 there were a total of only 426 mutual funds in the country, with total assets of $46 billion. By 2012 there were 7,596 funds with assets of over $13 *trillion*.[10] Large financial firms advertise aggressively, usually showing ordinary couples and families at various stages of life, perhaps playing golf or sitting on a beach as they enjoy the satisfaction of having invested wisely. The underlying message is that the investment firm in question, whether Fidelity, Vanguard, Franklin Templeton, or another, can deliver such prosperity and security, but only if you claim your share of the corporate growth that drives rising stock prices and mutual fund share value.

With the expansion of mutual funds, an entire industry has grown up around the idea of capitalizing on the perceived value of corporations. The financial services industry, which does not actually produce necessary goods and services in the traditional sense, now accounts for more than 20 percent of the U.S. gross domestic product, a share that is about double what it was in the 1970s and comparable to that of the federal government.[11] With so much money being poured into the sector, it's little wonder that lobbyists were soon applying enormous political pressure on legislators to deregulate the industry. And so they did, in various steps over the years, culminating in 1999, when Democratic president Bill Clinton signed an act lifting barriers that had previously prohibited the consolidation of banks, securities companies, and insurance companies. This deregulation, not surprisingly, was portrayed as "modernization" that would benefit consumers, with the enormous profits reaped by financial firms, of course, just incidental. Also unsurprising were the unscrupulous schemes that quickly emerged on the deregulated financial playground, resulting in wildly speculative investments—such as the dot-com bubble of 2000 that saw trillions of dollars evaporate—and the creation of investment vehicles that even professionals didn't understand, such as the mortgage-backed securities that led to the subprime crisis of 2008.

And as the financial industry continued to grow, more and more ordinary people became part of it. Whereas a financial advisor was once assumed to be a highly skilled individual, presumably with an MBA or something similar, by the 1990s mutual funds were being sold almost like Tupperware. One "financial advisor" who approached me in an attempt to sell mutual funds was a former truck driver, another had been laid off from a computer company, and another had majored in music in college. All had obtained the necessary licensing for this career change without so much as an undergrad business degree.

Thus, today's America is totally dependent on a stock market that is performing well, creating enormous pressure for short-term growth to please fund managers and large institutional investors. The entire economy has been constructed around the idea of corporate value—and, more specifically, the assumption that corporate values will continue to increase. Corporate value, meanwhile, as reflected in stock price, is based primarily on the perceived ability of a corporation to continue profit growth. Everyone has a stake in corporations and their profits, yet this measure of value fails to account for profits arising from unscrupulous and socially undesirable corporate activity. Moreover, few even acknowledge that the structure of the system, particularly the nature of corporations themselves, actually encourages such activity. If war, environmental destruction, mistreatment of workers or consumers, or other misdeeds are profitable, corporations will see them as desirable. If the system is not necessarily immoral, it is at best amoral.

SOCIETY CONFORMS TO CORPORATISM

Corporations have an interest in shaping society in a way that will maximize their pursuit of profit, and they will naturally try to do so unless stopped. It shouldn't be surprising, therefore, that we regularly see well-funded efforts to deregulate entire industries, to subsidize other industries through government spending (especially military spending), to limit unions, and so forth. The mere existence of corporations makes such efforts inevitable.

Their success, however, should not be considered inevitable. An alert and critically thinking public, capable of recognizing and opposing the corporate pursuit of power and profit, could use the democratic process to rationally regulate and control corporations, so that corporate institutions serve the public good without dominating government and all of society. Rather than deregulating banking to allow the consolidation of large financial firms, for example, there is no reason that America could not have instead, through sensible public policy, solidified the concept of community banking and local investment. We went the opposite direction, allowing the vast expansion and consolidation of multinational financial firms to the detriment of smaller community banks, because real humans are not in charge. We can have private ownership, capitalism, and free enterprise without handing over almost complete control of the system to corporate interests, but it will take effort.

The systemic obsession with short-term corporate profit is reflected in what Americans do as a people and how they shape their lives. For example, there is little reason for any bright young person in American society to go to medical school, when more money can be made with less effort by obtaining a master's in business administration. Only about 17,000 students graduate from medical school each year in America, whereas about 150,000 graduate with MBAs. Graduates from top business schools embark immediately for careers on Wall Street or with major corporations, usually earning far beyond what medical school graduates earn. The median first-year pay package for a Harvard MBA working in private equity, venture capital, or leveraged buyouts, according to a CNN/*Fortune* report in 2014, was $327,500.[12] Even the average MBA graduate from an ordinary school outside the top tier will earn close to a six-digit salary immediately, with income usually climbing steadily thereafter.

Medical school students, meanwhile, go to school longer, tackle highly demanding material, and typically graduate with debt between $150,000 and $200,000, sometimes much higher. For all of this, the reward is an average income that is hardly more enticing: The average salary for a resident is about $56,000, while a starting pediatrician can expect about $109,000 and an internist only slightly higher.[13] We can see why many of the best and brightest would pass at this option.

In fact, there are few positions in the American economy more financially rewarding than that of upper management in a publicly traded corporation. While such a position certainly requires intelligence and skill to perform well, any objective assessment would conclude that the compensation is disproportionate to the work performed. Average CEO pay among the top 350 corporations is over $14 million annually, a figure 273 times that of the average worker, according to the Economic Policy Institute. In the 1970s, the figure was less than 30 times average worker pay.[14] Few other careers offer rewards close to this, so it's understandable that top American students would choose business schools over science labs.

Great rewards await even those whose performance can be described as mediocre, such as that of JCPenney CEO Ron Johnson, whose 2011 compensation package of about $53 million was 1,795 times that of the average department store worker.[15] The pay is even more outlandish in light of his performance, which saw the company experience a disastrous

25 percent drop in sales in his first year, leading to his ouster.[16] This kind of exorbitance is by far most prominent in the United States, where CEO-to-worker pay ratios are higher than in any other country and a multiple of most (France is 104:1, for example, Britain is 84:1, and Japan is 67:1).[17] Even these countries, of course, are not immune from the undue influence of corporate power, and an argument could be made that even their rates of compensation are excessive, but the United States stands high above others in lavishing riches upon those driving corporate engines.

To anyone thinking critically, this system would seem to be one with misplaced values, but it would be a mistake to blame the situation on private enterprise per se. We can have relatively open markets, fair competition, and a wide array of consumer products and options without unleashing powerful corporate entities to do whatever they wish. Capitalism, like socialism, is a somewhat nebulous term, but it's clear that the system operating today in America is severely compromised from its idyllic version. American capitalism has become a form of instant gratification in which the single motivating force is not just profit itself—which would be bad enough—but *short-term profit.* The system lives and breathes to satisfy nonhuman, institutional interests run by managers whose concerns and visions rarely project beyond the next quarterly earnings report. Especially in a democracy in which the will of the people should be able to restrain other interests, there is no inherent reason that concentrated corporate power should be the tail wagging the dog.

HUMANS AS SECOND-CLASS CITIZENS

The systemic flaws just outlined also highlight an imperfect framework used by some who are fighting for rational, egalitarian policy. Popular rhetoric in recent years has focused on the enigmatic "one percent," a term popularized by the Occupy Wall Street movement but subsequently adopted by many others to signify the richest of the rich, the elite few who actually own and control so much of America. The intent is understandable, for those elite few certainly do stand apart from ordinary Americans who struggle to pay bills, worry about job security, and hold relatively modest hopes and expectations. But because language is important, we should realize that the "one percent" concept can actually be misleading and counterproductive.

Most important, the "one percent" framing, by vilifying a tiny slice of the overall American demographic, points the finger at the wrong place. The reason American public policy has lurched so far to the right is not a conspiracy of the wealthiest one percent of individuals, but because *large institutional interests* have gained the upper hand over *ordinary humans*. The problem is systemic—and it arises from corporate institutions, not individuals.

The wealthiest one percent of Americans would be a cross section of about three million individuals, some of whom (such as the Koch brothers) no doubt advocate for anti-egalitarian policy, but others of whom, such as Bill Gates and Warren Buffett, generally do not. Buffett penned a column in the *New York Times,* for example, headlined "Stop Coddling the Super-Rich," that was highly critical of tax breaks for the rich, pointing out that he paid a lower percentage of his income in taxes than did his secretary.[18] Gates is among dozens of wealthy Americans who in recent years have called for raising more revenue for the federal government through higher estate taxes. Some of these efforts have been organized by Responsible Wealth, a network of leaders in America's wealthiest 5 percent who, according to their Web site, "believe that growing inequality is not in their best interests, nor in the best interest of society."[19] It's easy and tempting to paint the richest individuals as the bad guys, and surely some of them have a hand in driving anti-egalitarian policy, but targeting these individuals can also be a wasteful distraction from the much deeper systemic issues relating to corporate power.

Importantly, as impressive as the wealth of the richest one percent of individuals might seem, it generally pales by comparison to the wealth of corporations. In his above-mentioned column, for example, Buffett reported paying income taxes of just under $7 million in 2010—17.4 percent of his taxable income, which therefore would have been just under $42 million. Before he started giving away much of his fortune to charity in recent years, Buffett's net worth was estimated to be around $64 billion. Most of us would be pretty happy with that personal balance sheet, yet it's a pittance when compared to those of many publicly traded companies. If Buffett, one of the richest individuals in the country, were himself a corporation, he would be about the size of one typical large-cap company, nothing particularly noteworthy. At $64 billion, his net worth even at its peak was far below the market capitalization of large publicly traded companies. (In terms of market capitalization, each of the top ten largest companies, for example, is well above $200 billion in value.)

Keeping in mind that there are literally tens of thousands of publicly traded companies out there, the error and futility of blaming bad public policy on a few rich individuals—when in fact an entire nonhuman corporate sector drives such policy—becomes clear. All of these companies are driven by the single goal of maximizing profit, they enjoy resources that are far beyond those available to ordinary humans, and most of them are owned not by humans but by other corporations that expect strong earnings reports each quarter. With this background, talk of the one percent becomes a distraction.

Faced with such a formidable foe, ordinary citizens stand no chance unless they actively promote their own human interests. Few would wish to return to pre-corporate days of low technology, and most realize that the answer to the problem of corporate power is not a government takeover of Apple or General Electric—so in that sense, corporate interests have made themselves indispensible. The only realistic solution, therefore, is to allow the corporations to stick around but with the understanding that they work for us, not vice versa.

This can be achieved by dispensing with the idea that corporations, as "people," enjoy rights equivalent to those of real humans. Corporations are entities that hold immense wealth—much more than real humans—and therefore their role must be strictly defined. The idea that corporate entities must enjoy the same level of constitutional protections as those afforded to real people is, in fact, a danger to real people. Humans become less influential and less powerful when institutional interests gain rights equal to theirs, particularly when those institutions hold wealth that far exceeds that of individuals. By giving corporate entities full constitutional protection, we create a class of "people" that dominates less powerful, flesh-and-blood humans. In essence, we have created a class structure whereby humans are second-class citizens in a society in which nonhuman people are the first-class citizens.

CONSERVATIVE FRAMING

Whenever progressives raise issues such as corporate power or wealth dispar-ity, conservatives inevitably shoot back with dreaded accusations of "social-ism," which for many is synonymous with "anti-American." Exemplifying the anti-intellectual atmosphere of the times, conservatives started hurling accusations of "socialist" at Barack Obama from the earliest days of his presidency, even on mundane issues.[20] For example, writing in *Forbes* (sup-posedly a respectable mainstream publication) on the subject of Obama's plan to raise taxes modestly on the highest income bracket, Peter Ferrara called Obama not just a socialist but a "Marxist," implying truly revolution-ary intentions. "So why does President Obama keep saying that the rich do not pay their fair share? Is he ignorant?" asked Ferrara, pointing out that the rich already pay more taxes than the poor. "The answer is that to President Obama this is still not fair because he is a Marxist. To a Marxist, the fact that the top 1% earn more income than the bottom 99% is not fair, no matter how they earn it." To Ferrara, this "is the only logical explanation" of Obama's proposal.[21]

This is alarmist enough, but it's even more bizarre when we consider that Obama's top marginal tax rates (35 percent) were well below Ron-ald Reagan's (50 percent for six of his eight years).[22] If this makes Obama a Marxist, his fellow travelers would include other notorious Bolsheviks such as billionaires Warren Buffett, Bill Gates, and Mark Zuckerberg, all of whom have called for higher taxation on the wealthy.[23]

One need not be a socialist to understand that a reflexive fear of the word "socialism" is both irrational and counterproductive—"so twentieth century," as my college friend might say. Of course, there are rational arguments for and against various governmental actions such as tax in-creases, regulation of business, and social programs like Obamacare, but a public that is going to be persuaded on such issues by wild accusations of "Marxism"—as if an uptick in the highest marginal tax rate is the first step down a slippery slope to totalitarianism—is in no position to ratio-nally discuss policy. The psychological dynamics are astounding: Fear has trumped critical thinking, and the debate is doomed.

The accusations of "socialism" that reflexively emanate from conserva-tive politicians and pundits are, in fact, an effort to limit the scope of debate.

Once corporations gained sufficient power and were capable of exerting great influence over society in general and government in particular, they naturally opposed any ideas and institutions that threatened their domination. Hence, any agenda that could be described as remotely socialistic—rights and fair wages for workers, regulation of corporate activity, higher taxes, or programs providing broad public benefits—is adverse to the corporate mission of maximizing profit. (Let's not even consider true socialism: the public takeover of businesses or industries.) For obvious reasons, corporations are not fond of egalitarian policies that benefit real humans but impinge on profits, and therefore it's not surprising that a corporate-dominated society denigrates such ideas. By first demonizing socialism and then allowing any pro-worker or pro-consumer idea to be labeled "socialist," the debate is framed in a way that works to the advantage of corporate interests.

UNNATURAL AND UNJUSTIFIED

Most Americans, if asked, would probably say that markets should determine wages and salaries, that any attempt by government to influence that process through legislation (other than a fair minimum wage) should be viewed skeptically. This may be true as a general notion, but it is yet another area where pragmatism and critical thinking can be very useful.

For one thing, the obscene compensation enjoyed by those on the high end of the pay scale is not the result of free market forces, but of government action. The richest of the rich generally achieve their status through the activity of corporations—as investors or as upper management, or both—and corporations are *unnatural* entities that can be created only through government action. It is not the "pure" capitalism of Adam Smith that we see playing out in the American system but a game in which the government is complicit. The most frequent winners are hardly the great scientific innovators or contributors but the individuals who have learned the rules of high finance and corporatism.

Investment bankers, Wall Street insiders, and corporate CEOs can hardly be compared to Jonas Salk. Any critical thinker would question whether their outrageous salaries are justified, because common sense raises the question of just what they contribute to society. Their value, unlike that of a doctor, scientist, or teacher, is derived almost entirely from the perceived value of corporate shares, which are in turn entirely reliant on government action for their very existence. The compensation packages that put them at the top of the economic food chain are made possible only by the government-created system that allows not just the creation of unnatural corporations but the public trading of the shares of those corporations. As such, it's reasonable to ask whether the social value of these top earners is even remotely commensurate to their pay.

This is not to suggest that government must institute policies that strictly regulate wages and salaries, but certainly a sober assessment of the more egregious aspects of wealth inequality calls out for rational measures. Bear in mind that much of the disparity—from the outlandish pay of the top earners who exploit corporatism to their advantage to the poverty-level pay of those at the bottom—is produced by corporatism, by the obsession with short-term profit growth inherent in the system. Just as corporate dominance enables those who assist the drive for short-term profits to reap huge rewards, it drives down the pay of those real people who stand no chance of competing with corporate power. Corporate dominance dismantles the power of labor unions that once helped working people get a fairer deal. Corporate dominance encourages the anti-intellectualism and anti-egalitarianism that is so prominent in American society, so that even modest egalitarian proposals are met with accusations of socialism. And of course, the combination of corporate dominance and widespread exaltation of religion helps assure that subversive influences—such as freethought and egalitarianism—remain at the fringes. Understanding the problem as such, we can hopefully start working toward answers that are fair to all.

ANTIREASON MAKES IT POSSIBLE

Both the consolidation of corporate power and the vilification of egalitarianism are achieved most effectively when the public involved can be easily manipulated. A vigilant public, facing an increasingly powerful corporate sector, would of course use any means within its ability—especially the means of democratic government—to check corporate power and ensure that public policy responds to real human needs, not necessarily the needs and desires of nonhuman institutions. But a public that has quashed freethought will be incapable of such vigilance.

We see this play out constantly, as much of the public accepts the spin from Fox News and other conservative media that any marginally egalitarian policy is anti-American. Obama may be proposing a modest tax increase on the wealthy—an unremarkable policy proposal in any capitalist system—but to millions of Americans, he may as well be reciting the Communist Manifesto or singing "The Internationale." After all, accusations of socialism emanate not just from the reactionary fringes of cyberspace but from national GOP leaders and respected publications such as the *Wall Street Journal*.[24]

The first step in addressing this mischaracterization is to acknowledge its absurdity. It should be beyond dispute, for example, that a strong social safety net is entirely consistent with a free market economy in a modern high-tech society. In fact, most sensible Americans know that a mix of free enterprise and government regulation and safety nets—neither laissez-faire capitalism nor socialism—is a formula for prosperity and social stability. Social Security, unemployment insurance, Medicare, food stamps, and similar programs can guarantee a minimum level of assistance to some of the most vulnerable within the population, benefits that can be provided without seriously inhibiting commerce and without placing an unfair burden on anyone. In fact, as anyone familiar with the lower end of the economic spectrum knows, most monetary benefits—whether a Social Security check, food stamps, or an unemployment check—get poured right back into the economy.

Although it would be a gross mischaracterization to describe such commonsense programs as being a first step toward Big Brother, this is the kind of fear that popular conservative media encourage. "Inside Every Liberal Is A Totalitarian Screaming to Get Out" declares the permanent banner of conservative Web site *FrontPage Magazine*, run by the David Horowitz Freedom Center.[25] Appearing on Fox News, commentator David Limbaugh described Obama's agenda as "totalitarian, socialist, and divisive."[26] Sarah Palin, echoing many other conservatives, told audiences that Obamacare would require bureaucrats to consider a patient's "level of productivity in society" to determine whether he or she is "worthy" of health care. The Orwellian nightmare Obama envisions, Palin warned, is "downright evil."[27]

Fairly considered, such claims would be recognized as baseless and ideologically driven. A review of the health care law by fact checkers revealed

Palin's warning, as well as claims that the law encourages euthanasia and counsels seniors to shorten their lives, to be completely unfounded, calling such claims "extreme" and "more like a science fiction movie."[28] It's not surprising that political opponents would misrepresent facts and make attempts to instill fear, but what's remarkable about policy discussion in America is the degree to which a gullible public accepts such claims.

HUMAN NEEDS OR INSTITUTIONAL NEEDS?

Often accompanying the "socialist" allegation in American politics is the claim that social spending, taxes, and regulations are signs of "big government." Thus, the argument goes, we can't let government grow into a behemoth under those taxing-and-spending liberals. The farcical nature of this argument becomes clear, however, once we look seriously at so-called conservative budget proposals, which almost always call for increases in spending in the one area that takes up by far the largest portion of the nation's discretionary budget—the military. A relatively insignificant government program to aid the poor, such as food stamps or heating assistance, is always "socialism," but far greater government spending on the military, no matter how exuberant or unnecessary, is beyond question. The debate between conservatives and liberals, therefore, is not really one of small government versus big government, but the age-old question of guns versus butter.

In American society for the last half century, guns have been winning over butter, thanks in large part to the suppression of freethought. Fear-based politics and appeals to nationalism and patriotism have resulted in a virtual blank check for the defense department and hostility toward almost all nonmilitary aspects of government. Millions support candidates who openly promise to dismantle government, deregulate Wall Street, cut taxes on the rich, eliminate social programs, and inject anti-intellectualism into schools and public life while of course continuing to ramp up military spending. This antihuman platform is justified by its proponents—who are well funded by corporate interests and enjoy wide grassroots support from networks of conservative churches and other organizations—as being true to American values, the best antidote, naturally, to creeping socialism.

In truth, the idea that government must be made to work for real people, not corporations, shouldn't be seen as radical. The choice Americans need to make is not one between capitalism or socialism—like most "isms," even the definitions of these terms are open to debate, and their interpretation and application in the real world make their meaning even more ambiguous—but between a society that complements *human* needs or the needs of *nonhuman* institutions.

Faced with this reality, freethinkers are skeptical of both government and corporate power and therefore realize that rational choices must be made with regard to each. Even though progressives generally see the wisdom of rational egalitarian policies that would regulate corporations, tax everyone fairly, and implement social programs, as freethinkers they also understand the need to remain skeptical of government authority, if only because of its potential for abuse. Their acceptance of government action is not based on a dogmatic belief that government is the best solution for all problems, but on the recognition that, rationally considered, intelligent state action makes sense in specific situations. Anyone who has waited for hours at the department of motor vehicles for something as simple as renewing a driver's license can understand the ranting of those who feel government can't do anything right. The truth is, however, that government does many things very well and in fact can be an excellent means of promoting general prosperity.

Even those who exalt liberty above all other values (usually the same crowd that attacks government) should realize that governmental action actually can promote both liberty and entrepreneurship. When I left a secure job with a large law firm years ago to open my own practice, one of my biggest concerns was providing health insurance for my family, since leaving my employer would mean losing my health insurance. If health care had been made available not as a benefit through my employer but as a *right of citizenship* via single-payer health care through the government, leaving my job and launching my business would have been made easier. Those who insist that government can only obstruct the enterprising spirit rarely consider how a public delivery of services can free individuals from the chains of reliance on private institutions, thereby enabling them to do more.

The freethinker has no sentimental attachment to Adam Smith or Karl Marx, recognizing that both are icons from past centuries and neither has a comprehensive answer to today's challenges. We can recognize the importance of markets without beatifying Smith, who wrote in the early days of the Industrial Revolution before the rise of corporate power, just as we can recognize the ugliness of concentrated power and the injustice of labor exploitation without deifying Marx. Both laissez-faire economics and classless societies can make for enjoyable theoretical discussion, but neither exists in the real world, nor is either likely to exist in our lifetime.

What practical freethinkers and progressives want is a system that is genuinely fair to all. Surely there will be disagreement over just how to define "genuinely fair to all," but that's why it's important to have critical thinking, intelligent public dialogue, and effective democracy.

EIGHT

NEW TRADITIONS

IN HIS FAMOUS "SEGREGATION NOW, SEGREGATION FOREVER" SPEECH of 1963, defiant Alabama governor George Wallace argued for continued separation of the races by repeatedly referring to both God and tradition. "We intend, quite simply, to practice the free heritage as bequeathed to us as sons of free fathers," Wallace declared, adamant that blacks and whites must work from "separate racial stations." This, he explained, was the "great freedom of our American founding fathers." Decrying liberals and the Supreme Court, railing against Harvard intellectuals and "ungodly government," and even stating, incorrectly, that "In God We Trust" was placed on American currency by the founders, Wallace framed the fight to keep the races separate as nothing less than a divine calling to defend America's cultural heritage, proclaiming: "God has placed us here in this crisis!"[1]

Such blending of religion and heritage is nothing new, of course, and the practice shouldn't surprise us. Since religion is part of the cultural history of almost every society, allusions to the divine and to tradition are to be expected, especially in defense of a long-standing institution or attitude. Defenders of all sorts of evils and prejudices—from racism to misogyny to homophobia—have pointed to both God and tradition, often simultaneously, as justification. The Ku Klux Klan frequently has claimed, and in fact still insists today, that it works merely to preserve the "heritage" of "White Christian America."[2] It's well known that the Bible was used to justify slavery in the South, as numerous passages in both the Old and New Testaments condone it, but what most people don't know is that even today some religious conservatives long for a return of the institution, still basing their position on religion and heritage. One such advocate, David Opperman of the online publication *Faith & Heritage,* attributed the fall of slavery, perhaps correctly, to the rise of "a secular humanist worldview." Because humanists value equality, Opperman complained, "slavery in any form must be discarded."[3] (The inclusion of "in any form" is particularly amusing, as if only bleeding-heart liberals would oppose slavery in *all* forms.)

Arguments for the oppression of women are predictably similar. From the refusal to educate girls to the shrouding of women in veils and burqas to the tradition of honor killing, social practices that keep women under control frequently are justified as being both religious and traditional. A more extreme example, female genital mutilation (which involves excision of the clitoris), still is practiced in about two dozen countries and is rationalized as being an "integral part of the societies that practice it, where patriarchal authority and control of female sexuality and fertility are givens."[4] This violent and barbaric disfigurement of girls, usually by someone with no medical training, is explained as a social practice that "reduces the uncertainty surrounding paternity by discouraging or preventing women's sexual activity outside of marriage."

Finally, we find the same dynamics at work in the treatment of gays and lesbians. "Traditional marriage" is the mantra of the vocal opponents of same-sex marriage, who claim to adhere to biblical tradition in insisting that marriage be between a man and a woman only. These arguments conveniently ignore that "biblical marriage" also treated women as chattel, included polygamy, allowed arranged marriages and the marriage of barely pubescent girls, and even called for women to marry their rapists.[5] Today's social conservatives easily discard these aspects of "biblical marriage," but the Bible nevertheless stands as firm authority in their minds when considering the rights of gays and lesbians. Folk artist Roy Zimmerman captures the hypocrisy of religious conservatives marvelously, as only a musician can, in his song "Defenders of Marriage," with the lyrics: "It's the Lord's holy word, my second wife said to my third!"

INVENTING A NEW HERITAGE

Understanding that tradition and heritage, often mixed with religion, can be used to promote injustice, it's no surprise that they pop up again in efforts to implement anti-egalitarian economic policy. Often such historical framing suggests that great wealth disparity is an important part of the fabric of American society. Thus, the Heritage Foundation, a conservative think tank (and note the use of "heritage" in the name), explains its mission this way: "We believe the principles and ideas of the American Founding are worth conserving and renewing. As policy entrepreneurs, we believe the most effective solutions are consistent with those ideas and principles."[6]

Oddly, however, if corporations were virtually nonexistent at the time of the nation's founding, it's hard to see how any economic system totally dominated by them, as America's is today, could be seen as "conserving" the nation's original "principles and ideas." Even though the framers gave no indication that they would be sympathetic to the idea of unrestrained corporate power, the Heritage Foundation's Web site provides one academic article after another attacking government efforts to rein in corporations through environmental regulation, food and drug safety measures, and rules for financial institutions. In the eyes of the Heritage Foundation, these measures are "burdens" that offend the tradition of the framers, who would have been sympathetic to concentrated corporate power and aghast at any kind of governmental authority.[7] Not surprisingly, reports indicate that the foundation, which was cofounded by the notorious conservative Joseph Coors (of Coors beer), receives much of its funding from right-wing benefactors and corporate interests.[8]

In fact, "heritage" is a wildly inaccurate descriptor of the extreme anti-egalitarian character of modern American public policy. Far from adhering to tradition, today's conservative extremists are blazing a new trail that reflects the wishes not of the founders, but of the corporate entities that now control the economy and, for practical purposes, the political system. The growing ratio of CEO pay to that of the average worker, mentioned in the last chapter, demonstrates that growing wealth disparity is a departure from tradition. That ratio has multiplied ten times since 1950, from about 20 to 1 to over 200 to 1.[9] More than 50 percent of all income in 2012 was taken home by the top 10 percent of earners, the highest percentage recorded since records were first collected in 1917.[10] These trends are not in keeping with the nation's heritage.

Yet defenders of anti-egalitarian policy insist not only that it is consistent with tradition but that it is biblical. "Capitalism, in my opinion, is a liberator," said Fox Business host Stuart Varney in describing the religious dimensions of free markets. "Society benefits most when people are free to pursue their own self-interest. I know that sounds like a contradiction, but it is not." We are all better off "financially and spiritually," Varney told his television audience, when we operate in an environment that encourages the selfish pursuit of our own material interests.[11]

What a happy coincidence that the road to salvation encourages unbridled greed! This is entirely consistent with the "prosperity gospel" mentioned earlier, the uniquely American theological movement that teaches material wealth is a sign of God's favor. Some of America's best-known preachers—Joel Osteen, Kenneth Copeland, Benny Hinn, Oral Roberts, and many others—have promoted this distasteful doctrine.[12] Although they're usually careful to avoid expressly accusing the poor of being deservedly so for some lack of righteousness, this is the quiet assumption. Also conveniently implied in the message is that the immense wealth of televangelists—mansions, private planes, the best of everything—is simply the just reward of theological correctness. This idea may contradict the common understanding of the theology of Jesus, but revisionism, as we've seen, is among the many talents of the Christian Right.

Of course, not all theologians approve of the hypercapitalistic Christianity of the prosperity gospel, and the conflict can be instructive even for those outside the flock. Pope Francis, for example, has been vocal in his criticism of capitalism, directly targeting the influence of high finance and the wealth disparity it creates. "While the earnings of a minority are growing exponentially, so too is the gap separating the majority from the prosperity enjoyed by those happy few," he said in 2013 in one of the first major writings of his papacy.[13] "This imbalance is the result of ideologies which defend the absolute autonomy of the marketplace and financial speculation. Consequently, they reject the right of states, charged with vigilance for the common good, to exercise any form of control. A new tyranny is thus born."

It's interesting that this high-minded and well-meaning rhetoric, while impressive, seems to have much less impact on American Catholics than does papal language criticizing abortion. Most Catholics wouldn't consider giving up their comfortable homes to combat poverty, let alone seriously challenge the capitalist system that their pontiff takes to task. Yet many passionately abide by every pro-life word, as if the papal dictate against abortion were the central theological principle of Catholicism.

Pope Francis's criticisms of the excesses of capitalism, combined with his statements implying a slightly higher tolerance than his predecessors for gays, have raised grave concerns among American conservatives. "He's had some statements that to me sound kind of liberal, has taken me aback, has kind of surprised me," said Sarah Palin in a television interview.[14] Indeed, concern for the poor and tolerance of gays are not characteristics that will endear one to the Religious Right.[15] Others were even harsher. "This is pure Marxism coming out of the mouth of the pope," charged radio host Rush Limbaugh. "It's sad because this pope makes it very clear he doesn't know what he's talking about when it comes to capitalism and socialism and so forth."[16] Note that Limbaugh tosses out that common alarmist fear—socialism—to his loyal followers, who accept it without question.

Pope Francis, a global figure, is proof that not all religious leaders associated with social conservatism are necessarily anti-egalitarian in their economic views, but he is a relatively rare exception. The vast majority of those who press the conservative social agenda, especially in American politics, also embrace the anti-egalitarian, pro-corporate economic policies that contribute to the wealth disparity that has been growing since the mid-twentieth century. And they will insist—wrongly—that they are carrying on the great American tradition of free enterprise.

CHANGING TIMES

One evident problem with appeals to tradition and heritage, regardless of source, is that today is not yesterday. The world has changed. Hence, even when both sides claim to carry the torch of preceding generations, in truth the present day would be unrecognizable to our forebears, and nobody can truly know what individuals from centuries ago would think today. The issue of church-state separation is a good example. We can only guess how

James Madison or John Adams would assess a nativity scene being displayed at a public park today, or a Ten Commandments monument in a courthouse, yet all parties in such disputes confidently claim that the framers would stand with them. It's possible that the framers would be divided on many of these issues, as they were on so much else in their day. Even if there were clear, unambiguous writings from them on these specific issues (which there aren't), the lapse in time and the staggering social, economic, demographic, and technological changes that have occurred in the interim would make their opinions largely irrelevant today anyway.

Regardless of what the framers thought, to compare their America with ours is a useless analogy. The entire country's population, according to the first census in 1790, was only 3.9 million, or smaller than the Phoenix metropolitan area today, and its religious population was relatively homogenous. The nation was not only almost entirely Christian but Protestant: Only 1.6 percent were Catholic.[17] Thus, even if the framers exhibited some tolerance for religiosity in government—and in truth, they exhibited very little—it shouldn't be surprising, given that religious diversity was quite limited. To suggest that whatever toleration they exhibited should be precisely the level that we tolerate today, even though less than half of Americans today are Protestant (and one in five has no religious affiliation at all), makes little sense.[18] Times have changed, the nation has changed, and much greater diversity calls for a different standard. Just as attitudes and laws relating to race, gender, and sexual preference have evolved, so too with religion.

But the urge to have the founders on one's side is clearly compelling. Personally, if they could magically be transported by time travel to modern America, I tend to believe that the founders would be too overawed by technology to pay much attention to questions of law, at least initially. One could imagine Jefferson spending months digesting all of the scientific and technological advancements—indoor plumbing, biology and genetics, electronics, automobiles and jets, space exploration, and everything else—before it would occur to him to inquire about government and law. Of course, we'll never know—and that is the real point here.

The same point applies when we attempt to claim tradition and heritage with regard to economic matters. Preindustrial America was a world that modern Americans would find unrecognizable. Subsistence farming, small merchants, crude technology, no large industries, and relatively little trade—while much nostalgia about life back then is more mythological than reality based, the common quip that those were "simpler times" is misleading at best. Consumer products were almost nonexistent, limited to basic commodities and necessary tools that were almost always manufactured nearby. Transportation, if not by foot, was by horse or boat. The most sophisticated communication medium was the newspaper. Medicine was primitive—there was no knowledge of cells, viruses, genes, or vaccines—and sophisticated diagnostic tools such as X-rays, MRIs, and the like were still generations away. Many experts believe that George Washington was bled to death by his physicians, who saw bloodletting as a legitimate treatment for many ailments. Yes, simpler times.

Compare this to modern America, where we zip around town—and across the country—in sophisticated machines guided by technology that uses satellites orbiting many miles over the earth, where we can communicate in real time with individuals hundreds or even thousands of miles away. The Internet, television, and numerous high-tech devices, most of which were manufactured far away by multinational corporations, are in our homes, even usually the homes of the poor. All of this would have been unimaginable in the founding era.

Keep these facts in mind when any politician or other opinion leader claims the legacy of the founders when advocating for particular public policy, including economic. Jefferson did indeed advocate for small government, for example, but that hardly supports an argument for stripping today's federal government of the ability to regulate multinational corporate interests. Again, it's an apples-and-oranges comparison.

Claims of tradition and heritage become only slightly less facile when we move into the industrial age. It is true that in the early days of industrialization, government did little to regulate businesses or protect ordinary workers and citizens, but it was also a world of exploitation and squalor, hardly what we mean when we refer to the "good old days." It was a transformational time when economic changes resulted in severe injustices, inequities that eventually forced political change. Nineteenth-century industrialization spurred great waves of immigration to America, and those demographic changes eventually gave rise to democratic demands for more egalitarian public policy, but progress came slowly. Thus, America's early industrialization isn't a sentimental reflection of free enterprise but rather another chapter in the clash of egalitarian and anti-egalitarian forces—and an important one.

.SEPARATE AND UNEQUAL

The latter decades of the nineteenth century, sometimes referred to as the Gilded Age, were a time of rapid industrialization and the growth of great concentrations of wealth—John D. Rockefeller in oil, Andrew Carnegie in steel, the powerful railroad conglomerates, and the emergence of Wall Street financial interests. It was also a period in which America took a sharp turn in the direction of anti-egalitarianism.

When the Civil War ended in 1865, the country was poised for great economic expansion. It had abundant natural resources, no serious external enemies, the necessary levels of technological advancement, steady streams of immigrant labor, and social, political, and economic systems in place to allow growth. Even from the earliest days, America's political and legal systems were greatly influenced by the nation's wealthiest sectors—the founders, after all, were rich establishment men, not fringe radicals seeking to overturn the economic order—but in the late nineteenth century the nation's power dynamic was redefined. To accompany the nation's growing industrialization, a new vehicle emerged for the concentration and accumulation of wealth at levels far beyond anything previously seen: the corporation. And because neither social nor economic egalitarianism served the interests of the increasingly powerful corporate sector, both faired poorly during this era. Hence, ironically, although we think of the Civil War as having been fought in the name of egalitarianism—what could be more egalitarian than the abolition of slavery?—the postwar period was one of the most anti-egalitarian in history.

Immediately after the Civil War, there were a few efforts to ensure civil rights for the freed slaves in the South, but they were largely abandoned within just a few years. Most historians date the end of the so-called Reconstruction era to 1877, when the federal government removed the last of its troops from the South, thereby enabling white supremacists to reestablish control of state and local governments. The Confederacy had lost the war, but anti-egalitarianism would define the culture in Dixie for generations to come. Jim Crow laws institutionalized segregation and excluded blacks from holding office and even voting, ensuring second-class citizenship. Despite the high-minded rhetoric about freedom and equal rights that accompanied the drive to abolish slavery and defeat the South, the postwar realities reflected little concern for the plight of African Americans.

The segregated South naturally becomes a focal point when discussing American racism in the late nineteenth and twentieth centuries, but in fact racism was rampant throughout the country. The white population of the North, while opposing slavery, nevertheless generally saw African Americans as less than equal, and often even educated individuals simply could not overcome long-standing, deeply rooted racial biases. What we find is not that the South was racist while the rest of the country wasn't, but only that racism in the old Confederacy was simply more extreme and overt. When Theodore Roosevelt invited Booker T. Washington to dine at the White House in 1901, four decades after the Civil War, it was the first such invitation to a person of color, and it created a national controversy that especially enraged the South. The *Memphis Scimitar* called the dinner "the most damnable outrage ever," and Mississippi politician James K. Vardaman said the White House had become "so saturated with the odor of the nigger that the rats have taken refuge in the stable."[19] If there was any question whether Vardaman's comments were outside the mainstream in his home state, they are put to rest by the fact that he was subsequently elected to terms as both governor and senator.

But whereas Vardaman, who advocated lynching as a device to maintain white supremacy, represented a brazenly racist view that was widespread, even the more enlightened Roosevelt had a ways to go.[20] Roosevelt's attitude toward African Americans was "contradictory," writes biographer Nathan Miller. "Like most white Americans of the day, he accepted the view that as a group blacks, in terms of education and social attainments, were inferior to whites, but felt that discrimination, with its attendant lynchings, antiblack riots, and poverty, was morally wrong." Miller, whose depiction of Roosevelt is generally favorable, describes Roosevelt's view toward blacks as "paternalistic," which is instructive when we consider that Roosevelt was on what would have been considered the liberal, enlightened, egalitarian end of the spectrum among whites of his day on the issue of race.[21] Between Vardaman and Roosevelt sat the vast majority of white Americans, many of whom were working-class immigrants who had never interacted in any significant way with people of color and who often carried vile racist views as part of their social and cultural baggage.

If jurisprudence is any indication of the national consciousness, the anti-egalitarian tendencies of the period are reflected in the landmark 1896 Supreme Court case of *Plessy v. Ferguson,* which upheld racial segregation in public facilities. The seven-to-one decision, famous for the doctrine of "separate but equal," would give official sanction to the second-class citizenship of blacks, validating racist attitudes that would inhibit social progress for generations. In confirming the legality of a Louisiana statute requiring racially segregated railroad cars, the majority opinion of Justice Henry Brown was candid in its acceptance of anti-egalitarianism, arguing that only *political* equality was required by the Constitution, not *social* equality: "A statute which implies merely a legal distinction between the white and colored races—a distinction which is founded in the color of the two races and which must always exist so long as white men are distinguished from the other race by color—has no tendency to destroy the legal equality of the races." The Constitution, the court ruled, "could not have been intended to abolish distinctions based upon color, or to enforce social, as distinguished from political equality, or a commingling of the two races upon terms unsatisfactory to either."[22]

The invidiousness of the *Plessy* decision is staggering in historical hindsight, but at the time the opinion was hardly controversial. Even some important African American leaders, such as Booker T. Washington, addressing the separate-but-equal issue, focused more on the importance of the separate accommodations being truly equal (which they were not) than on the underlying wrongfulness of the doctrine itself.[23] But egalitarian voices surely could be found, as in the dissenting opinion in *Plessy* of Justice John Marshall Harlan, a former slave owner who understood the motivations behind segregationist laws. "The thing to accomplish was, under the guise of giving equal accommodations for whites and blacks, to compel the latter to keep to themselves while travelling in railroad passenger coaches." Insisting that "in the eye of the law, there is in this country no superior, dominant, ruling class of citizens," Harlan famously declared: "Our Constitution is color-blind. . . . The arbitrary separation of citizens, on the basis of race, while they are on a public highway, is a badge of servitude wholly inconsistent with the civil freedom and the equality before the law established by the Constitution. It cannot be justified on any legal grounds."[24] For the cause of egalitarian public policy, it was most unfortunate that such forceful language was that of the lone dissenter.

CORPORATE POWER GROWS

While the specter of racism made social egalitarianism impossible in America in the generations following the end of slavery, economic dynamics were also at work in shaping the culture. Most important, the role of the corporation as the dominant institution in American society, ultimately more influential than either the government or the citizenry itself, was being solidified. This was predictable, since corporations now employed millions, produced vast wealth for investors, and provided the foundation for much economic activity. As steel, mining, oil, railroad, and banking interests became the backbone of the economy, they wielded enormous social and political power; governments, from small municipalities to the halls of power in Washington, responded to their wishes, and individuals and families increasingly depended on them.

An excellent example of the power of corporate interests, as well as the futility of democratic efforts to restrain that power, is the Sherman Anti-Trust Act, a statute passed by Congress in 1890 in an effort to control the monopolies and cartels that were so obviously coming to dominate the nation. In the midst of the Gilded Age, public concern over the corruption and inequality that seemed to accompany growing corporate power had slowly given rise to progressive and populist reform efforts, and the Sherman Act was a manifestation of that sentiment. The law declared illegal any monopoly and any "contract, combination in the form of trust or otherwise, or conspiracy, in restraint of trade of commerce." Senator John Sherman of Ohio, author of the law, said its purpose was "to protect the consumers by preventing arrangements designed, or which tend, to advance the cost of goods to the consumer."[25]

Unfortunately, however, in an astonishing example of what concentrated wealth can accomplish by utilizing the available political and legal processes, this noble piece of consumer protection legislation subsequently was used for the exact opposite purpose. Rather than restraining monopolies and placing ordinary citizens on a level playing field with corporate interests, the Sherman Act instead was used as a weapon by corporations to crush unionization. An effort to use the act against a monopoly that controlled 98 percent of the nation's sugar output was unsuccessful, for example, but the law was used with drastic effect when a hat manufacturer that was resisting a unionization effort sued the hatters' labor union for calling a boycott of the company's products. The Supreme Court sided with the company, saying the boycott was an unlawful restraint on interstate commerce, and ordered punitive damages against the union.[26]

The hatters' case, with the utilization of the Sherman Act as a weapon *for* corporate interests rather than as a bulwark against them, demonstrates why the effective regulation of corporations is so important. With their ability to hire expensive lawyers, lobbyists, advertisers, and public relations professionals, commercial corporations are much better equipped to use the courts, influence the government, and shape public opinion than any individual could possibly be. Big law firms in this country rarely work for you and me; instead they are in the service of America's corporate and industry interests. Washington and the state capitals of America are filled with lobbyists, almost all on the payroll of corporate interests.

Resistance to unionization was typical of business sentiments in the late nineteenth and early twentieth centuries, as it still is today. Though labor eventually would see some victories in America, peaking in the middle of the twentieth century, the endgame has not been good. Membership in labor unions in 2012 was at an all-time low, at just 11.3 percent of the workforce overall and only 6.6 percent in the private sector.[27] This is a cataclysm that would not have occurred if the public had been better engaged, thinking critically, and in a position to demand egalitarian policy. Instead, corporate interests have gotten what they wanted, proving to be far more influential than labor interests, courtroom opponents, or democratic reform efforts.

The trajectory of history could have been different, even though today's anti-egalitarians will insist that corporate power is as American as apple pie. In fact, although corporate interests have been winning the war so far, there have been progressive victories, sometimes even significant ones, throughout the American narrative. The so-called Progressive Era, a somewhat dubious name for the period from the late 1890s through the first two decades of the twentieth century, was a political response to the excesses of the Gilded Age and saw a number of positive developments, including child labor laws, workers' rights, consumer protections, and democratic political reforms. By this time, however, the corporatist system was so deeply entrenched that it could withstand such occasional waves of progressivism.

A good example of how the law had been framed to favor anti-egalitarianism is the 1905 Supreme Court case of *Lochner v. New York,* in which the court struck down a state statute that limited the number of hours a baker could work a day (to ten). Such regulation of business, the court reasoned in its five-to-four decision, was an unconstitutional restriction on the "liberty of contract," which could not be violated by state laws aimed at protecting petty concerns such as workers' health and safety.[28] With *Lochner,* we see the nineteenth-century exaltation of unrestrained business activity clinging to life and a sharply divided court striking down a modest effort to regulate the workplace. The same liberty of contract was cited by the Supreme Court in the 1915 case of *Coppage v. Kansas,* upholding so-called yellow dog contracts in which an employer hires an employee only on the condition that the employee agree not to join a labor union.[29] In these and many other cases, the courts of this era showed little concern about the relatively unequal bargaining power between an employer and prospective employee; rather they looked on the right to contract as an almost sacred concept that could not be disturbed by government action.

The rare instances when government action was upheld usually involved women and children, two classes of citizens seen as requiring special protection from the paternalistic state. Thus in 1908, just three years after the *Lochner* court refused to regulate bakers' work hours, the Supreme Court in *Muller v. Oregon* upheld a state law imposing a ten-hour workday on employers of women. The court's reasoning would be alarmingly sexist by today's standards. "That woman's physical structure and the performance of maternal functions place her at a disadvantage in the struggle for subsistence is obvious," the unanimous, all-male court declared. A lengthy workday "tends to injurious effects upon the body, and as healthy mothers are essential to vigorous offspring, the physical well-being of woman becomes an object of public interest and care in order to preserve the strength and vigor of the race."[30] The unanimity of the opinion, whereas the *Lochner* court had been sharply divided, illustrates how the fragility of women was one subject on which liberal and conservative men could agree.

The movement to end child labor gained momentum during the Progressive Era, but even here we see the Supreme Court hesitate to regulate business. Although state laws regulating child labor were generally understood to be valid, the Supreme Court in 1918 struck down a federal law that attempted to address the issue. Because federal laws need a basis in the Constitution for validity, Congress based the federal child labor law in question on the constitutional provision allowing the regulation of interstate commerce, thereby prohibiting the sale by interstate commerce of products made by child labor. The Supreme Court, however, skeptical of federal attempts to regulate the sacred realm of commercial activity, found this connection to interstate commerce too tenuous and therefore struck down the law.[31]

Thus, in the early twentieth century, we find courts resistant to democratic efforts to promote egalitarian legislation that would protect workers and other ordinary citizens against more powerful commercial interests, often large corporations. One could argue that this judicial resistance acknowledges some kind of "tradition" or "heritage" of governmental noninterference with commercial matters, but this view doesn't survive scrutiny. It is true that few legal protections existed for the waves of immigrants during the Industrial Revolution in the nineteenth century, but this was not due to any tradition. America had no tradition of corporate manufacturing at all, as the country was making a transition from an agricultural to an industrialized economy. The conditions faced by nineteenth-century industrial workers—men, women, and children—were not traditional and are no basis for nostalgia.

There are many ways to portray historical development, and no interpretation can be wholly objective, but there are serious problems with the depiction of anti-egalitarianism as the only true American tradition. This is where knowledge of history and an ability to think critically are valuable. Attempts to label rational progressive efforts as un-American or socialistic should be sharply rebuked, because there is certainly nothing subversive about egalitarian, human-centered policy. In hindsight, we can see most of the progressive legislation of the early twentieth century as sensible and pragmatic, aimed at ensuring some degree of protection for the health and safety of ordinary people. At the time, those modest measures were met with virulent objections from conservatives, who insisted that any defense of workers' rights or attempt to regulate business was an offense to tradition, even the first step down a slippery slope to communism. We hear the same ranting today.

NOT SO PROGRESSIVE

What is perhaps most noteworthy about the Progressive Era, however, is its moderation. Proving remarkably resilient, anti-egalitarian interests emerged from the era relatively unscathed or even stronger. Rockefeller's Standard Oil empire was dismantled in 1911 under the Sherman antitrust law, and a few legal protections for workers and consumers were passed, but otherwise corporate interests faced no serious threats. The nation, having entered the First World War behind the supposedly reformist Woodrow Wilson (who had won reelection in 1916 by promising to keep the nation out of the war), was feeling a surge of patriotism and a suspicion of foreigners and radical ideas. With the Palmer Raids and the nation's first red scare following the Russian Revolution of 1917, dissent had become dangerous. If the pendulum had swung in the progressive direction for a few years, it was time to reconfirm that acceptable political boundaries must acknowledge the predominance of governmental and corporate power.

After the right of women to vote was secured by ratification of the Nineteenth Amendment in 1920, the American appetite for progressive reform had been fed just enough red meat, and corporate interests, more secure in their place than ever, were finding the environment quite satisfactory. The 1920s would be a decade of three Republican presidents—perhaps best represented by Calvin Coolidge, who famously stated that the business of America is business—and relatively unrestrained corporate activity, including an unregulated stock market. It would take the crash of 1929 to move the pendulum back toward human-centered, progressive public policy.

NINE

SAME OLD DEAL

IF YOU CAN IMAGINE AN AMERICA WHERE EVERY PERSON HAS A RIGHT to a good job, a decent home, health care, education, and comfort in retirement, you're not the first. In fact, you'd be in the company of Franklin D. Roosevelt.

Speaking to Congress and the nation in 1944, with the Second World War still raging in Europe and the Pacific, FDR was already looking ahead to the postwar world, and he proposed a new Bill of Rights—aimed at assuring economic security for all—to supplement those that had been ratified in the founding era. Unlike the *political* rights assured by the constitutional framers—free speech, free press, religious freedom, the right to a jury trial, and others—the rights proposed by FDR would guarantee a certain level of *economic* well-being. "We have come to a clear realization of the fact that true individual freedom cannot exist without economic security and independence," he said. "People who are hungry and out of a job are the stuff of which dictatorships are made."[1] Thus, having witnessed poverty give rise to a fascist nightmare, FDR's call for a guaranteed level of economic security was no exercise in idealism, but was profoundly practical.

FDR was a pragmatist who understood the realities of the modern world. The political rights of the founding era were both enlightened and radical for their time, certainly sufficient for an agrarian society that was severing ties with a distant monarchy, but the definition of "self-evident rights" had changed in the intervening century and a half. "As our nation has grown in size and stature—as our industrial economy expanded—these political rights proved inadequate to assure us equality in the pursuit of happiness," Roosevelt explained. "We have accepted, so to speak, a second Bill of Rights under which a new basis of security and prosperity can be established for all—regardless of station, race, or creed." What FDR was proposing was a kind of egalitarianism, an economy based on vibrant private enterprise but with strong social safety nets that would ensure a level of prosperity, or at least security, for all. His was not a vision of a state-controlled, planned economy, but simply a system in which commerce could be conducted fairly, a society that assured "the right of every businessman, large and small, to trade in an atmosphere of freedom from unfair competition and domination by monopolies."

Roosevelt had entered office over a decade earlier, offering the American people a New Deal in the midst of a severe economic depression—a domestic program that promised a proactive government that would not sit idly by as market forces and reckless corporate activity left much of the nation out of work, hungry, and destitute. Roosevelt would regulate banking, securities, and other industries; initiate large public works programs; guarantee collective bargaining rights and encourage unionization; and launch the Social Security program, all of which would invigorate the economy. Although economists and historians continue to debate the overall success of the New Deal, the general consensus is that these initiatives helped the nation recover from the devastation of the Great Depression. Most also agree, however, that the massive government spending associated with the Second World War—the ultimate Keynesian priming of the pump—was what permanently boosted the American economy out of the downturn.

FDR's critics didn't hesitate to accuse him of being a socialist, even a communist. Publisher William Randolph Hearst, one of the most powerful opinion leaders in the nation with his chain of newspapers and magazines, was among the most vocal. One 1936 front-page editorial that ran in Hearst's newspapers accused FDR of being backed by "Karl Marx Socialists" and other "radicals" and "revolutionists," but such alarmist rhetoric didn't faze the American people, who that year reelected Roosevelt in the biggest landslide to date.[2]

Roosevelt, of course, was no communist or even socialist but a pragmatist who believed that economic and technological progress should enable all people, not just an elite few, to live well. This kind of pragmatism, how-ever, depends on a public that shares an enthusiasm for modernity, a will-ingness to think critically and embrace the future without fear. That this vision has not yet been realized in America is a testament to the strength of anti-egalitarian influences, particularly the combined forces of anti-intellectualism, conservative religion, and corporate interests.

NEWLY EVIDENT RIGHTS

It's worth asking why, if the rights enumerated in Roosevelt's second Bill of Rights were so self-evident, the framers didn't include them when they drafted the original document in the late eighteenth century. If rights to employment, housing, and health care were not self-evident to Adams, Jef-ferson, or Madison, it seems a bit presumptuous of modern generations to suddenly see them as so. Conservatives could argue that we are inventing such rights as we go along.

And we are.

This fundamental concept—that rights are inventions of humans and not a gift from God—is one of the key philosophical differences in the so-called culture wars. It raises the question of whether rights—and, implicitly, morality—are absolute or relative, and it forces us to seriously consider just how we choose to understand history, modernity, and the human condi-tion itself. That is, we must decide whether rights are carved in stone and handed to us by God, as religious conservatives would argue, or are subject to revision and editing as we progress as a people, as the more modernist view holds. It is an important debate, with arguments that are counterintui-tive even to many liberals, but it's essential to an understanding of how the American train of progressivism was derailed and how we can put it back on track.

Conservatives love to talk about absolutes. Former Pennsylvania senator Rick Santorum, a Catholic, in describing his willingness to disregard his church's teachings on issues such as welfare reform, war, immigration, tor-ture, and the death penalty, has explained that such matters do not involve "moral absolutes," whereas strict opposition to abortion, birth control, and gay rights—areas where he is consistent with his church—apparently do.[3]

When morals are absolute, factors such as time, place, and prevailing social standards have no bearing on the rightness or wrongness of particular actions. Claiming to believe in moral absolutes allows one to sound righteous, even if one is vague about which morals are in fact absolute and even if one is far from perfect in adhering to them.

Former South Carolina governor Mark Sanford, caught in an elaborate extramarital affair in 2009 in which he secretly flew to South America to spend time with his Argentine mistress, nevertheless assured the public that his worldview remained biblical: "There are moral absolutes, and God's law is indeed there to protect you from yourself, and there are consequences if you breach that."[4] Thus Sanford, faithful to God if not to his wife, used moral certainty to rehabilitate his image, and it paid off politically. After divorcing his wife and taking some time off, he won a South Carolina congressional seat in 2013.

People don't like to hear, particularly from politicians, that morality is relative, because there is a security in knowing, or at least believing, that human behavior is governed by fundamental, objective standards. Voters want their leaders to know the difference between right and wrong, and firm talk of moral absolutes conveys that assurance. As we function in our day-to-day lives as individuals and as a society, even if we disagree about some issues—abortion, military spending, and numerous others—there are certain standards that, for practical purposes, are pretty much absolute. Homicide, rape, and child abuse are wrong by the standards of American society and most of the rest of the world, and it's unimaginable to most of us that there could be any relative circumstances that would make them right.

The public's desire for certainty and absolutes can make the issue of morality especially difficult for progressives and freethinkers, who often argue on an intellectual level that morality is in fact relative, that there are no God-given commandments or standards. If we take divine dictates out of the equation, we eventually must conclude that we determine right and wrong among ourselves, not by any stone tablets or holy books. To many, even some liberals, this makes human morality seem somehow less solid, less authoritative, more wishy-washy; it also explains why modernity can seem so threatening. To the righteous believer, if modern society tells us that premarital sex is acceptable, this proves that society has turned away from God's law. In this view, a sexually active single woman who uses birth control is not liberated nor a sign of social progress, but instead is clear evidence of our failure to acknowledge moral absolutes.

Yet conservatives, for all their talk of absolutes, rarely accuse George Washington—who owned slaves—of being an evil man. Washington lived in a different time, of course, in a society in which slavery was an ingrained social and economic institution, but in pointing this out, conservatives rarely acknowledge that they are arguing moral relativism. That is, the wrongness of Washington's slave ownership is defined to some degree by his place and time. Even to those who are less forgiving of Washington—those who legitimately point to his slave ownership as just plain morally wrong—most would agree that he should be judged differently from a hypothetical modern Virginia landowner who tries to enslave agricultural workers. Time and circumstances are factors in defining degrees of evil.

If we accept that moral standards change, we can understand why the rights enumerated in Roosevelt's second Bill of Rights were not expressed in the eighteenth century by the constitutional framers. Times change, so our concept of rights can change as well. This view, that rights evolve and are invented by humans as a means of remedying wrongs, is inherently secular and is described in some detail by Harvard law professor Alan Dershowitz in his 2004 book, *Rights from Wrongs: A Secular Theory of the Origins of Rights*. In this view, rights are not divine, nor do they exist in nature waiting to be discovered; instead, they are concocted and applied by humans for real-world ends. Even the political rights set forth in the original Bill of Rights were a practical means of addressing existing wrongs. The wrong of government censorship, for example, is remedied by the invention of the right of free speech; the wrong of religious oppression is remedied by freedom of religion; the wrong of unfair prosecution is remedied by the guarantee of a jury trial, protections against unfair searches and seizures, the right against self-incrimination, and others. "There are no divine laws of morality," Dershowitz writes. "It is we who create morality, for better or worse, because there is no morality 'out there' waiting to be discovered or handed down from some mountaintop. It is because I am a skeptic that I am a moralist."[5]

Seen this way, the notion that the citizens of a highly technological society have a right to economic security—a right that didn't exist in previous societies—is much more understandable. Just as Jefferson and Madison shaped a society that recognized rights of religious liberty, free speech, and free press that their ancestors never enjoyed, so do we have an opportunity to build a society that sees a job, a home, and an education as rights that are necessitated by the standards of our day. These new rights remedy wrongs that we see in modern society: poverty, unemployment, crime, homelessness, lack of health care, and others. The constitutional framers did not live in a society that had the economic or technological ability to guarantee such standards—consumer goods were simple and few, the economy was primarily agrarian, and institutionalized health care and education were almost nonexistent—so the values set forth in FDR's Bill of Rights would have seemed foreign to them. It's no coincidence, however, that the political rights they did assert perfectly addressed the wrongs that they had experienced as subjects of the British monarchy.

GETTING CIVILIZED

The expansion of how we define rights can be seen as a part of a civilizing trend that has been ongoing for much of human history. This development is discussed in detail in evolutionary psychologist Steven Pinker's 2011 book, *The Better Angels of Our Nature: Why Violence Has Declined,* which documents the intriguing fact that societies around the world have become less prone to aggression as the human animal has marched into modernity. Given all the violence seen in the world nowadays, from wars all over the globe to the constant stories of murder and mayhem delivered to us by television and other electronic media, Pinker's thesis may seem counterintuitive, but he provides extensive data showing that violence has, in fact, been declining.

Human history reflects a process of pacification, Pinker shows, as our chronology reveals a more or less steady progression from cultures of violence toward those that value and practice nonviolence. The chances of violent death decreased markedly when humans moved from pre-state societies to states and have continued to decrease as history has moved forward. These rates apply to virtually all kinds of violence, from homicides to genocides to warfare, and the decreases are not nominal but dramatic. Examining historical hunter-gatherer societies from all around the world, for example, Pinker estimates average rate of violent death at around 14 percent, whereas even the *most* violent societies in modern times—for

example, Europe in the first half of the twentieth century, with two world wars—had rates of around 2 or 3 percent.[6]

Biologically, the human animal has not changed much over the course of the last few thousand years, so it's interesting to consider how and why standards of decency have changed. Violence, though certainly feared, was an accepted (or at least expected) part of life in most human societies throughout history—domestic violence toward women and children, honor killings, duels, public executions even for nonviolent crimes—but generally is considered abhorrent in more developed societies today. Just a few generations ago, many Europeans entertained themselves by torturing cats, whereas doing so today would land them in jail. If our biology hasn't changed, there must be environmental factors at work that are causing us to view violence differently—social, technological, economic, and political factors.

If there's any doubt that standards have changed, consider the saga of Molly, a three-year-old dog that suffered four broken legs and other serious injuries when she was struck by a snowplow in Manchester, New Hampshire, in 2013. Molly's owner was unable to afford the surgery that could save the dog's life and in fact could not even pay to have her euthanized, so he instead planned to take her home to die. When local news outlets told of Molly's plight, however, things quickly changed, as word spread through social media and a Web site was set up to raise money for her. Within days, over $40,000 had been raised from all over the country, easily covering Molly's surgery and canine physical therapy. This kind of activity, of course, would have baffled our ancestors, who were far too worried about their own survival to even consider expending resources for complex medical care for an insignificant, faraway dog. Clearly, while our genes have not changed, our values and behaviors have.[7]

And we see it in other areas as well. Although racism and homophobia have hardly been eliminated in modern society, anyone proposing violence based on such criteria today would be considered brutish. Not long ago, police frequently ignored domestic violence simply because it was domestic, but intervention is expected today. The reasons for this pacification and civilization are complex and even somewhat debatable—wider literacy and mass media, the expansion of commerce, the accumulation of knowledge, the appreciation and application of reason, and others—but the phenomenon itself cannot be denied. Whereas a schoolmaster would not have hesitated to take out a ruler to discipline a child even a generation or two ago, today it would be almost unthinkable. Gays and lesbians who would have been cruelly bullied yesterday can apply for marriage licenses today. As we look to the future, we now ask whether even nonhuman animals such as chimpanzees should have rights, and it's conceivable that technology such as lab-grown meat someday might allow us to feed the entire population without slaughtering innocent animal life, thereby making the killing of animals universally immoral.[8]

Viewed this way, the continuing evolution of social standards and rights is not part of any grand ideology but a practical consequence of the changing environment in which humans find themselves. Economic security becomes a right not because some Marxian historical process of dialectical materialism has played out, not because proletarians have risen up to cast off their chains, but because technology has enabled us to provide such security, and because other factors—our better innate impulses, to be sure, but also pragmatic considerations—impel us to make it a right.

To utilize a term coined by author and scientist Richard Dawkins, each evolving definition of rights, or for that matter morality, can be seen as a new *meme*—a concept that will live or die in the marketplace of ideas according to whether it has survival value. Dawkins used the term to draw an analogy between cultural phenomena (ideas, behaviors, styles) and genes, pointing out that both self-replicate, mutate, and respond to selective pressure.[9] Like a living being, or more accurately like a gene, a new idea that has emerged will live or die according to its ability to survive in the particular environment in which it appears. The idea that no person should live in involuntary servitude, for example, would have gained little traction in ancient Greece or Rome or, for that matter, most other ancient societies; the same is true of most of the other rights that we consider fundamental and self-evident today. As conditions change, however, memes can replicate, survive, and even thrive, eventually becoming predominant—as did the relatively modern concept of personal freedom, resulting in the view, now accepted around most of the world, that slavery is abhorrent.

We see this process playing out constantly in popular culture as well, as ideas and trends develop, are replicated, and gain popularity or not; and they survive and continue to replicate according to their ability to adapt to the constantly changing environment. Whether the meme is a song, a particular style of art, a word, an entire language, or a concept of fundamental rights within a given society, it replicates (or not) in a way that is analogous to a random mutation in a biological gene pool.

THE IMPORTANCE OF BALANCED VALUES

If there's one meme that's the favorite of today's conservatives, it's the concept of liberty. In right-wing semantics, the principle of liberty is often used to justify public policy that leaves corporations unregulated and the rich untaxed while dismantling social safety nets. Of course, everyone claims to value liberty, but its use as an anti-egalitarian weapon demonstrates the danger of exalting one important value over all others.

The multitude of values that many modern human societies consider important—liberty, equality, tolerance, pluralism, empathy, compassion, justice, and the like—require balance and, in fact, often conflict with one another. Tolerance and appreciation of cultural differences are wonderful values, for example, but few Americans would suggest that these values should extend to toleration of domestic violence. Even if a particular subgroup has a long-standing cultural acceptance of it, if they wish to be part of American society we expect them to abide by our standards. The same goes for any other cherished value: No value is so singularly important that it must always be exalted above all others. As the philosopher Isaiah Berlin explained, "[U]ltimate human values are objective, but irreducibly diverse, . . . they are conflicting and often uncombinable."[10] As such, we can appreciate freedom, pluralism, and cultural tolerance, but not necessarily when they conflict with other values, such as the safety and security of women and children.

This conflict of values explains the futility of ideologies—philosophies that place one value over all others (often to the *exclusion* of all others). The libertarian exaltation of freedom is one example, but there are many others. Overemphasis on patriotism and national pride, for example, can lead to disastrous outcomes, as we've seen throughout history, and the exaltation of equality and collectivism over all other values is equally dangerous. All are symptomatic of a tunnel-vision mentality that fails to consider the need to balance values. A more pragmatic and less ideological approach would assess the current state of affairs in any given situation, define realistic goals, and develop reasonable means of attaining those goals—all while being mindful of the need to balance *all* of the important values that define us as people and as a society.

This balance of values is not only pragmatic, it is consistent with the high standards of skepticism demanded by freethought, and it can help progressives find common ground with opponents. For example, so-called socialistic proposals often are criticized for empowering government at the expense of individual freedom, as if any increase in government activity is a step toward Big Brother. Rather than dismiss such worries outright, it would behoove progressives to fairly consider them and address them. To a freethinker, after all, the notion of questioning the involvement of government in any area of life is not outlandish. By assuring that appropriate checks and balances can be put into place to control government bureaucrats and regulators, while also demonstrating a sincere commitment to civil liberties, progressives can alleviate concerns that government action is a slippery slope to totalitarianism.

With all the emphasis on reason being made in this book, right-wing opponents could accuse me of exalting that value over all others, but this would be incorrect. In fact, reason and rational thinking are more often a *means* of attaining other values than *ends* in themselves. If one has flawed values—greed, vanity, or anything else—one can then use rational thinking to fulfill those ends. Similarly, if a nation has a goal of global conquest, the bombing of foreign cities might be a rational means to attaining that end. If an oil company has a goal of short-term profit, suppressing knowledge of global warming is a perfectly rational action. Thus, it's critically important that we as individuals and as a society think about our values—all of them—and balance them properly. At that point, the application of reason becomes important in achieving those values. In America today, not only are our values too often out of line, but we are incapable of applying reason in determining them or achieving them.

Of course, rational discussion is sometimes easier said than done. If liberals were suggesting the nationalization of companies such as Google, Microsoft, Boeing, General Motors, and General Foods, one could legitimately sound an alarm that socialism is on the march in America, but of course that's not the case. When efforts to provide basic services such as health care, to raise revenues via modest tax increases on the wealthiest strata of society, and to regulate commerce are met with cries of "Marxism" and "socialism," a critically thinking public would laugh it off. The fact that such alarmism actually garners support in modern America—and is promoted by major media outlets—should give pause to every rational thinker.

IDEAS WITH SURVIVAL VALUE

It's worth noting that truth is no guarantee that a meme will have survival value, nor is the fact that it is right or just. In fact, in the latter half of the twentieth century, Roosevelt's notion of an economic Bill of Rights was a meme that did not go on to thrive in American culture. On the contrary, his egalitarian vision eventually fell into disfavor, and if we examine what happened we find that the usual suspects—anti-intellectualism, conservative religion, and corporate power—are to blame.

The corporate interests that exercise so much control over government had few reasons to support FDR's economic Bill of Rights and many reasons to oppose it. That is not to suggest, however, that the corporate sector was necessarily averse to all aspects of FDR's broader agenda. As we'll see, certain New Deal policies were able to survive because relevant factors in the environment allowed them to do so, whereas others simply could not. Roosevelt's economic Bill of Rights was in that latter category, a meme unfit for the hostile landscape on which it was spawned.

Most historians are quick to point out that the New Deal was largely left intact in the post-Roosevelt years, that even the Republican administrations of Eisenhower and Nixon did little to challenge the basic concept of an active and engaged federal government. For decades after the Second World War, many of the central concepts of New Deal liberalism were not only accepted but expanded on. Civil rights legislation, Lyndon Johnson's Great Society programs, and even Richard Nixon's domestic agenda indicated a consensus view that accepted government activism. Even in this atmosphere, however, anti-egalitarian influences were quietly being put into place that eventually would destroy many of the gains. Those influences were unleashed with the Reagan revolution of 1980, and they would proceed to push the country steadily to the right for decades thereafter.

But even the post-1980 conservative tide was not a complete negation of the New Deal. In fact, a return to the 1920s was never the goal, as there was much about Roosevelt's expanded federal government that some of the strongest anti-egalitarian sectors found quite desirable. Huge military budgets, for example, were very much to the liking of corporate interests. Even increased business regulation sometimes worked to the benefit of large corporations, by creating a complex and burdensome barrier for smaller potential competitors seeking to enter many industries.

Thanks again to the sheer power of the corporate sector, it could dismantle the parts of the New Deal that it disfavored (labor rights, for example, and undesirable regulations) and leave in place or even expand on the parts it liked (enormous federal contracts, desirable regulations). While there were aspects of the New Deal that certain corporate interests would find unappealing—regulated securities markets irked the financial sector, for example—such issues could be targeted individually. (And they would be, as financial deregulation would become a reality in the 1990s, with eventual disastrous results.) But aside from these individual issues, anti-egalitarian interests were hardly trying to turn the clock back.

These details, in turn, only demonstrate the importance of checking the power of profit-obsessed corporate institutions. It would be overly dramatic to suggest that corporate executives in the 1950s joined together to draw up an explicit plan to wreak havoc on the environment, unleash global warming, obstruct democracy and human rights in the developing world, and dumb down the population in America in the decades to follow, but this was the unfortunate and inevitable result of their pursuit of profit.

EGALITARIANISM QUASHED

By the 1970s, the New Deal had been part of American culture for four decades, and even if FDR's economic Bill of Rights hadn't yet become a reality, it still seemed possible that policy would move in that egalitarian direction. The fact that it didn't—and that society instead veered hard to the right with the Reagan revolution—was the result of a number of factors.

First, the power centers in American society saw little value in economic egalitarianism. The corporate sector had much to gain from some forms of government spending, but general economic fairness and security for the population—guarantees of jobs, higher education, housing, and health care—held little benefit to the nonhuman interests that were really in control. If anything, such benefits to real humans would only result in higher costs and tax burdens to corporations. Short-term profit growth— the primary concern of publicly traded corporations in America—would be better served by low taxes and minimal government safety nets for the human population.

Also, as mentioned in chapter 4, racial factors in the South had provided a strong resistance to many liberal policies, from national health care to civil rights, holding back both economic and social egalitarianism and eventually proving to be an affirmative resource for activist conservatives. When Ronald Reagan gave a key campaign speech in 1980 at a site in Mississippi near where three civil rights workers had been murdered in 1964, filling his speech with "states' rights" language that had once been the rhetoric of segregationists, he was sending a not-so-subtle signal to Southern whites and the entire nation: Reagan and the GOP were not above playing the race card.

Thus, although the New Deal, the civil rights movement, and other factors gave liberal, egalitarian public policy some momentum in the middle years of the twentieth century, the tide turned sharply in the later decades. With Reagan in 1980, corporate-friendly conservatism was packaged in a populist manner and sold to the public more effectively than anyone would have dreamed possible even just a few years earlier. Reagan played the tune perfectly, convincing the public that liberals wanted nothing more than to raise taxes on working people in order to hand out welfare checks, stroking national pride and fear to boost military spending, brazenly playing the race card, and jumping enthusiastically on the social conservative bandwagon on the side of "morals and values" in order to shore up a large base of voters. His successors would carry the same message and expand on it, as they still do today.

In hindsight, it should not be surprising that economic anti-egalitarians finally discovered the value of social conservative voters. If anything, the surprise is that it took as long as it did, since socially conservative elements were always present and visible in the culture even in the heydays of economic egalitarianism. The postwar years may have seen Truman's Square Deal, record levels of union membership, and Johnson's Great Society, but symptoms of sharp rightward tendencies—God-and-country patriotism, McCarthyism, the Cold War, and racism and resistance to civil rights—were never far from the surface. Even when the mainstream flowed a bit to the left, America still had strong contrary undercurrents.

A common element in those undercurrents was fear. Long before the Reagan shift in 1980, fear acted as a driving force behind social conservatives, who apparently never got FDR's message that there was nothing to fear but fear itself. If racial differences and the communist menace alone weren't enough reason to be afraid, social conservatives could turn their attention to the hedonistic, material, liberal forces of modernity that were so visible everywhere in popular culture. Rock and roll, the women's movement, youth culture, and reproductive freedom would give social conservatives much reason to see postwar America as a contemporary Sodom. Pastor David Noebel, writing in 1965, reflected the sentiments of many when he wrote that the Beatles were part of a communist plot "to destroy our American form of government and the basic Christian principles governing our way of life." Denouncing the Fab Four's "ability to make teenagers take off their clothes and riot," Noebel insisted that rock music is not an art form at all but a "destructive process" aimed to produce "a generation of young people with sick minds, loose morals and little desire or ability to defend themselves from those who would bury them."[11]

Conservative politicians in the postwar years realized that social conservatives offered potential, but none until Reagan were able to utilize that potential to drive forward an anti-egalitarian economic agenda on a national level. (Nixon exploited social conservatives to get elected but never even tried to champion a conservative movement as Reagan did.) For forty years after the New Deal, America had clung to liberal, egalitarian values to varying degrees—at some times more than others, and in some places better than others, but never completely letting go. With Reagan, however, the nation finally did let go, as social conservatives leaped onto the bandwagon of an agenda that would be openly subservient to corporate interests. Newly mobilized religious conservatives—a demographic that by no mere coincidence substantially overlapped with the white Southern population that had decried desegregation—had created a tipping-point opportunity for Reagan in 1980, and he seized it.

FDR's vision of an economic Bill of Rights was dead.

TEN

A HIGHER COMMON DENOMINATOR

RICHARD HOFSTADTER'S *ANTI-INTELLECTUALISM IN AMERICAN LIFE* became an instant classic when it was published in 1963, earning the author a Pulitzer Prize the following year, but it's arguably even more instructive today. Over half a century after its publication, we unfortunately see not only how little America has advanced in the area of intellectualism, but how it has in many ways regressed.

Hofstadter wrote at a time, in the midst of the Kennedy years, when there was cause to be optimistic about intellectualism in America. The 1950s had been difficult, as McCarthyism and the Red Scare cast a cloud of suspicion over academia and even President Eisenhower scoffed at "eggheads," memorably defining an intellectual as "a man who takes more words than necessary to tell more than he knows."[1] The new Kennedy administration, however, was overflowing with academics and intellectuals, and it was well known that the young president welcomed new ideas and vigorous debate.

Perhaps inspired by this development, Hofstadter wrote that "intellect has taken on a new and more positive meaning and intellectuals have come to enjoy more acceptance."[2] He felt that, although more progress was needed, an important intellectual plateau of sorts had been reached. In discussing the Scopes trial of 1925, for example, in which a Tennessee teacher had been prosecuted for teaching evolution, Hofstadter referred to the controversy over evolution as more or less a purely historical phenomenon. "After the trial was over, it was easier to see that the anti-evolution crusade was being contained and that the fears of intellectuals had been excessive."[3]

This statement, read from the standpoint of today's America, is beyond remarkable—it is stunning and depressing. Writing in 1963, Hofstadter was suggesting that the anti-evolution movement had been essentially defeated many years earlier! "Today the evolution controversy seems as remote as the Homeric era to intellectuals in the East," he wrote.[4] Hofstadter acknowledged that anti-evolution sentiments could still be found in America even in the 1960s, that large segments of the population still rejected the notion that humans had evolved from lower life-forms, but he believed that such thinking was limited to remote rural outposts and was largely irrelevant.

We can only imagine what Hofstadter would think of today's America, where organized, well-funded efforts to teach creationism in public schools are widespread, and not only in the rural Bible Belt. Litigation was needed in Pennsylvania in 2005 to reverse a devious plot by creationists to promote anti-evolution "Intelligent Design" in science curricula, and similar controversies have occurred all over the country. The organization leading the charge against evolution education—not the only group by any means, but among the most visible—is the Discovery Institute, which is based not in the Deep South but in Seattle.

Describing itself as a "public policy think tank," the Discovery Institute is just one example of the kind of relentless antireason mobilization that simply did not exist half a century ago. Founded in 1994, the institute is committed not to science but to religious ideology and has been sharply criticized by legitimate scientists and humiliated in court for its unscrupulous efforts to promote antiscience creationism. In the 2005 case of *Kitzmiller v. Dover Area School District,* a federal court ruled that Intelligent Design was religion, not science, chiding the defendant school officials, who had been working with the Discovery Institute, for their dishonesty. In its written opinion the court said, "It is ironic that several of these individuals, who so staunchly and proudly touted their religious convictions in public, would time and again lie to cover their tracks and disguise the real purpose behind [Intelligent Design] Policy."[5]

The Discovery Institute is also responsible for the infamous Wedge Document, which enunciates a grand strategic plan to infiltrate American public life with religious conservatism, carefully promoting "a broadly theistic understanding of nature" to combat the "materialist" approach of modern science. The document starts by declaring: "The proposition that human beings are created in the image of God is one of the bedrock principles on which Western Civilization was built" and goes on to describe in detail how religious ideas can be nurtured and advanced through educational programs, media production efforts, sophisticated publicity materials, legal campaigns, and other actions.[6]

Originally drafted in 1998 but not intended for public viewing, the Wedge Document was leaked to the public in 1999, and it offers a glimpse of the siege mentality of many activist religious fundamentalists. We see a determination that is motivated by a sincere and genuine fear of modernity. "[A] materialistic conception of reality eventually infected virtually every area of our culture, from politics and economics to literature and art," the document explains. "The cultural consequences of this triumph of materialism were devastating." The devoutly religious personalities driving the creationist movement see rampant moral decay in modern society, and this reaffirms their commitment to social-political religious advocacy.

The Discovery Institute runs an annual budget of over $5 million—modest when compared with other Religious Right organizations—pursuing its mission of defeating "materialistic" science.[7] Answers in Genesis, for example, just one of numerous other groups committed to the futile goal of using creationism to debunk evolution, has an operating budget of about $20 million.[8] Answers in Genesis is run by Ken Ham, a vocal proponent of young-earth creationism, which posits the earth is just a few thousand years old. The group operates a grandiose monument to anti-intellectualism in Kentucky known as the Creation Museum (which most qualified observers would not consider a museum at all, since it presents falsehoods as facts). Opened in 2007 at a cost of over $27 million, the Creation Museum includes high-tech displays that present the biblical creation story as science. According to its narrative, humans rode on dinosaurs, carbon dating is useless, and the abandonment of biblical literalism has led to sins such as birth control, divorce, murder, and gay marriage. Before Adam's sin, visitors are told, not only was there no death or disease, but neither were there any weeds or snake venom. With its own spin on geology, paleontology, biology, and other scientific fields, the facility attracts hundreds of thousands of visitors each year, often via busloads of student groups and church groups, while legitimate science museums struggle.[9]

Discovery Institute and Answers in Genesis are just two of numerous organizations strongly committed to propagating creationist ideas in American society, but there are many others. In fact, at the Web site run by Creation Ministries International, where visitors are told that "the account of origins presented in Genesis is a simple but factual presentation of actual events and therefore provides a reliable framework for scientific research into the origin of life, mankind, the Earth, and the universe," over 150 American creationist organizations are listed.[10] Clearly, pro-religion, antireason interests in America have made a conscious decision not to sit quietly while awaiting the events prophesied in the Bible, but instead to participate actively in America's cultural mishmash.

RELIGION AND ANTI-INTELLECTUALISM

It's noteworthy that Hofstadter, in discussing anti-intellectualism in America, dedicated about one-third of his book to the topic of religion. The connection between religion and antireason has been well established for centuries, and it is not unique to America. The Vatican's seventeenth-century persecution of Galileo for promoting the Copernican notion of a heliocentric universe is a prime example, and there are many others. But as Hofstadter points out, the American manifestation of anti-intellectualism is unique. Historically, the American religious experience has been especially hostile to intellectualism, whereas in Europe and elsewhere, at least in more recent times, strong intellectual characteristics often can be found within religion. Instead of viewing religion as being at least potentially consistent with reason, Americans have more often chosen to see it as a wholly separate realm, as "an affair of the heart" that is "intuitive," Hofstadter explains. For that reason, religious Americans have been more inclined to perceive the rational mind as "irrelevant or worse."[11] The result is a posture that not only fails to understand science and reason but often affirmatively opposes them.

A number of factors, many of which are still debated today, may have led to this outcome in America. Some have argued that America's lack of a state religion created a free marketplace of sorts wherein various faiths had to compete, thus enabling the more marketable among them to thrive in a

manner similar to other businesses. As it turned out, if religions are products to be sold in the marketplace, the more anti-intellectual of them have
had more marketing appeal. There's probably some truth to this, but it is
also likely that other factors—the characteristics of the people who settled
here, for example, and their socioeconomic conditions—also played an
important role. It's noteworthy that the first Great Awakening, a religious
revival characterized by intensely emotional services that had little use for
rationalism, swept colonial America in the 1730s and 1740s, before the nation was founded. This suggests that it was not constitutional separation of
church and state, which of course didn't come until decades later, that laid
the groundwork for America's anti-intellectual religiosity.

The experience of the first Great Awakening would not only be repeated after the nation's founding, it became part of a regular cycle in
American culture, making the revivalist, apocalyptical, evangelical strain
of religion increasingly prevalent. Whereas at the time of the revolution
the three largest religious denominations were Anglicans, Presbyterians,
and Congregationalists—all relatively sober and restrained faiths—by 1850
the entire landscape had changed, with populist evangelicals (mainly Bap-
tists and Methodists) becoming the largest Protestant traditions.[12] The new
dominant faiths were more fervent, emotional, and, most strikingly, anti-
intellectual. "There is a hell and when the Bible says so don't you be so
black-hearted, low-down, and degenerate as to say you don't believe it, you
big fool!" preacher Billy Sunday (1862–1935), one of the most popular of
his era, told audiences. "Thousands of college graduates are going as fast as
they can straight to hell. If I had a million dollars I'd give $999,999 to the
church and one dollar to education," said Sunday. "When the word of God
says one thing and scholarship says another, scholarship can go to hell!"[13]

This is a sentiment that would come to define a large segment of the
American population, not just fire-and-brimstone clergymen. "If we have
to give up either religion or education, we should give up education," declared William Jennings Bryan, who was among the most prominent public
figures in the early twentieth century, having served as secretary of state
and run three times as the Democratic nominee for president (losing each
time).[14] A lawyer, Bryan also famously represented the anti-evolution side
in the Scopes trial. As organized and mobilized Christians today overtake
school boards, rewrite textbooks, and otherwise obstruct education, they

are simply continuing—and to some degree expanding on—this anti-intel-lectual tradition.

GORE: TOUGH ON BUSH, SOFT ON RELIGION

A particularly instructive view of the connection between American anti-intellectualism and religious fundamentalism was provided by former vice president Al Gore, whose razor-thin loss to George W. Bush in the presidential election of 2000 was largely due to religious conservatives who heavily favored Bush. Since that election Gore has become a vocal advocate for evidence-based public policy, particularly with regard to climate change. His 2007 book, *The Assault on Reason,* discussed the increasingly prominent effect anti-intellectualism has had on modern public policy, and he was quick to point out the role of fundamentalist religion. He criticized, for example, the tendency of Bush to portray conflict in stark, God-laced rhetoric of good versus evil, always with great certainty and an aversion to complex analysis. "There are many people in both political parties who worry that there is something deeply troubling with President Bush's relationship to reason," Gore wrote. "Moreover, during times of great uncertainty and public anxiety, any leader who combines simplistic policies with claims of divine guidance is more likely to escape difficult questions based on glaring logical flaws in his arguments."[15]

Gore seems to have the problem clearly identified, but as his analysis proceeds, he makes a fascinating disclosure that reveals much about the attitude of many American liberals toward religion and government. In criticizing Bush's simplistic, Manichean view of conflict, Gore argues that it "does not really represent Christian doctrine" and he even calls it "heresy."[16] Thus, as Gore explains it, the problem was not so much that Bush was overly reliant on religion, but that Bush didn't correctly *understand* Christian doctrine. Gore claims to be arguing for reason—and to his credit, much of his book does precisely that—but it is interesting that he takes a detour to argue that Bush *misinterpreted* scripture. This, of course, suggests that reliance on faith might not be so bad if one correctly understands doctrine. It is abundantly clear that, at the very least, Gore is hesitant to criticize religion and even feels compelled to defend it as he chides the religious Bush.

At one point Gore even assures readers, "I consider Jesus to be my savior also"—as if, in the context of a book on the importance of reason, this statement somehow gives him and his arguments more credibility! Gore then proceeds to exonerate religion altogether by describing Bush's flaws as arising from other sources. "Make no mistake: It is the president's reactionary ideology, not his religious faith, that is the source of his troubling inflexibility."[17]

Such an eagerness to excuse religion shouldn't surprise us, coming from a man who spent a career in politics, and in fact it's fairly common among many who otherwise favor rational, evidence-based public policy. The mistaken assumption is that religion as a subject is itself sacred, that it *must* be seen as a force for good, even if sometimes it is misused or wrongly interpreted. With this mind-set, it is almost unimaginable that a mainstream religious view could be harmful; instead, any flawed public policies motivated by religion must be the result of inept individuals, such as Bush, who misunderstand scripture and misapply faith.

Few would suggest that Gore had a duty to attack religion in his analysis, but affirmatively defending it weakens his own credibility. This protective view of religion should be problematic for all rational citizens— believers and nonbelievers—because it necessarily creates a landscape that gives religion-based views an undeserved special status. If religion must be seen as a force for good, then those who lack it are more likely to be suspect. If religion must be seen as a force for good, policies based on religion (assuming the theological interpretation is correct) must be good. If religion must be seen as a force for good, the entanglement of religion and government might not be so bad. And if religion must be seen as a force for good, we presumably want political candidates who adhere to some kind of religion and belong to a church. Today, conservative and anti-egalitarian interests just love such talk.

Very importantly, from a theological standpoint, Bush's interpretation and application of scripture—seeing clear right and wrong as he considers the world, understanding himself to be in a battle against evil—is no less legitimate than Gore's. In fact, Gore is simply engaging in the timeless and somewhat amusing practice of claiming to know the meaning of scripture better than his opponent. The question is not whether Bush's actions were motivated by faith *or* ideology, as Gore suggests, for it is clear that *both* faith and ideology were factors. Bush's neoconservative ideology was in large part defined and validated by his fundamentalist religion. To dismiss the religious faith factor and instead blame Bush's flawed worldview on ideology alone is an attempt to guard religion from criticism—an exercise in sugarcoating reality, and certainly a disservice to Gore's claimed goal of objectively analyzing the assault on reason in America.

A fairer assessment of the relationship between Bush's religious faith and his disastrous policies can be found in Susan Jacoby's 2008 book, *The Age of American Unreason*. Stating that she took Bush at face value when he claimed to consult God before making major decisions such as launching the war in Iraq in 2003, Jacoby correctly noted that "a religious hypocrite might make a less dangerous president."[18] A politician who puts on a religious act from time to time in order to impress voters, going to church with the family or throwing in some religious rhetoric in speeches, might be relatively benign, unlike a true fundamentalist believer who sees foreign policy as an opportunity to expedite the Second Coming of Jesus.

To be sure, Hofstadter, Gore, Jacoby, and most other observers recognize that numerous factors contribute to American anti-intellectualism, even as they disagree on those factors and their relative weight. Hofstadter clearly felt that the nation's religious tradition in many ways helped create its anti-intellectual tradition, but he also pointed to deep historical factors, such as America's preference for the practical over the abstract, the democratic over the elitist, and even geographic and economic factors. Gore, writing more recently, places great emphasis on mass communication—and particularly the changing ways Americans have gotten their information and shaped their opinions—as a significant factor contributing to the decline of reason. In days past, he argues, healthy public discourse seemed to be assured through traditional publishing, journalism, and freedom of the press, but the increasing importance of electronic media over the last century—first radio, then television, then the Internet—radically changed the way Americans absorb information and discuss public policy, and not necessarily for the better. Jacoby, though seeing the role of religion differently from Gore, also lays much of the blame for the dumbing down of American discourse on evolving media, what she calls "the pacifiers of the mind that permeate our homes, schools, and politics."[19]

I don't expect to resolve questions about the relative importance of these and other factors, but there can be little doubt that the situation has gotten dire, especially in the realm of politics, where ignorance and anti-intellectualism often seem to be assets, not liabilities. Because anti-intellectualism is such a strong force in American culture, and especially in politics, many aspects of public policy are negatively affected. If the problem were limited to creationism in public schools it would be bad enough, but it goes far beyond that, contributing to wealth disparity, corporatism, militarism, and a general environment of anti-egalitarianism.

LOWBROW EGALITARIANISM

The fact that modern anti-intellectualism contributes to anti-egalitarianism is significant, because in the past this was not always the case. In fact, anti-intellectualism in America has some roots that are decidedly egalitarian, appearing at a time when the realm of politics was expanding to include the common man. America's founding politicians, of course, were the intellectuals of their day, men who were informed and inspired by the Enlightenment. They were generally well read in classical literature and philosophy, multilingual, abreast of the latest advances in science, and firm believers in the power of reason. But after the founding generation, egalitarian tendencies moved America away from leadership by intellectuals and toward a more populist form of democracy that disfavored those who exuded higher learning or elitism.

Democratic, egalitarian trends in the early nineteenth century eased restrictions that had limited the right to vote to those who owned land, opening up the realm of politics to the broader free male population, and it was in this atmosphere that the era of Jacksonian democracy arose in the 1820s. Andrew Jackson, elected the nation's seventh president in 1828, epitomized the anti-elitist sentiment that would come to define American politics and culture. Born on the frontier, with little formal education, rough and tough by nature, "Old Hickory" was the antithesis of the philosopher-statesman, a man who proved his smarts and abilities by his actions and strength of personality, not personal refinements. This, to his supporters, was a great virtue, as Jackson had "a judgment unclouded by the visionary speculations of the academician" but instead exhibited "that native strength of mind, that practical common sense, that power and discrimination of judgment which, for all useful purposes, are more valuable than all the acquired learning of a sage."[20]

It was during the Jackson presidency that Alexis de Tocqueville visited America from France and traveled widely, subsequently writing his classic work, *Democracy in America,* with its insightful observations of American society. Tocqueville, who came from an aristocratic family but was sufficiently modernist to hold liberty in high regard, was fascinated by the American experiment in democracy while wary of its potential shortcomings. One problem, he said, was a "depraved taste for equality" that worked not just to lift up the low but also to bring down the high.[21] The virtual elimination of aristocracy, Tocqueville observed, meant an intellectual leveling of society: "There is no class, then, in America . . . by which the labours of the intellect are held in honour. Accordingly, there is an equal want of the desire and the power of application to these objects."[22]

Lowbrow egalitarianism would continue in American politics long after the Jacksonian era. The aforementioned William Jennings Bryan, the three-time unsuccessful Democratic nominee for president (in 1896, 1900, 1908), is a good example. Despite being ardently fundamentalist in his religion, publicly opposing evolution education, Bryan's politics were generally egalitarian, as he railed against corporate power and advocated for "free silver" instead of the gold standard, a position understood as favoring ordinary people over the financial establishment. (And it's noteworthy that when egalitarianism conflicted with corporate power, as it did with Bryan, corporate power usually won.)

Anti-intellectual tendencies, in one form or another, would become a defining characteristic of American politics, where the "regular guy" is consistently favored over the intellectual. We see the theme played out with the saga of Lincoln and his log-cabin birth and backwoods upbringing, with the aristocratic Theodore Roosevelt emphasizing his tough-guy outdoorsman qualities (despite the fact that he was indeed an intellectual), and even nowadays with modern media ignoring substantive issues to instead poll voters on which candidate would make a better drinking buddy.

Thus, ironically, America's anti-intellectualism, which today is a vital part of the coalition that delivers anti-egalitarian policy, was nurtured by egalitarian tendencies. The dumbing down of American politics has roots in egalitarian impulses, because the earliest attempts to widen the net of democracy necessarily opened the door for men (but not yet women) whose experiences, economically and intellectually, were far removed from those of the elites of the nation's founding generation. As we see, however, by exalting the regular guy and scorning the intellectual, America eventually set the stage not for egalitarianism but its opposite.

HIGHER-BROW EGALITARIANISM

Realizing this, perhaps it's time for a new approach. That is, there should be an understanding by now that anti-intellectualism is no longer an effective means of reaching desirable egalitarian ends, because a modern society that drifts toward the lowest common denominator, as we have seen, is one that abandons rational public policy. Truly egalitarian public policy requires both intelligent public officials and a general public that values intelligence, questions concentrated power and wealth, and expects rational, evidence-based policy. This doesn't mean that abstract, highly intellectual thinking should dominate the public sphere, but it does mean that the environment cannot be defined by the exaltation of anti-intellectualism.

One thing to consider is what might happen if the level of discourse were raised to a higher common denominator; if efforts to instill fear were unsuccessful because the citizenry is unfazed by such tactics; if fundamentalist religion had little or no impact on politics or policy; if corporate power in government were minimal and government instead responded to the needs of real humans; if science, reason, and education were highly regarded American values, not merely areas that receive occasional lip service from politicians; and if public policy was consistently based on evidence and facts. In such a scenario, there would still be plenty of room for debate over issues, but certain assumptions and elements present in the public discourse today would not be so prominent. Fear-mongering, government as a cash cow for corporate interests, absurdly oversized military budgets, accusations of socialism and Marxism, deregulation of major industries to appease Wall Street, righteous claims of biblical morals and values—a critically thinking electorate would quickly dismiss such notions.

Keeping in mind that progressive, rational Americans have been able to win elections in this country, we must ask why, despite this apparent political power, they haven't been able to implement public policy along the lines just outlined. Here there are two factors. One is that even with some progressive electoral success around the country, the overall level of public discourse in America remains too low, at times pathetic. In much of the country the public willingly elects right-wing candidates who assure that a significant portion of the ruling class, sometimes even a majority, will include a strong anti-intellectual element. The second factor is that even the supposedly liberal, left-leaning candidates are often far from progressive. These "Wall Street liberals" reflect the power of corporate interests to favorably structure the political spectrum regardless of who wins.

The good news here is that we can visualize the solution to the problem—a rational population that demands a high level of discourse and progressive, human-centered policy—but this is also the bad news, because mighty forces are opposed to these ends. Simply by enunciating the goal, however, we make its attainment more plausible. For too long, progressives have had good intentions but little unity and cohesion, because the focus has been on individual areas of concern—labor, abortion, health care, fair taxation—that often have no obvious relationship to one another. Little attention has been paid to the macro-issue that does indeed tie all of these issues together: the need for a high level of discourse and rational, evidence-based, human-centered policy. It's time to vocally proclaim that goal rather than accept the lowest-common-denominator approach of traditional American politics.

This larger issue necessarily requires recognition that certain kinds of authority have little or no weight in the course of rational debate in a pluralistic democracy—religious authority, for example, or appeals to tradition that are otherwise unsupported rationally—and that institutional interests, particularly those of profit-seeking corporations, cannot be more influential in a democracy than the voices of real humans. It also requires a constant awareness of arguments that are grounded in fear and other emotional impulses, not reason.

OPPOSITION TO RATIONAL DISCOURSE

Of course, the Religious Right will never be willing to set aside its theological worldview in the course of public policy discussion. This is a political reality that progressives must confront head on. Most progressives, for their part, believe strongly, and correctly, that religious conservatives have a right to free exercise of religion and a right to participate in the democratic process. But progressives too often go even further by accepting the notion, exemplified by Al Gore's argument, that religion itself must be "respected." As such, we've gone from the sensible notion of *respecting people* to the irrational notion of *respecting ideas*. As we'll see, there is no reason that an *idea* should deserve respect just because it happens to be religious. (To be fair, I'll also mention that no idea deserves respect just because it's *not* religious.)

If we are to raise the level of discourse in America—and this is a goal that all rational Americans, religious or nonreligious, should recognize as necessary—then it is incumbent upon us to call out blatant reliance on irrationalism in public debate. For example, it's fine to discuss abortion by pointing out that women should have a right to control their own bodies, but it is also necessary to point out that the theology upon which abortion opponents base their position (and the vast majority of abortion opposition is religion-based) deserves absolutely no weight in the public discourse of a pluralistic democracy. We can discuss the facts and the science of abortion, but theology has no place in the debate over public policy. Your religion can be a valid personal reason for not getting an abortion yourself, but it is not a legitimate basis for denying other women the right to control their own bodies. The proper role of religion in public life must become a topic of conversation in America, because otherwise it will continue to carry undeserved credibility and influence. (Inevitably in the abortion discussion, someone will point out that a few nonreligious voices can be heard opposing a woman's right to choose. Although this is true, what's noteworthy is how few those voices are. If we remove the vocal religious factor and rely solely on rational and factual arguments, the debate is overwhelmingly lopsided in favor of choice.)

As more people realize that religion can be challenged when it enters policy debate, we are seeing new efforts to immunize religion from criticism, even on the international level. With the Internet and social media, information revealing the implausibility of religious claims has become far more widely available than in the past, so efforts to quash debate over religious questions are increasing. In the United Nations, for example, the concept of "defamation of religion" has gotten some support, particularly from Muslim countries that do not wish to see Islam publicly criticized. Under this concept, *criticism* of religion—which in the developed world is usually understood as a free speech right—becomes *defamation* of religion. These same societies sometimes use blasphemy laws—a concept that any civil libertarian should find appalling—to silence dissent. Progressives and freethinkers must push back by pointing out that only *people* can be defamed. *Ideas,* however, religious or otherwise, should never be immune from criticism.

Social conservatives oppose rational, evidence-based policy because it so frequently contradicts their positions. Evolution is scientific and evidence based, whereas creationism is not; comprehensive sex education deals in biological facts and has been proven to be more effective in preventing teen pregnancy than abstinence-only programs, which are filled with misinformation and almost always are religiously motivated; opposition to school-sponsored prayer is based on values of inclusion and pluralism and principles of church-state separation, whereas support for it is, of course, rooted in religion. Similar analyses can be applied to other issues, such gay rights and even environmentalism.

Thus, the larger issue that is rarely discussed in the back-and-forth of American debate—and the issue that exposes a great vulnerability for social conservatives—is the preliminary question of whether public policy must be rational and evidence-based rather than emotionally driven or theology-based. Before engaging with social conservatives who argue that their faith and values compel a certain position on an issue, the question to consider first is whether the religion of social conservatives must be given any "respect" in public debate. Social conservatives deserve respect because they are *people,* but their theological *beliefs* are merely ideas and, as such, deserve no mandatory respect.

Keeping in mind that even many progressives are religious, and even those who are not have been raised in an American environment that suggests we must give great deference to religion, there is an understandable tendency among many to avoid a head-on confrontation with conservatives over their use of religion in political discourse. Nobody wants to appear intolerant, and sometimes it's not clear where the line is drawn between legitimate criticism of conservatives and an improper attack on religion.

In truth, however, the line is usually very clear, because almost any reference to one's religion as a basis for public policy that would affect anyone else's rights is illegitimate. There is almost no valid reason for raising one's religious beliefs in the context of a debate over policy that would affect non-adherents of that religion, and if those beliefs are raised, they become fair game for criticism.

For example, even though I think that a belief that the world is only 6,000 years old is incredibly misguided, I also believe that it would be rude, in most social contexts, to ridicule a person who holds that belief. However, if that person pushes a political position based on that belief—such as, for example, opposition to rational environmental policies (a common fundamentalist Christian position, based on biblical interpretations that conclude God gave men dominion over the earth to exploit)—I then have every right to scrutinize and criticize that theology. Shame on anyone who would place all of society at risk based on personal religious beliefs that can't be supported by evidence while simultaneously rejecting irrefutable facts.

It's also worth remembering that when religion is used as a basis for policy positions, it's often to disguise other motives. Today's social conservatives are the direct political descendants of those who, like former Alabama governor George Wallace, mentioned earlier, most vehemently defended segregation and other unseemly policies, with frequent references to God and religion. As they used religion, along with "tradition" and "heritage," to defend invidious practices, they also showed a willingness to engage in stunning logical fallacies. The 1967 Supreme Court case *Loving v. Virginia,* which declared laws against interracial marriage unconstitutional, provides a good example. Defending the racist anti-miscegenation laws, social conservatives argued that such laws were fair because under them whites were prohibited from marrying blacks, just as blacks were prohibited from marrying whites. To them, this was *equality,* not discrimination! The same social conservatives, and devout Christians, who made these arguments in 1967 would energize the Christian Right a little over a decade later, as their successors do today.

Like religious conservatives, corporate interests often have no interest in a well-informed citizenry, intelligent public discourse, or rational public policy. The reason for this is very simple: Corporations have only one interest, and that is profit. From time to time corporate profit growth can be consistent with rational public policy, and when that occurs there will be no problem; but what we often find is that such instances are random and incidental, that more often corporate interests are inconsistent with such lofty values. Because of this, the corporate sector uses its resources to shape the culture to conform to its wishes, to the detriment of ordinary people.

It's hard to imagine, for example, a rational citizenry, after intelligent public debate, concluding that military budgets approaching or exceeding those of the rest of the world combined are necessary year after year; thus, the contractors that benefit from such budgets have great interest in fanning patriotic sentiments, instilling irrational fear, and otherwise distracting the public from that discussion in one way or another. In fact, much of America's consumer culture—a public that buys things it doesn't need with money it doesn't have—is heavily reliant on irrationality and emotion, and corporate interests know this. A rational, intelligent public is unlikely to comfort itself with needless purchases, worry about appearances to the point of obsession, or waste enormous blocks of time with mindless entertainment—so the multibillion-dollar interests behind these industries have no interest in nurturing critical thinking. Unlike the real humans who populate the country, corporate interests are sharply focused on exactly what they want—profit—and collectively they have the financial means to shape the culture to fit their desire.

A SERIOUS QUESTION

Now that we have not only spotted the problem but apparently identified an important part of the solution—a better-informed public with a higher level of discourse and more rational policy making—a legitimate question might still be asked: Are we dreaming? One could certainly look around and reasonably conclude that the general public is unlikely to suddenly adopt critical thinking and vigilant engagement as new favorite pastimes. Many people simply have no interest in analyzing public affairs, dissecting the issues of the day, or thinking about such subjects at all. Many people are just lazy. Others are just disinterested. And that will never change.

This isn't just social commentary, but a valid concern in discussing strategy. Such passivity is exactly what the opposition counts on, and it presents a legitimate obstacle to achieving human-centered policy. In the next chapter we'll take a look at the issue of vigilance to consider who has it, who doesn't, and why.

ELEVEN

IMPOSSIBLE VIGILANCE

CONTRARY TO POPULAR BELIEF, THERE IS NO RECORD OF THOMAS JEF-
ferson saying that the price of liberty is eternal vigilance.[1] In fact, the quote
didn't originate in America at all but appears to have been coined by an Irish
lawyer and statesman, John Philpot Curran. "It is the common fate of the
indolent to see their rights become a prey to the active," Curran warned in a
Dublin speech in 1790. "The condition upon which God hath given liberty
to man is eternal vigilance; which condition if he break, servitude is at once
the consequence of his crime and the punishment of his guilt."[2]

It's not surprising that Americans, thinking they invented (or at least
perfected) the notion of liberty, have misattributed the quote to one of
their own founders. The common myth is that the concepts of individual
freedom and inalienable rights would never have occurred to the rest of the
world had it not been for us. Of course, the ideas and actions of the American revolutionaries did help inspire democratic sentiments elsewhere (the
French Revolution being the obvious example) and have continued to do
so even centuries later, but self-congratulations can lead to a diminished—
and erroneous—assessment of the rest of the world. Enlightenment ideas
of liberty and democracy (arising in Europe, not America) had taken
root among intellectuals long before the Declaration of Independence
was drafted, and the American Revolution can be seen most accurately
as not causing those ideas but resulting from them. Nevertheless, many

Americans today, despite generous evidence to the contrary, feel we are in a position to lecture the rest of the world about the concepts.

But if attitudes of exceptionalism are typically American, eternal vigilance is not. The Irishman Curran was spot-on in noting that freedom will not last among those who do not affirmatively defend it. Human interaction is such that individuals and the institutions they create tend to pursue interests that naturally encroach on the interests of others, and those who do not stand ready to defend themselves are likely to get steamrolled by others who are more assertive.

Historically, in most civilizations only an elite few have ruled, and generally only those same few would enjoy some degree of what we might call individual liberty and prosperity, while the masses would toil in some kind of servitude. The mark of an enlightened modern society is a system that allows the wider population, not just the elites, to participate in government and enjoy fundamental liberties and prosperity. Experience has shown, however, that such an environment doesn't come easily, and we know that vigilance is required to create and maintain it. As such, we need to consider who has—and who has not—been vigilant in protecting their interests in American society.

VIGILANT INSTITUTIONS

If there is any doubt about the powerlessness of average people, consider the way government works in real life. Washington, DC is a city filled with lobbyists and lawyers, but almost none of them are working for the interests of average voters. Sure, there are a few nonprofits that advocate for various real-human interests, such as environmental protection and the rights of minorities or ethnic groups, but the overwhelming majority of paid influence in Washington works for the corporations that can afford it. The big law firms and expensive lobbyists with plush modern offices just a few steps from the Capitol are subsidized almost exclusively by corporate players, and those professionals and their clients are uninterested in what average humans want or need. These interests all have links to Wall Street, and to them the existing American political system, a republican democracy in theory, is little more than an external condition that must be managed as a business expense.

And manage it they do. Proving to be much more vigilant than average working people, corporate interests pour millions upon millions of dollars into the system to shape public policy to their benefit. For average citizens with busy lives, democratic participation means nothing more than voting every couple of years and following the headlines to the extent possible, and even this is not always easy when there are jobs, kids, and bills that require more immediate attention. Corporate "people," however, are eager to participate in politics and policy making around the clock, for maximum profit demands influence in government, where the rules are written that will affect the bottom line. With assets and cash flows (not to mention time) far exceeding those of real humans, corporations and industries—or, more accurately, their lobbyists and lawyers—are there for every stage of the sausage making. Vigilance pays.

Such vigilance gives rise to groups such as the American Legislative Exchange Council (ALEC), an interest group that literally writes legislation for conservative lawmakers to introduce in legislatures around the country, to the great benefit of corporate interests. Though officially described as nonpartisan and nonprofit, ALEC has been an arm of the conservative movement since its founding in 1973 as a "membership association" for state lawmakers, promoting "limited government, free markets, federalism, and individual liberty."[3] This sounds innocent enough, but investigations reveal that dues from lawmakers comprise less than 2 percent of ALEC's budget, whereas 98 percent is funded through tax-deductible donations from corporations, such as ExxonMobil, Coca-Cola, PepsiCo, McDonald's, Wendy's, Intuit, and Procter & Gamble; trade groups, such as the pharmaceutical industry's PhRMA; and pro-corporate foundations, such as the Charles G. Koch Charitable Foundation.[4] ALEC raised over $21 million from such sources in one recent three-year period, while dues from lawmakers in the same period totaled about $80,000 each year.[5] The corporate money is used to fly legislators to elaborate ALEC meetings, where they are wined, dined, introduced to potential campaign donors, and "educated" (ALEC, after all, describes its mission to the IRS as "research and educational"[6]) about conservative positions on a wide array of issues.

At its meetings, ALEC presents model legislation to the legislators but, without blushing, insists that this activity is not lobbying, even though industry representatives are also present to "discuss" the model legislation. ALEC conventions are expensive and technically lose money, but they're plenty valuable for all involved. Lisa Graves, writing for the Center for Media and Democracy, reports, "ALEC conventions are not close to break-even operations, financially, but they are a bonanza for marrying state legislators with the wealthy captains of industry (and their lobbyists) at luncheons, dinners, golf outings, skeet shooting, boat rides, cigar smoking parties, and other events to help politicians and corporations bond."[7]

Until recently, only the lawmakers and their bedfellows knew what really happens at ALEC events, but in 2013 a Wisconsin state representative, Chris Taylor, attended an ALEC conference and reported to the public. Her findings were not comforting. ALEC "melds together rightwing think tanks, corporations and legislators," she reported to constituents and anyone else who would listen. "This ménage a trois has created a policy-making machine that produces a corporate agenda to elevate private profits over the needs of most people."[8]

No contemporary political issue seems to escape ALEC's attention: education (ALEC advocates vouchers and privatization), taxes (cuts for the wealthy), labor and employment (reduce workers' protections), the environment (antiregulation), and a host of other issues. Legislators and other attendees are told that the Endangered Species Act threatens the economy, carbon dioxide isn't harmful to the environment, the tort system needs "reform" (since tort lawyers suing corporate wrongdoers usually work on a contingency basis, this is one of the few areas where ordinary citizens can afford lawyers), and professors work just three hours a week.

As lawmakers and corporate representatives discuss these issues, they are presented with model legislation that addresses the perceived problems in a way that satisfies corporate interests, and these models frequently become real law. A 2013 report found that 139 ALEC-modeled education bills were introduced in 43 states and the District of Columbia in the previous year alone, and 31 of them became law. The same report found that 117 ALEC-backed bills affecting wages and workers' rights had been introduced that year, along with 466 promoting "polluters, privatizers and profiteers."[9] When George W. Bush became governor of Texas in 1995, one of the first bills he signed into law was an ALEC measure to give immunity to corporations that break environmental rules.[10] Laws for school vouchers, banking deregulation, and privatization of government services all have origins in ALEC model legislation.

Bear in mind that ALEC is just one of many cogs within the vast corporate influence machinery. The U.S. Chamber of Commerce, for example, lobbies, advertises, funds campaigns, and otherwise advocates politically on behalf of conservative, anti-egalitarian interests. The chamber spent over $74 million in lobbying alone in 2013 and millions more on outside spending and contributions. As a nonprofit business association, the chamber does not have to disclose its donors, yet it is an influence powerhouse, making or breaking candidates with its ability to throw money around in any congressional district. In 2014 records from OpenSecrets, a nonpartisan project tracking money in politics, none of the chamber's outside spending was for Democrats, while the vast majority was for Republicans. (Since it can also spend money to advertise *against* candidates, it spends some money opposing Democrats and some opposing a few unlucky Republicans who weren't sufficiently pro-chamber.) Once candidates actually are elected, the chamber stays connected through its extensive lobbying activities.[11] And again, aside from ALEC and the chamber, numerous other industry and corporate groups are knocking on your legislators' doors.

If corporations were real people, you'd have to commend them for their vigilance in pursuing their interests. They participate in the democratic process at a level far beyond that of most living, breathing humans. Most of us try to stay on top of current events, keeping informed about issues and political candidates, but we could never hire in-house professionals to closely follow all the regulatory developments that affect us, nor could we hire lobbyists to traverse Capitol Hill seeking to influence legislation, nor outside law firms to litigate the legal issues that we care about.

Ever-vigilant corporations and industries can even manufacture science in order to create a lack of scientific consensus on issues that affect their profits. The tobacco industry's resistance to medical evidence linking smoking to lung cancer exemplifies the level of vigilance—and dishonesty—that only wealthy corporate interests can exercise, delaying public health efforts to eradicate smoking and thereby causing untold suffering. Corporate interests similarly obstructed efforts to inform the public about the dangers of lead in the 1960s, delaying for years the elimination of toxic lead in gasoline.[12] And, of course, the oil industry is at the center of efforts today to create a lack of consensus on the link between fossil fuels and climate change.

The resources at the disposal of corporate interests, as compared to those available to ordinary citizens, are difficult to exaggerate. The oil industry's approach to legal challenges is a good example. One ExxonMobil board member is quoted describing the company's approach to litigation this way: "It's very much a take-no-prisoners culture. We will not settle to avoid a struggle. . . . [W]e will use our superior resources to fight and appeal for as long as possible, and when the case is over, your house may no longer be standing. Think twice before you take us on."[13] This is what ordinary citizens are up against if they challenge the corporation's position on not only climate change but oil spill cleanup responsibility, chemical regulation, or anything else—and somehow Americans have come to believe that such corporate power (and citizen powerlessness) exemplifies effective democracy and free enterprise.

Multinational corporate interests demonstrate their vigilance in all these ways and more. They even shape their own images through paid advertising and public relations—a power that most real humans realistically lack. Moreover, since corporations are essentially immortal, they can outlast anyone. Senators Bernie Sanders and Elizabeth Warren can joust with Wall Street in an effort to hold corporations accountable to the public interest, but in some form or another, ExxonMobil, Bank of America, General Motors, and IBM will live on long after Sanders and Warren—and you and I—are gone.

This level of vigilance is simply impossible for ordinary humans. It's little wonder that these corporate "people" have supplanted real humans as the central focus of government, especially given their role as the entities that employ almost everyone and drive the economy. In light of all this, the one power still retained by ordinary humans—the power to vote—seems rather quaint by comparison. That right to vote, however, shouldn't be dismissed too quickly. In fact, as we'll see later, it leads us to the issue that should be a primary focus of the progressive movement going forward.

TEMPORARY VICTORIES

If there were any doubt about the vigilance of corporate interests, consider the Glass-Steagall Act. Passed in 1933, in the early days of the New

Deal, Glass-Steagall regulated commercial and investment banking, separating higher-risk securities activities from the realm of commercial banking. Considering the devastation that had occurred due to the stock market crash of 1929, the need to regulate banking and securities could hardly be questioned, although of course bankers and stockbrokers were highly critical of efforts to do so. Thus, after the act passed, attempts to overturn it began immediately, as the vigilance of the profit-seeking corporate sector was ignited. With its resources, there was no limit to the creative ways that the law could be attacked: in the courts, legislatively, through influence within regulatory agencies that interpreted the law, and through persistent public messaging that was critical of government activity in general and regulation in particular.

Real humans, meanwhile, had less day-to-day interest in the law, even though their lives indirectly benefited from its stabilizing impact. To the extent that some ordinary citizens may have cared about the law on a conscious level, none had resources to counter the multipronged attack on the law from the corporate sector. Thus, it shouldn't be surprising that corporate interests slowly got what they wanted, first through looser interpretations of Glass-Steagall from regulatory agencies, then through minor legislative victories, and finally culminating in the act's repeal in 1999 via passage of the Gramm-Leach-Bliley Act. A triumph for Wall Street, Gramm-Leach-Bliley was a deregulatory green light for the consolidation of securities firms, banks, and insurance companies into huge "financial services" conglomerates that would become the tail that wags the dog in the American system and beyond.

And within a decade, the economy was in complete collapse.

The lesson to be learned here, besides the obvious need to regulate securities, is that the relentless vigilance of corporate interests must be checked. Every high school civics class sings praise to the system of checks and balances within the American *governmental* structure—each branch holding power to check the others so that no one branch can wield too much—but there is little discussion of the need for checks and balances of *external* power centers. The awesome power of the corporate sector, which was nonexistent at the founding of the nation but today carries resources and influence that totally eclipse the voice of ordinary people, needs counterbalancing. This

notion is not socialist, nor is it an offense to freedom; it is simply a pragmatic, commonsense response to obvious realities.

There are many great ideas floating around Washington nowadays, and it's
conceivable that some of them might even make their way into law. But like
Glass-Steagall, any legislative victory for progressives must be considered
only temporary if it conflicts with corporate interests, because corporate
opposition will not rest until it's repealed or otherwise neutralized. Worker
protections or other industrial regulations can be passed this year, but those
laws will be met with opposing legislative initiatives and court challenges
next year.[14] The defense budget may be reduced this year, but a manufactured crisis to justify increased defense spending will be a certainty next
year, as will relentless lobbying by the corporate sector. With the current
power dynamics of the system, all progressive victories are temporary.

THE BIG ISSUE

The reason corporate and industry interests can be so vigilant is because
their status as "persons" with rights equal to real humans allows it. And that
is why progressives should direct their energies, first and foremost, at the
corporate personhood issue.

Until corporations are returned to their place as instruments that *serve*
the public interest—as vehicles that enable commerce but do not dominate politics and government—human-centered public policy will remain
largely elusive. Occasional victories will occur, and some of them may even
result in long-term positive outcomes for average citizens, but all activity
nevertheless will take place on a field where corporations and industries
are the real players. A regulation passed in the public interest one year will
be revised or repealed by vigilant special interests the next; a tax on corporations subsequently will be watered down with loopholes, exceptions, or
subsidies passed through lobbying efforts; a measure to protect consumers
will be attacked through well-financed public relations and litigation until
it is repealed or weakened beyond recognition. Thus, if real humans want
to be something other than spectators in an American system that caters to
the concentrated wealth and power of the corporate sector, they must go
for the jugular.

Closely related to the issue of corporate personhood is the issue of election reform, where the vast majority of Americans—as high as 90 percent in some polling—favor major overhauls to the existing system of campaign finance.[15] Even in this age, when Americans seem so divided over so many issues, they overwhelmingly agree that the current system of electing their leaders is broken. A 2013 Gallup poll found that even the most radical election reform option—complete government funding of federal elections, with all contributions from private groups and individuals banned—was favored, with 50 percent approving and 44 percent disapproving (6 percent with no opinion).[16]

With such widespread support for reform, one would think that a responsive democratic government would deliver it, but such is not the case. Efforts to legislate election reforms typically meet stern resistance, and even when occasionally successful they are repeatedly set back by court rulings declaring that such legislation violates First Amendment guarantees of free speech. This first occurred in the 1970s when, in the post-Watergate era, Congress passed several measures to regulate and finance elections, only to see most of them struck down by the Supreme Court on the theory that spending money on elections is constitutionally protected "speech."[17]

Little progress was made in subsequent years until, in 2002, a bipartisan effort led by Senators John McCain (R-AZ) and Russ Feingold (D-WI) finally resulted in a new campaign finance law that sharply limited fundraising by political parties and candidates. Subsequent developments, however, particularly the *Citizens United* decision of 2010, have revealed that law to have no real teeth. The Supreme Court further weakened campaign finance regulation with a 2014 ruling that declared the aggregate limit on personal donations to candidates, political action committees, and parties to be unconstitutional.[18] And to the extent any rules remain, wealthy donors and corporations that funnel money into elections can easily avoid them in a variety of lawful ways. For example, donors (including corporations and their shell front groups) can put unlimited funds into issue-oriented ads that clearly support one candidate over another without expressly saying so. The end result is virtually unrestrained election spending.

And the numbers tell the story. The likelihood of winning election in America has become increasingly contingent upon raising huge sums of money. From 2000 to 2012, the amount spent on congressional elections more than doubled, from \$1.6 billion to \$3.6 billion, while presidential campaign spending rose from \$1.4 billion to \$2.6 billion.[19] The average winner of a congressional race in 1990 spent about \$407,000—a significant sum, to be sure—but that figure would more than triple over the next two decades, to over \$1.4 million. On the Senate side, by 2012 the average winning candidate had spent over \$11 million to get elected.[20]

These figures don't even include money spent by so-called super PACs—the powerful new vehicles that have sprung up since court rulings, including *Citizens United,* effectively allowing limitless political spending.[21] Super PACs can accept donations of any amount from corporations, other groups, and individuals, and they can advocate in ways that effectively support one candidate and oppose another. While they cannot directly contribute to a candidate or a party, their advocacy essentially makes them a part of the campaign of the candidate that they support. According to OpenSecrets, the 1,300 super PACs that sprang up for the 2012 electoral cycle alone spent over \$600 million.[22]

With numbers like these, it's little wonder that the public policy emanating from Washington lacks a human focus. The notion that the system is "of the people, by the people, and for the people," while commendable, seems to apply only to *corporate* people, not humans.

If effective campaign finance reform has been made impossible by corporate personhood and Supreme Court rulings that strike down efforts to legislate reform, the necessary first step toward a solution becomes clear: constitutional amendment. Without a constitutional provision that unambiguously puts corporations in their proper place, any efforts to legislate electoral reform are doomed. If relentless lobbying from the corporate sector doesn't repeal or water down such legislation, court challenges will. Without a constitutional amendment, well-intentioned progressive reformers are fighting a hopeless battle against a better-funded opponent that never sleeps and has the law on its side.

True progressives in Washington now recognize this reality, which is why leaders such as Bernie Sanders have supported a constitutional amendment to end corporate personhood. "There comes a time when an issue is so important that the only way to address it is by constitutional amendment," Sanders said in introducing a proposed amendment in the Senate in

2011. "Nobody I know thinks that ExxonMobil is a person."[23] Introducing a companion measure in the House chamber, Representative Ted Deutch (D-FL) expressed similar sentiments. "The dominance of corporations in Washington has imperiled the economic security of the American people and left our citizens profoundly disenchanted with our democracy," he said.[24] Another measure, although not directly addressing corporate personhood, would have amended the Constitution to expressly give Congress the authority to regulate campaign finance, effectively overruling court decisions that rely on constitutional free speech protections to strike down electoral reform legislation. None of these measures, unfortunately, has come anywhere near passage—yet.

Similar efforts will continue to meet similar fates until the various sectors of American progressivism realize that a constitutional amendment to redefine corporate personhood must be the unifying issue around which all can rally, the issue on which almost all other priorities eventually rely. Until the issue of corporate personhood is won, corporate influence in government and politics cannot be brought under control. Redefine the role of corporations and remove the corrupting influence of big money from elections, and the road is paved for all other progressive reform. This is why I refer to it as a jugular issue: If progressives can strike with a constitutional amendment, the corporate Goliath falls, and all the other battles become winnable.

DEMOCRATS: WHICH WAY TO GO?

Garnering the necessary political will is the real challenge, for even the Democratic Party is beholden to the hypnotic allure of corporate money. Although there can be no doubt that the GOP stands as the party that is effectively owned and operated by corporate influence, the Democrats are not far behind. Even prominent Democrats have pointed this out, as when the late Minnesota senator Paul Wellstone, a staunch progressive, noted that he represented the "Democratic wing of the Democratic party."[25] The party's embrace of corporatism, when it supposedly stands as the party of average working people, is undoubtedly one of the great failings of American politics, a fact recognized by many progressives. "Both major parties are out of touch with American values," declared Kaitlin Sopoci-Belknap, spokesperson of the group Move to Amend, which has led the call for a constitutional amendment to end corporate personhood or, as the group says, an effort to "legalize democracy."[26] The group and others were highly critical, for example, of the Democratic Party's acceptance of millions of dollars in corporate money to pay for its 2012 national convention, despite promises that corporate money would be kept out.[27] These convention perks were minor, however, compared to the money flowing through super PACs and other vehicles.

An important spokesperson for the progressive wing of the Democratic Party is Elizabeth Warren, the senator from Massachusetts who has emerged as the most outspoken critic of corporate power. Elected in 2012, Warren was a noted consumer advocate who helped create the Consumer Financial Protection Bureau, the federal agency designed in the wake of the 2008 financial collapse to oversee consumer protection in the financial services area. Warren was seen as the obvious person to lead the newly created bureau, but financial institutions, the GOP, and even some Democrats with Wall Street connections (such as Treasury secretary Timothy Geithner) opposed her.[28] As a result she never led the agency, but revenge was sweet when she was elected to the Senate to sit among the lawmakers and power brokers who had obstructed her nomination.

As a senator, Warren has been the leading voice for progressive reform, using her extensive knowledge of banking and finance to expose the inherent systemic flaws that work in favor of corporate interests. From her seat on the Senate Banking Committee, for example, she has cross-examined banking regulators by asking simple questions that have never been put forward by others. At her first Banking Committee hearing in February 2013, pointing out that regulators have the job of overseeing Wall Street (never known for its high standards of ethics), Warren asked regulators a straightforward question: "When was the last time you took a Wall Street bank to trial?" The regulators fumbled to avoid answering the question directly, but Warren pressed and eventually got the answer: Never. Through Warren's questioning, we learned that *no* Wall Street bank has *ever* been brought to trial for criminal behavior, despite the abundance of instances when banks have been involved in egregious criminal behavior. Federal regulators, resolving Wall Street malfeasance cases instead through plea bargains, settlements, and consent decrees, have helped make criminal wrongdoing a simple business expense for these very flush financial institutions.[29]

Warren's harsh criticism of Wall Street has shed light on the gap between the progressive wing of the party and more centrist, pro-corporate Democrats. "Nothing would be more disastrous for Democrats," wrote a centrist think tank, Third Way, than to embrace the economic populism of Warren and others like her, such as New York mayor Bill de Blasio.[30] It shouldn't be surprising that the Democratic anti-Warren argument appeared in the editorial pages of the *Wall Street Journal*, always known for its defense of corporatism and firm opposition to progressivism. The Third Way authors, Jon Cowan and Jim Kessler, argued the case against Warren as zealously as any Republican. Calling progressive policies "reckless" and "fantasy-based," Cowan and Kessler warned against "unrestrained entitlements" and predicted that the "Warren wing" of the party could never appeal to average Americans.

Progressives may disagree with Cowan and Kessler, but the questions they raise—whether the politics of the "Warren wing" can gain popularity across the country, even in the heartland and in so-called red states—are worth asking. Surely, even if we leave aside the extreme social conservatives who vote for right-wing candidates for obvious reasons, we still are left with many Americans who find something appealing about the messaging of the Republican Party. Thus, to consider the viability of progressivism as a national phenomenon that can appeal even to moderate voters, we'll have to examine the mind-set of some of those average Americans who currently align against it.

TWELVE

SARAH PALIN'S MASSACHUSETTS

I HAD NEVER TALKED POLITICS WITH BOBBY, BUT HE ALWAYS SEEMED like a reasonable guy, and I would have expected his political views to match that character. He wasn't a close friend, just a casual acquaintance, mainly because he occasionally repaired office equipment for my suburban Boston law practice. We'd see each other a few times a year, usually at my office unless I happened to bump into him in public, and we'd typically chat briefly about business-related topics with a little light conversation thrown in. He always struck me as an intelligent person with a sensible outlook.

Imagine my surprise, therefore, when I saw Bobby leave my office one day in 2009 and get into his SUV—a vehicle with a "Sarah Palin 2012" bumper sticker on the back!

Now, it wouldn't have shocked me to learn that Bobby was a Republican, or even that he might have voted for John McCain in the election of 2008. My personal feeling was that the GOP had long ago jumped off a cliff of irrationality, but I know there were still many decent people who just didn't see it that way. If Bobby's vehicle had been adorned with a "McCain-Palin" sticker left over from 2008, I wouldn't have looked twice.

But Palin 2012? *Palin?*

Surely by 2009 even McCain must have realized the enormity of his mistake in putting Palin on the ticket, and I was certain that every rational American must have seen her as a wing nut. She gave one impressive speech—accepting the vice presidential nomination at the Republican convention immediately after McCain selected her—but her image quickly tarnished as the public got to know her better. She made a series of bizarre statements in succession, her religious views made many people uneasy, and her high-profile televised interview with Katie Couric was an unmitigated disaster as Palin bungled one answer after another. In an exchange that's painful to watch, she couldn't even tell Couric what magazines and newspapers she read to stay informed. Here's a sample of her eloquence from the interview:

> That's why I say I, like every American I'm speaking with, were ill about this position that we have been put in. Where it is the taxpayers looking to bail out. But ultimately, what the bailout does is help those who are concerned about the health care reform that is needed to help shore up our economy. Um, helping, oh, it's got to be all about job creation, too. Shoring up our economy, and getting it back on the right track. So health care reform and reducing taxes and reining in spending has got to accompany tax reductions, and tax relief for Americans, and trade, we have got to see trade as opportunity, not as, uh, competitive, um, scary thing, but one in five jobs created in the trade sector today. We've got to look at that as more opportunity. All of those things under the umbrella of job creation.[1]

This kind of senseless rambling was standard Palin by 2009, and I was baffled as to how Bobby could possibly endorse it.

Having grown up in Massachusetts, I've long known that the state's reputation for liberalism is somewhat exaggerated. Yes, the Bay State is home of the Kennedys, and it was the only state to vote against Nixon in 1972, and of course there's Harvard and Cambridge with their liberal reputations—but there's another side to the state that the media and pundits tend to ignore. After all, Reagan carried Massachusetts in both 1980 and 1984, and Republican governors sat for 16 straight years recently, from 1991 to 2007. Maybe it's a hotbed of liberalism when compared to the rest of the country—but that says more about the rest of the country than it does Massachusetts!

In fact, while I can say with confidence that Sarah Palin will never carry Massachusetts, voters like Bobby are not so unusual. They are highly skeptical that government can do anything right, and terms such as "freedom," "free enterprise," and "private sector" resonate with them. They recognize that huge corporations are powerful, sometimes too powerful, but they never even consider the possibility of trying seriously to rein them in. When they think of bad guys, they think of drug dealers and other common criminals, and they rarely consider corporate malfeasance. They are proud patriots and naturally assume that American military power must extend around the globe, although individual overseas entanglements sometimes can be questioned. Someone like Bobby may or may not own a gun, but even if he's not a hunter, surely some of his buddies are, and these guys are suspicious of any schemes to restrict gun rights. That said, Bobby's not an absolutist on gun rights either, and he will listen to commonsense ideas on the issue. On questions of race, Bobby is typical of many suburban white guys: He is critical of ignorant prejudice, but he also nods his head when affirmative action is portrayed as "reverse discrimination." Frankly, he just wishes everyone would get along. And don't ask him about religion, because he doesn't want to talk about it—and he doesn't want *you* to talk about it either.

To a liberal, the voter I just described might seem conservative. But on the American spectrum, such voters are not considered conservative but moderate. They are the voters in the middle who can go either way. They may not sympathize with Republican positions on social issues, but they are persuaded by GOP rhetoric espousing free enterprise, small government, getting tough on crime, patriotism, and strong national defense. Packaged in an appealing way with the right candidate, such messaging can be sold to Middle American voters. This is why Bobby liked Sarah Palin: He thought she had spunk and would stir things up. In a similar case of personality politics, these Bay State voters surprisingly elected Republican Scott Brown to the Senate in 2010, filling the seat held for decades by Ted Kennedy. Brown was a regular guy who drove a pickup truck, a pro-choice Republican who seemed like a moderate, the kind of guy you'd want to have a beer with. (Or, as they say at Harvard, "the kind of guy with whom you'd want to have a beer.")

The good news is that these Middle American voters are, for the most part, reasonable people. The mess we're in today is largely due to an attack on reason, but the voters who can take the country back are not immune to reason. In fact, since moderation is often a defining characteristic of American swing voters, progressives need to realize that their inability to sell their agenda is due in large part to posturing that portrays progressivism as extreme. If Democrats truly were interested in promoting a progressive agenda, they would make serious efforts to demonstrate that progressive policies are wholly consistent with the *moderate* views of Middle America. Instead, however, elected Democrats too often abandon progressive policy in favor of what they perceive as "moderate" policies, which in fact are policies that cater to Wall Street and other conservative sectors.

In his 2004 book *Don't Think of an Elephant!,* linguist George Lakoff argued that progressives for years had been outmaneuvered by conservatives in message framing. Conservatives had seized the moral high ground by talking about values and moral principles, and they had mastered the sound bite to convey their messages in a few understandable words. Liberals, meanwhile, more often talked about details and specific programs instead of core values and beliefs, an approach that turned off many voters. Democrats have adjusted some of their framing in subsequent years—talking about "equality" instead of "gay rights," for example—and have seen some successes, but they have largely failed to enunciate the progressive position in a way that challenges the entrenched institutional interests that obstruct a progressive agenda.[2]

Yet the values and principles of progressivism are entirely consistent with the core values of average, reasonable people. Unfortunately, selling the progressive agenda politically amounts to a constant battle against conservative interests that effectively control the system and shape public opinion. The fact that many Democrats accept conservative framing makes it even harder. To get anywhere with voters, first we must unmask some blatant conservative deceptions.

To see how the right-wing pitch works, consider the conservative obsession with privatization. Corporate interests pound away at the issue of privatization with a few common messages: Government can't do anything right. Free enterprise is the backbone of America. Private industry creates jobs. Government is wasteful. Hearing these mantras, average Americans reflexively nod their heads in agreement, and as a result we see corporate interests creeping into ever more areas that were once under public control, often with disastrous results. Two examples are all we'll need.

PROFITABLE PRISONS

Along with the military, police departments, fire departments, and public schools, few institutions are more commonly understood as a government function than prisons. When individuals are accused of committing crimes, it is only the government, through the court system, that can convict them, and it is only the government that ultimately can take away their personal liberty. Despite this, however, a growing trend in recent years has state and county governments delegating the task of imprisoning convicted criminals to private prison corporations. These large, publicly traded corporations, such as Corrections Corporation of America (CCA), operate on a business model that depends on the incarceration of individuals. If we keep in mind that *growth* is the primary goal of all publicly traded corporations, one quickly realizes how these private prison companies can expect to see increasing revenues and profits: *Incarcerate more people!*

This is not an opinion but a fact: Business is good in the private prison industry when more individuals are being imprisoned and when sentences for crimes are made harsher. In a 2010 financial report, CCA told shareholders that "demand for our facilities and services could be adversely affected by . . . leniency in conviction or parole standards and sentencing practices."[3] Indeed, since repeat offenders can be seen as repeat customers at private prisons, these corporations actually have an interest in encouraging recidivism.

The private prison industry, not surprisingly, strongly backs tough-on-crime legislation, since such legislation ensures continuing revenue streams. Through ALEC, the policy group mentioned in chapter 11 that brings together corporations and lawmakers and actually drafts model legislation, the prison industry has promoted mandatory minimum sentencing and three-strike laws that result in a steady flow of inmates. "ALEC has been a major force behind both privatizing state prison space and keeping prisons filled," writes Alan Greenblatt in *Governing* magazine, reporting that about 40 states have passed versions of ALEC's model Truth in Sentencing bill requiring prisoners to serve out entire sentences without parole.[4]

The boldness of the industry is shocking. One report found that about two-thirds of private prison contracts actually contain language wherein the state *promises* that prison occupancy will be maintained at high levels, usually 80 to 100 percent.[5] Imagine owning a hotel and then signing a contract in which the government guarantees that it will keep 80 percent of your beds filled—that's essentially the bargain that these corporations have made for themselves. These sweetheart deals, together with America's obsession with incarceration, have helped make private prisons a booming industry. CCA reportedly has seen revenues increase 500 percent in two decades.[6] This results in big payoffs for Wall Street, as from 2011 to 2013 the corporation's stock price (ticker symbol CXW) more than doubled.[7]

Private prisons are an excellent example of what happens when reason is absent from public discourse and policy making. Here we see many of the factors mentioned previously combining to create a perfect storm of disastrous public policy. We have an emotionally charged issue—crime—that plays to the fears of the general public, fears that are stoked by corporate media that emphasize and sensationalize crime news. As such, we have a public that is responsive to simplistic tough-on-crime talk from politicians who have few constructive ideas for reducing crime rates. Next, we have corporate interests—not just the private prison corporations themselves but the Wall Street investment firms that demand good returns—with the resources to lobby and otherwise advocate for privatization of prisons and policies that benefit them. And finally, we have a political system that allows those corporate interests to exert undue influence. The public has already been sold on the notion that government is wasteful, that private enterprise can do things cheaper and more efficiently, so prison privatization is often an easy sell. Once that's done, the task of lobbying for tougher criminal laws that result in more and lengthier sentences—another pitch that the public will accept easily—is a piece of cake.

As a result, the United States has the distinguished title of being the incarceration capital of the world, with imprisonment rates far exceeding those of most other societies. As most Western developed countries have rates around 100 or fewer per 100,000, America locks up its citizens at a rate of over *seven times* that figure.[8] This might be arguably justifiable if it somehow resulted in lower crime rates, but of course crime statistics in America are just as unenviable.

If this mess is attributable in large part to the abandonment of reason, we can also see that the remedy is an application of rational, sober thinking that is not motivated by fear or other emotional hot buttons. The first step is to realize that some functions simply do not belong in the private sector, particularly in the realm of powerful corporate interests. The conflict between the public interest and the innate corporate drive for revenue and profit growth is direct and undeniable, and there is simply no room for conciliation.

For this reason, the American conversation must include more frequent reference to the nature of corporations, their proper role in society, and the need to regulate them, because without wider understanding of these issues, the concept of privatization is too easily sold. Americans must understand—as objective truth and not just a product of liberal spin—that corporations, especially publicly traded corporations, are entities totally absorbed in their own self-interest (a fact that, as mentioned previously, is central to the ideas of even conservative economists).

From that starting point, if we consider the private prison issue objectively, we can see that the blame for the mess is not really the corporation's, since the corporation truly cannot help itself. Blaming corporations here is like blaming a lion set loose in a public park when it kills someone. The unrestrained animal is only doing what it does naturally, and any blame would rest with those who are responsible for keeping the beast contained and controlled. With regard to corporations, that responsibility rests with public officials and, ultimately, the public itself.

As if we needed more proof that privatized prisons are a bad idea, consider the scandal that became known as "kids for cash," in which two Pennsylvania judges were convicted in 2011 in a scheme to funnel children to two for-profit prisons in return for kickbacks.[9] Not only were the judges secretly involved in getting a private detention center built through a developer and leased to the county, but business was assured as thousands of juveniles were quickly found guilty and sent away for minor and first-time offenses. "Things were different in the Luzerne County juvenile courtroom, and everyone knew it," reported the *New York Times*. "Detention center workers were told in advance how many juveniles to expect at the end of each day—even before hearings to determine their innocence or guilt."[10] Fortunately, this deplorable scandal was uncovered, and the judges involved, Mark Cia-varella and Michael Conahan, were convicted and given lengthy prison terms of their own (28 years and 17.5 years respectively), but not before thousands went to jail unnecessarily.

Obviously, corruption can occur in the public sector even without the involvement of corporate interests, and certainly prisons and criminal justice in general present a challenge for any society, but it should be obvious that injecting profit-driven corporate interests into the sphere is only asking for trouble. Of course, even with a publicly run prison system there are certain factions that might support undesirable criminal justice policy out of self-interest. Institutions and bureaucracies naturally seek increased funding, so police departments, corrections facilities, and even prison-guard unions might support tough-on-crime legislation if they see it as benefiting their cash flow. Yet these interests, while noteworthy, are insignificant when compared to the enormous weight that Wall Street and high finance bring to the equation through private prisons. Police and corrections officials, as government employees, ultimately answer to the public and do not have unlimited resources to peddle influence, but publicly traded corporate interests that are backed by institutional investors and intensely focused on revenue, market share, profit, and growth, do. Incentivizing incarceration in the marketplace is a huge mistake.

SOCIAL INSECURITY

Wherever the privatization song is sung, similar themes echo. Just as private prisons are sold to the public by playing up the wisdom of free enterprise and bemoaning the evils of government inefficiency, so is the argument to privatize Social Security. Texas governor Rick Perry once called Social Security a "Ponzi scheme," and Representative Paul Ryan made Social Security privatization a key element in his budget proposal entitled "Roadmap for America's Future," which defined him as a visionary for the GOP and eventually led to his being selected as Mitt Romney's running mate in 2012.[11]

Republicans have had their eyes on Social Security for years, for just as its name suggests, the system epitomizes the notion that government can and should help provide long-term security for its citizens, and this notion directly conflicts with the antigovernment sentiments of the GOP's core. Thus, conservatives portray Social Security as a badly broken system and yet another example of government ineptitude, hoping to convince the public that complete failure is inevitable.

In truth, however, Social Security is arguably the most successful government program ever, providing older Americans with a foundation of economic stability that has allowed them to live with some degree of comfort and, yes, security. Cries that the system is collapsing are greatly exaggerated, since most estimates show Social Security staying in the black well into the 2030s. Despite the best efforts of extremely powerful interests to dismantle the system, Americans, to their credit, have consistently rejected privatization. "Social Security is going broke," declares a headline on Ryan's official House Web site, but even he insists that "one of my top priorities is to preserve the Social Security safety net and make sure the program remains solvent for future generations."[12] It reveals much about the popularity of Social Security that even a legislator who is among those striving hardest to dismantle the system feels that he must use language claiming his goal is to "preserve" it.

Rational Americans should ask themselves why the attacks on Social Security—which is not going broke but merely will need some modest tweaking over the next two decades to keep it from operating in the red in the 2030s and beyond—are so persistent, especially given that it is such a popular program among the general population. For a minimal tax that most of us hardly notice (a tax that is separate from the ordinary federal income tax and placed immediately in a fund that is outside the federal government's regular operating accounts), we are assured a guaranteed income in old age that serves as a foundation for retirement. Without getting ideological about the issue, the system just seems to make sense.

Yet the opposition to Social Security is indeed ideological and also profit driven. Ideologically, the notion of a successful government program is abhorrent to the Right. Few Americans are truly ideological in their antigovernment views, but many are sympathetic to sound-bite messaging that is critical of government in general. The mantra of "government wastefulness" is accepted by most Americans without question and was a tactic used by Ronald Reagan to sell conservatism in the 1980s as he criticized bureaucratic procurements of $436 hammers and $640 toilet seats (while nevertheless increasing military spending and doing little to stop such procurements).[13]

This is where conservative individuals and institutions find their opening: Surely we can't expect government to do anything right. If it overpays for toilet seats, how can it be trusted to provide a secure retirement for an entire population? And this is where the profit-driven element comes in. As many Americans nod their heads in agreement, sympathetic to criticism of the federal government, Wall Street licks its chops at the thought of having access to billions upon billions of dollars of "privatized" Social Security funds. Ultimately, the debate about privatizing Social Security is little more than an effort by corporate interests, with the help of ideologues, to raid the retirement coffers of America's working population.

As conservatives talk about downsizing government and privatizing programs in the name of free markets, it's noteworthy that the effort to transform Social Security would do nothing to make government smaller or eliminate government programs. The Ryan plan, as well as other Social Security privatization plans, simply would allow those paying into the system to reallocate their payments to the stock market, benefiting primarily the financial firms that would enjoy the added revenues. There are two huge problems with this plan, however. First, the Social Security system is structured so that the incoming money, which Ryan would divert to private accounts, is needed to pay the benefits of today's retirees, so the privatization plan is, in effect, a way of defunding current benefits. Therefore, although even conservative estimates have Social Security staying afloat for two decades, if privatized it would go broke almost immediately. Second, whereas Social Security currently provides a guaranteed income that retirees can rely on as they leave the workforce, a foundation that can be supplemented by other retirement savings (for those fortunate enough to have such savings), privatization would leave millions of Americans totally dependent on the stock market alone for their retirement security. If a person is unfortunate enough to retire at the time of a great stock market collapse, such as those of 2000 and 2008, when many mutual funds lost 50 percent or more, tough luck.

Obviously, this scenario isn't appealing to anyone who actually saw their retirement nest eggs evaporate during the stock market collapses. At least now such individuals have their Social Security checks to fall back on, but under privatization that wouldn't be the case. Instead, those crashing stocks would in fact be their Social Security.

Conservatives either don't understand such details or don't care about them. Oftentimes, we'll hear them scorn programs such as Social Security as "nanny state" policies, as if somehow we are becoming soft by subjecting ourselves to government coddling. Most Americans know better, however, and realize that there is a practical benefit to having a definite foundation of economic security for everyone in retirement. Indeed, since we all fund the system we are hardly getting a free ride, but rather we are utilizing a rational means of achieving a practical end. Perhaps conservatives feel that we all should fight and scrap our way through life, thereby entering retirement only with whatever we are able to save along the way—but without question that would inevitably result in millions of retirees having close to nothing. By implementing a practical program like Social Security, we are, it is hoped, ensuring as a society that we don't have elderly citizens living in the streets due to poor planning or bad investment choices.

Thus, the debate over privatization is a philosophical disagreement, but it would be a mistake to portray it as a clash of ideologies. The conservative view is indeed ideological, because it puts forth certain principles as virtually absolute. In the conservative view, we repeatedly see the concepts of free markets, liberty, and unrestrained capitalism being touted, with the flip side being that government is hopelessly wasteful and inefficient. We can see this in the rhetoric of politicians and in the policy proposals of think tanks and activist groups such as Cato, the Heritage Foundation, and ALEC. Interestingly, the exaltation of the principle of corporate power is never mentioned in conservative rhetoric, but it is the unspoken principle that the conservative agenda serves. The progressive side, meanwhile, is not at all ideological but instead simply pragmatic, seeking practical ends rather than bowing to any fundamental abstract principle. We want humans to live comfortably and securely. We don't want government to exercise control over the population, nor do we want real humans to be at the mercy of corporate institutions.

MOVING PEOPLE TO THE AGENDA

George Lakoff certainly has valid points when he criticizes progressive messaging in American politics, but the failure of progressivism cannot be explained merely by tactical shortcomings. Ineffective communication might be part of the explanation, but an honest assessment of America's lurch to the right since 1980 would conclude that the elected representatives who would be expected to advocate for progressive, human-centered policy—namely, the Democrats—have been too quick to abandon progressivism for policies favoring institutional interests. This is partly because there is a perception that the middle voters—the Bobbys of America—expect such conservative policies and would be unwilling to accept progressive policy, but it's also because powerful corporate interests are exerting undue influence. In fact, even to the extent that many middle voters seem to accept conservative assumptions, that's often the result of nonstop messaging by corporate interests.

This explains why the Democratic Party, despite its reputation as the home of American liberalism, is in fact a centrist or even center-right party when considered on a global political spectrum. The failure of progressivism in America, therefore, can be understood as resulting from the decision of many Democrats to move their party rightward rather than try to bring voters to the left. Although there certainly are differences between the parties, Ralph Nader struck a chord with many when he described the Democrats and Republicans as Tweedledum and Tweedledee in the election of 2000. Any progressive success, therefore, requires beating back not just the overt ideological conservatism of the GOP and its various backers, but also the corporate interests that too often control the Democratic Party.

There can be no doubt that Democrats have seen some electoral success while embracing centrism, but it would be a mistake to assume that center-right positioning was necessary for that electoral success. The fact that they frequently use ardent progressive rhetoric to win elections, only to move to the center when actually crafting policy, indicates that the centrism is more often an effort to appease powerful interests, not voters.

At first glance, with regular guys like Bobby sporting Sarah Palin stickers even in Massachusetts, the Democratic strategy of moving toward the

center-right might seem shrewd. In truth, however, such conciliatory positioning is just another example of how conservative, pro-corporate interests
are so effective, how they have so shifted the playing field that even when
they lose, they win. By convincing Democrats that the Bobbys of America
demand certain conservative assumptions, conservatives are assured that the
basic paradigms of corporatism will be accepted even when Democrats win.
Politically, this is masterful.

But it's also wrong. In fact, while voters like Bobby might get fired up
by Sarah Palin's give-'em-hell talk, they are just as impressed by the way
Elizabeth Warren rips up the bankers who wrecked the economy. Bobby
might be impressed by a gal who hunts, but he's also impressed by a senator who stands up to powerful corporate executives. The terrible error for
Democrats in recent years—besides the obvious error of willingly accepting
corporate power and influence within the party and within the lawmaking
process—has been the assumption that average voters like Bobby would be
unwilling to accept progressive public policy.

Progressives must do a better job of explaining their broad vision to
America's middle voters, but that statement in no way suggests that, once
elected, they must move to the center-right. As we'll see in the next chapter, if the truly important strategic issues can be isolated and focused on,
progressives indeed can shift the landscape back in the direction of reason
on all issues. But to do this, strategic thinking is essential. We've taken time
already to understand why corporate interests act the way they do, why
they have no choice in doing so, and how they make such a mess of things;
next we'll consider how we can take control of them effectively for the
public good. Doing this will require some consideration of both political
demographics and political mechanisms. Moreover, it may even require us
to think a bit about how we define success, as individuals and as a society.

THIRTEEN

TAKING CONTROL

IT'S FITTING THAT REPRESENTATIVE PAUL RYAN, A SHINING STAR IN today's Republican Party, calls his proposed agenda the "Roadmap for America's Future." Considering that almost nobody uses road maps anymore, the metaphor perfectly illustrates how out of touch the GOP is with real life. Surely, if we are to navigate out of our current mess, it will take reason and critical thinking, not the right-wing corporatist ideas of a man who would not allow a rape victim to terminate her pregnancy. Therefore, as Ryan and his companions struggle to fold their road maps, twenty-first-century American progressives must consider how to best put forward an agenda of human-centered public policy.

To do this, it helps to recap the perfect storm that created today's conservative predominance. Corporate interests have posed a realistic threat to democracy in America for well over a century, but for most of that time those interests were somewhat restrained by countering forces: labor unions, interest groups, activists and intellectuals, and other opinion leaders. The situation was far from perfect, and the balance usually tipped in favor of corporate interests even in the most progressive of times; but things got worse in the later decades of the twentieth century, as we saw a conservative political steamroller arise via the teaming of corporate interests with politically mobilized religious fundamentalists and social conservatives. If a critically thinking public is necessary for effective democracy, this new dynamic ensured that a sizable portion of the electorate would reject reason, vote against its own interests, and march in lockstep with a severe anti-egalitarian agenda.

THINKING STRATEGICALLY

Rather than sulk as we deconstruct this recent conservative success, progressives should realize that a correct diagnosis is the first step in finding a cure. In fact, amid this sorry scene, there is reason for optimism. It's helpful to remember that much of the policy generated at both state and federal levels leans well to the right of the public's center of gravity. Most Americans don't oppose higher taxes on corporations and the wealthy, for example, and two-thirds either support the Affordable Care Act or would prefer an even more progressive version of universal health care.[1] Further, over 90 percent of voters consider regulating Wall Street either "important" or "very important," according to polling.[2] Clearly, special interests—mainly corporate and industry interests—keep policy well to the right of where real, flesh-and-blood persons want it.

It's also worth recalling that conservative success would not have been possible without critical liberal strategic failures. These would include, for example, the Democratic Party's complete mishandling of the issue of corporate power. Too often have major party leaders willingly accepted conservative framing, including an acquiescence to corporate predominance, while real progressives within the party have failed to communicate effectively with the public about the true nature of corporations and the pragmatic values underlying human-centered policy. A second progressive failure has been the response to the Religious Right, particularly the doomed decision by many liberals not only to *accept* the notion that America is a very religious country that expects public displays of religious faith but to *promote* such religiosity through their own actions and rhetoric. This unwise exaltation of religion, and the implicit marginalization of secular Americans that accompanies it, has empowered the Religious Right, giving it much more credibility and efficacy than it otherwise would have had.

Perhaps most important, however, progressives have done a poor job prioritizing and seeing the big picture. As they've fought individual battles, sometimes winning (as with gay rights) but usually losing, rarely have they thought or acted as an integrated movement with a coherent message. Even within the Democratic Party, where one would expect various progressive factions and interest groups to unite for a common agenda, there has been almost no focus on the critical strategic issues that must be addressed for long-term, transformational change. Instead, progressives have tended to focus only on their specific areas of interest, paying little attention to broader progressive strategy.

As a result, we now have a Democratic Party that distinguishes itself from the GOP only in ways that don't threaten the corporatist agenda. Social issues, which usually don't pose any serious threat to corporate interests, are the area in which Democrats are most consistently and directly at odds with Republicans, and this is where the party attracts many progressives. On economic issues, meanwhile, Democrats as a party stay just nominally to the left of the GOP, without challenging Wall Street in any meaningful way. This will continue to be the case until progressives unite to give priority to the critical strategic issues needed for real change.

It's important to distinguish between those key strategic issues and ordinary political issues. The unique thing about strategic issues is that *the long-term success of any progressive movement actually relies on them.* By their nature, strategic issues *redefine the playing field* so that nonhuman, anti-egalitarian interests can no longer dominate policy making. This new environment, in turn, makes long-term success possible on all other progressive issues—fair taxation, social safety nets, reproductive rights, education, LGBT rights, environmental protection, peace, and everything else.

By distinguishing strategic from ordinary issues this way, the implication is not that the former are more important, only that they are a *necessary precondition* for long-term progressive success. Nobody is suggesting that progressives disregard ordinary issues, since such issues certainly stand as valid in their own right and directly affect the lives of millions each and every day. But advocates for the poor, women's rights, racial equality, universal health care, and other progressive causes all should realize that strategic progressive thinking has been ignored for too long. Put another way, if strategic issues are not won as a preliminary matter, any victories on ordinary issues should be considered temporary and easily reversible.

RETHINKING CORPORATE POWER

As we saw with the relentless corporate vigilance that chipped away at the Glass-Steagall Act regulating banking, and as we see with persistent attempts by Wall Street to dismantle Social Security in favor of privatization, corporations have not only unlimited resources but unlimited patience. Their interest in public policy is more intense than that of ordinary citizens, their focus is sharper, and their commitment is greater. This means that corporations will dominate government and policy making unless real humans—for whom the government is supposed to be working—take steps to protect their own interests.

Democracy and healthy debate are important, but allowing publicly traded, multinational corporations to participate in democracy in a way that overwhelms and silences the voices of ordinary humans is *not* real democracy or healthy debate. Thus, from a strategic standpoint, long-term progressive success depends first and foremost on ensuring that corporate interests are permanently controlled. The word "permanently" is critical here, because any restraint that can be easily removed via millions dollars of lobbying or influence peddling should be considered temporary. Ambitious regulations, or even grand statutes such as Glass-Steagall, often are little more than nuisances to major corporations and industries, since eventually most can be changed, watered down, or litigated away.

For this reason Americans need a new dialogue on the subject of corporate power, and progressives and freethinkers should be leading the conversation. Rather than accept corporate behemoths in their current form—as omnipotent entities that control the policymaking infrastructure—Americans need to realize that corporations are created by law and should be controlled by it as well. Corporations should act in the public interest, and any suggestion that we must allow them to control the nation's policymaking apparatus should be rejected outright.

Such rethinking shouldn't be seen as radical but as an attempt to put control back where it belongs. Humans still do the voting in America, but all other aspects of the political and governmental processes—shaping public opinion, controlling the economy, funding political campaigns, lobbying for policy, utilizing the courts—ultimately are dominated more by corporate persons than by real humans. One is hardly a communist if one suggests that such a system makes a mockery of democratic ideals.

Thus, the first step in any strategy for long-term progressive success in America must be to educate the population about the nature of corporations and to initiate a discussion about their proper role in society. Unfortunately, such thinking is not even on the radar screen of average Americans or their political leadership, but that must change. By telling the truth about corporate power, progressives can offer an empowering message: Average citizens, instead of feeling helpless in a system that is obviously dominated by institutions far more powerful than themselves, should see that those institutions must be subservient to the public interest.

CONSTITUTIONAL AMENDMENT

The Supreme Court's 2010 *Citizens United* ruling made one fact very clear: Americans will never control corporate power without a constitutional amendment. We can bicker about other issues and details, but the need for a constitutional amendment is undeniable.

Citizens United and other rulings show that corporations have so endeared themselves to the American system that they now stand on equal legal footing with real human beings, enjoying most of the same rights and liberties. In fact, having the added advantages of great wealth and no human concerns (such as family, physical health, or moral impulses), corporate entities focus solely on self-enrichment 24/7 and thereby exert much more control over the system than do real humans. "We the people" can pass laws intended to control corporations, but *Citizens United* and similar cases show that those laws will be rejected by the courts if they encroach on the "rights" of corporate persons. This being the case, the only realistic way to override this judicial interpretation is to amend the Constitution to properly define the limits of corporate power.

Constitutional amendments sometimes are seen as changing the original framework of the nation, but such would not be the case with an amendment overriding the *Citizens United* interpretation of corporate power. We've seen that corporations did not even exist in their current form at the time of the nation's founding, and to the extent they did exist, they were highly regulated and allowed to operate only in the public interest. Since it would be preposterous to suggest that the framers somehow envisioned today's corporate predominance, an amendment restraining corporate power should be seen as restoring the original relationship between corporations and government (and, indirectly, real humans), not departing from it.[3]

We saw previously that there are philosophical debates over the origin of human rights—whether rights come from God, exist naturally, or are invented by humans—but there is no such debate over the origin of rights for corporations. We can all agree that the rights of corporations are endowed by their creators—and *humans* (i.e., governments of laws) are the only *creators* of corporations. Thus, all discussion of *corporate rights* should begin and end with what real humans consider to be in the best public interest.

This issue must be seen as central to the success of any progressive agenda, because until it is resolved, everything else will remain volatile. Progressives might have a good political run at some point—perhaps passing budgets that reflect reduced defense spending and fairer taxation—but corporate interests always will loom in the background, plotting their inevitable comeback. Real humans stand no chance of long-term success in opposing corporate power until legal steps are taken to force the corporate sector to submit to the public interest. To do this, a constitutional amendment is necessary.

Various efforts to put forward constitutional amendments addressing the issue of corporate power have been made in recent years, as mentioned previously, but with little success because progressives have not given the issue the priority it deserves. The proposed amendment mentioned in chapter 11 that was put forward by Senator Bernie Sanders and Representative Ted Deutch, called "The Democracy Is for People Amendment," would effectively overturn *Citizens United* by forbidding corporate financing in elections and allowing campaign finance legislation.[4] This amendment would solve the legal problem that effectively dismantled the McCain-Feingold Act, a rational effort to regulate campaign finance that was overturned by a court ruling that money is speech for First Amendment purposes. Similar proposals have been introduced by representatives Jim McGovern and Adam Schiff, and others in Congress. Perhaps the most ambitious proposal, put forward by Representative Richard Nolan of Minnesota and backed by an activist group called the Move to Amend Coalition, would not only address the area of campaign finance but expressly affirm that corporations do not have *constitutional* rights.[5] Such deprivation of corporate constitutional rights would not mean that the people could not grant corporations various rights, but only that such rights would not be embedded constitutionally—corporate rights would be determined democratically, by real humans according to the public interest.

As we can see, the issues of corporate personhood and campaign finance reform are deeply intertwined. There are many reasons to rethink the pervasive nature of corporate power in America, but few are more compelling than the need to reestablish real democracy. By interpreting money as speech and essentially allowing unlimited funds to pour in to elections, often from undisclosed sources, *Citizens United* and related cases have extinguished any hopes of meaningful campaign finance reform. Ironically, by expanding the concept of fundamental rights so that large, powerful non-human institutions enjoy them, the law actually disempowers real humans and subverts the democratic process.

Taming corporate institutions that exert so much control over American society would have a direct impact on campaign finance reform, but it would go further as well. With corporate power under control, there would be greater consideration in public policy for the rights of workers, consumers, and even smaller businesses. Debates over health care and education, for example, would focus on the best interests of the human population, not corporations. In the world of business, it would not be outlandish to suggest that co-determination laws, requiring large corporations to give employees a significant say in the management and operation of the business, might gain traction. Such laws are common in Europe, but they are currently considered off-limits in American policy debate. In Germany, for example, up to half the seats on the board of directors of large corporations must be filled with employee representatives, a measure that ensures that the interests of workers are seriously considered in decision making. It's not that American workers oppose such measures, but Wall Street does—and that ends the discussion.

How far to go in reining in corporate power is open to debate, but what's troubling is that the topic is not even a serious part of the conversation in

America. If the issue were in the forefront, we would see it as a key plank in party platforms and a major topic of debate. Instead, the public at large passively accepts corporatism, oblivious to the fact that real humans need not be helpless in the face of institutional power. Faced with this general passivity, progressives should see the value of freethinking, with its healthy skepticism and tendency to question authority, because a wider appreciation of freethinking surely would awaken the public to the need for action.

DEFINING SUCCESS

In October 2013, with its stock price up about 20 percent for the year and near an all-time high, the pharmaceutical giant Merck announced 8,500 job cuts. The market responded by sending the stock price up another 2 percent the same day.[6] No rare phenomenon, this is the norm when big corporate layoffs occur. A couple of months earlier, Cisco Systems had announced 4,000 layoffs, then shortly thereafter gave its CEO a bonus of $19.9 million in cash and stock, an award for bringing its stock price up 18 percent for the year.[7]

Companies understand public relations, so they know they must outwardly depict employees as assets and part of the corporate team, but employees are a huge liability on real-world balance sheets. Thus, when a firm can continue to do business with fewer employees (or cheaper employees through overseas outsourcing), Wall Street typically responds with great enthusiasm. As the company's former employees march toward the unemployment office, management is applauded and institutional investors celebrate. There are few better examples of the inconsistency between the interests of real humans and those of corporate persons.

On paper, national leaders define success in strict economic terms, using figures such as gross domestic product (GDP), stock market indexes, inflation and unemployment rates, housing starts, and other raw data. All of these figures may be seen as relevant to a thorough analysis of society, but they don't paint the entire picture, and in fact overreliance on them paints a downright inaccurate picture. Too often, the key yardsticks used by politicians to assess the state of society are tied not to the health and well-being of humans but to corporate persons; and therefore, public policy discussion often ignores the quality of life of the humans who comprise society. As we see with Merck and Cisco, corporate success does not always equal success for human employees.

Overreliance on GDP is a good example of these misplaced values. The problem with GDP, which measures only raw production by totaling the dollar value of all goods and services produced within a society, is that it is blind to the effects of any given element of production, or even the reasons for production. Thus, constructing a huge parking lot by destroying vast, ecologically important wetlands would reflect positively on GDP. And if a neighborhood is devastated by fire or other natural disaster, GDP would reflect an uptick for the spending associated with any reconstruction but no downtick for the destruction. The effect on GDP is the same whether a company invests in inefficient oil burners or spends the same amount on solar panels. Social outcomes are irrelevant.

Even the economist primarily responsible for developing the idea of measuring national income in the 1930s, the Nobel laureate Simon Kuznets, warned that "the welfare of a nation can scarcely be inferred from a measure of national income."[8] Nevertheless, when politicians talk seriously about "the economy," the key figure cited is GDP. The dreaded term "recession" is even defined as "two consecutive quarters of negative economic growth as measured by a country's gross domestic product (GDP)."[9]

Although few would argue that GDP is irrelevant, many are coming to realize that the obsession with growth must be balanced with a greater concern for overall societal health. As such, alternative yardsticks have been developed, such as one index called the Genuine Progress Indictor (GPI), which weighs factors such as pollution, resource depletion, military spending, leisure time, and crime rates. Based on GPI, social health has deteriorated rapidly in the United States since 1970, despite rising GDP.[10] Another comprehensive measurement of social well-being, called the Index of Social Health (ISH), measures 16 factors, such as rates of poverty, infant mortality, teen suicide and drug abuse, and housing and health care costs. As with GPI, the ISH analysis shows that American social health has declined since the early 1970s, though not as significantly as rates shown in the GPI.[11]

Social health indicators have been criticized as requiring some degree of value judgment, and this is true. One could question, for example, whether rates of infant mortality should be weighed equally with rates of teen drug abuse (or numerous other factors) in defining "social health." Importantly, however, value judgments also are made by using GDP as the primary means of assessing economic health in the political arena. The political climate often is determined according to how "the economy" is perceived as doing, and "the economy" is largely defined by GDP and similar indicators. Thus, mainstream news organizations report these figures with great emphasis, as if the quality of lives of ordinary citizens actually correlates to such measurements. As we see with the laid-off workers whose former companies soar to all-time high valuations on the stock market, such is not the case.

In the process of crafting public policy, we should accept that value judgments are inevitable and necessary. Thus, we can't criticize social health indicators merely because they include value judgments, but rather we need to have a serious discussion about what our values are as a society.

HOW SHALL WE LIVE?

As we grapple with questions of economics and politics, it can be instructive to step back and consider issues from a big-picture standpoint. A really big picture.

Unlike other animals, modern humans have the ability to think in great detail about how they will live, personally and socially. Our intelligence, our complex linguistic abilities, and our technological advancements place us in a position, at least when under the right social and political conditions, to decide among a wide range of possible living conditions: urban, suburban, or rural living; career and education options; hobbies and interests; social relationships; and countless other life choices. Of course, life involves compromises, and factors outside our control seem to make many of these choices for us, but the fact that we can have a great amount of discretion about how we shall live sets us apart from other animals.[12]

For most of human history, such options have not existed. Our species, *Homo sapiens,* reached anatomical modernity at least 200,000 years ago (with millions of years as prehuman primates before that), and for almost all of our history our ancestors roamed about much like other animals, hunting, gathering, and struggling for survival. Only in the last few thousand years have humans lived in what we consider civilizations, with permanent settlements, governments, and written languages that would allow for knowledge to be preserved and built upon from generation to generation.

And it is only in the last few *hundred* years—a sliver of time amounting to just a handful of generations—that the accumulation of knowledge has reached a tipping point, resulting in an explosion of technology that has radically changed our environment and the character of human existence.

From an evolutionary standpoint, our intelligence has so far resulted in great success for our species, as our population now exceeds 7 billion and we inhabit almost all corners of the globe. It's noteworthy that our closest biological cousin, the chimpanzee—with whom we share a common ancestor that was swinging through the trees roughly 5 million years ago—shares over 95 percent of our DNA. Yet unlike humans, the world's entire chimp population is estimated at only about a quarter million, or less than the population of Lincoln, Nebraska.[13] Chimps have survived so far to modernity—but barely.

Most would agree that human evolutionary success can be credited in large part to our intelligence, but more accurately it can be attributed to our adaptability. Unlike chimps, humans have shown themselves capable of living in almost any environment on the planet. Anthropologist Rick Potts of the Smithsonian Institution posits that this adaptability too often gets overlooked in discussions of evolution. "[I]t's not the survival of the fittest in any one environment but the survival of the more versatile, the more general and flexible creatures that would really persist over time."[14] Importantly, however, from a political standpoint, one thing human adaptability has shown is that humans do not need democracy and freedom to survive and thrive as a species. After all, most humans have lived without such luxuries throughout history, and the human animal continues to propagate quite successfully in unfree societies like North Korea and Saudi Arabia even today.

We have a tendency to think, correctly, of free, open, and democratic societies as a sort of pinnacle of human progress, but we should be mindful that such societies are not the inevitable direction of human history. As we've seen, the human animal is quite capable of living in conditions that are much less optimal (and in fact almost always has). A free and open society can be attained only through affirmative efforts to ensure that existing social, political, and economic conditions allow for it. It's that vigilance thing again—if we let down our guard, institutional interests will most assuredly push our human interests aside.

This, in large part, is what has happened in America, where corporate interests have come to dominate, resulting in economic conditions that squeeze the human population. Fair wages and generous benefits would mean reduced profits for the corporate entity, so real humans just don't get them—and this phenomenon repeats itself over and over throughout the system. Because corporations have all the bases covered in controlling the system and shaping public policy, they are always in the stronger bargaining position relative to real humans, and the entire system reflects it. And sadly, those corporate interests have much of the general population believing that corporate dominance is simply the way it has to be.

There are some who will quickly point out that America is no North Korea, that we live in relative comfort and freedom, but this is hardly the standard by which we should judge ourselves as a society. The real question is whether the status quo is adequate. To the progressive and the freethinker, the fact that we are not North Korea does not end the debate over whether we should be doing much better.

And we can do much better. Once the corporate beasts have been tamed, first by constitutional amendment and then by a rational, ever-vigilant public that stays aware of the need to place human interests over those of nonhumans, real people will control the system that is rightfully theirs, and policy can align to their aspirations. Instead of working for a temp agency for a minimum wage below poverty level with no benefits, working people could have secure jobs with good pay, decent benefits, and adequate time for vacations, leisure, and creative pursuits. Families could send kids to college affordably, without remortgaging their homes, not because government is giving handouts but because our values dictate that higher education should be widely available and affordable.

That last statement raises another important point. The progressive vision is not one that claims government has a duty to provide citizens with a fulfilling life. It does assume, however, that a practical, intelligent citizenry can create an environment that provides the resources needed for individuals to attain such fulfillment: education, good jobs, and health care as a foundation, and beyond that a wide variety of outlets for creativity and other pursuits. Given our technological advancement, such ends are achievable so long as we don't allow outside institutions to overtake the system.

Of course, major differences of opinion will persist, and heated political clashes can be expected as we disagree over policy, but the environment will be much different from what it is today. With the rich, narcissistic corporate "people" put in their place—regulated, removed from politics, and serving the public interest—real humans can discuss and debate policy in a fair, intelligent manner, without undue influence from the corporate sector.

FOURTEEN

REASON FOR WINNING

WE'VE SEEN THAT THE RIGHT-WING AGENDA IS FUELED IN LARGE PART by an attack on reason, and therefore logic dictates that those striving for progressive, human-centered policy should work to nurture a cultural trend that appreciates rational, critical thinking. Such a trend would naturally carry over to politics, where the higher standards of the electorate would question institutional power and demand fact-based discourse and human-centered policy. Of course, mass appeal still would be needed for political success, but woe to the candidate who assumes that the masses are too stupid to listen to intelligent ideas and analysis. Any political tactics based on such assumptions would be seen as insulting.

One sure sign of a more enlightened electorate would be a political landscape with less nationalistic rhetoric. By refraining from chest-pounding patriotism and allusions to militarism, politicians would be showing the public a new level of respect. Constant pandering, repeatedly telling voters that they live in the greatest nation on Earth, distracts from the actual issues that deserve attention. To an intelligent audience, excessive talk of American exceptionalism from politicians is not flattering but demeaning.

The religious connection to patriotism, usually via the commingling of religious and nationalistic semantics, is especially important, for it points to a demographic issue that is vital to progressive success. Ever since the rise of the Moral Majority in 1980, liberals have been trying to drive home their own religious credentials—with two disastrous outcomes. One is that the entire political spectrum has shifted rightward, so that now even the Democratic Party is at best a center-right party. The other is that a huge, important part of the American population—those who are personally secular, either nonreligious or nontheistic—have been politically invisible. The isolation of this demographic, and its exclusion from the national conversation, is a devastating handicap for progressivism, even though, of course, many progressives are religious.

THE FENCE OF PIETY

Follow any national political campaign, and you'll inevitably hear the pundits talking about religious conservatives as a voting bloc, analyzing what the socially conservative segment of the electorate will think about particular issues and candidates. The media will repeat long-accepted myths without question, such as the worn-out notion that Americans are a very religious people. Nobody mentions that only 37 percent of the nation attends religious services on a weekly basis or that at least one in five has no religious affiliation.[1] Even on the central issue of God-belief, a significant minority are skeptics. According to the 2008 American Religious Identification Survey, a highly respected academic analysis of religious demographics, only about 81 percent of Americans actually affirm a belief in God (69 percent believe in a personal God, 12 percent in a "higher power"). The remainder fall into categories that would be described as atheist or agnostic ("don't know," "not sure," or "there is no such thing") or refusing to answer.[2]

Thus Americans, while on average somewhat more religious than the populations of most other developed countries, are hardly as devout as pundits and politicians suggest. Unlike truly religious societies, where religious beliefs and doctrines dictate the laws and define the culture, America is a pluralistic society in which religion is relatively insignificant to many, if not most. Despite this, every talking head on cable news—liberal, moderate, and conservative—nods with approval when the nation is described as deeply religious, and all discussion proceeds from there.

Despite the obvious secularity of everyday life for many Americans, a fence of piety has been constructed around the realm of politics, suggesting we all expect great religious devotion from our leaders. This lie comes with a heavy price. If conventional wisdom insists that politicians must pander to a religious population, it necessarily validates politically active conservative religion. After all, nobody can outdo the Christian Right when it comes to claiming religious credentials. This exaltation of religion also pushes seculars out of the mainstream and toward the fringes, making it virtually impossible for nontheistic and nonreligious candidates to get elected, especially to higher offices. This means that many intelligent, thoughtful individuals will be kept from public office (or, at least, will hide their true views if they seek office). Given that seculars tend to lean progressive, the exaggeration of the importance of religion effectively isolates many progressives from the electoral process and does great damage to the cause.

The fence of piety surrounding American politics handicaps progressives in another way. Because any perceived disrespect for religion is assumed to be unacceptable, progressive lawmakers and candidates are prohibited (or at least inhibited) from simply calling out fundamentalists for relying on senseless theological doctrines in policy debates. As lawmakers consider environmental policy on Capitol Hill, for example, those on the progressive side, out of respect for religion, never simply state the obvious: that their opponents are fools who think the world is only 6,000 years old. Instead, they dance around that powerful fact, avoiding any suggestion that religion is playing a role in obstructing rational policy. By giving policy positions based on theology immunity from rational scrutiny, Americans again tip the playing field to the advantage of conservatives.

Most other developed countries, and even some developing ones, routinely elect nonbelievers to high office, but in America only one open atheist has ever won a seat in Congress: Pete Stark, a Democrat from California, now retired. It's noteworthy that public policy in most other developed countries is well to the left of America's, with smaller military budgets, stronger social safety nets, and tighter regulation of corporate power. Just imagine how the complexion of Congress—and the policy flowing from it—would change if an Atheist-Humanist Caucus existed on Capitol Hill to offset the Congressional Prayer Caucus (which is an actual caucus formed in 2005, now with about 100 members, that advocates for more religion in government), with openly secular lawmakers serving as a constant reminder to right-wing fundamentalists that a significant portion of the population is not only not Christian, but not even religious or theistic.

From a strategic standpoint, the exaltation of religion and the vilification of secularism have been killing progressivism, and no long-term turnaround is likely until American attitudes mature. Those attitudes, although improving in recent years, still reflect a shocking level of ignorance and intolerance toward personal secularity, as surveys find atheists among the least admired and least trusted groups in the country.[3] Regardless of one's religious beliefs, it is important to recognize that the public's bias against atheists hinders progressive policy by feeding the righteous attitudes of God-and-country conservatism and validating anti-intellectualism.

Moreover, it is simply wrongheaded to discriminate against a demographic group that doesn't deserve it. If secularity led to lawlessness and immorality, perhaps prejudice against it could be defended, but in reality the opposite is true. Rates of violent crime, sexually transmitted disease, teen pregnancy, racial prejudice, ethnocentrism, and homophobia are consistently lower among secular individuals and societies than among religious ones. Such outcomes are found *internationally* (when the more religious United States is compared with less religious developed societies, such as those of Western Europe) and *domestically* within the United States (when more religious states are compared with less religious ones).[4]

One could correctly argue that the strong correlation between religiosity and social problems doesn't prove causation, that the social ills in question arise from other socioeconomic factors—poverty, education levels, and others. That may be true, but even so it seems clear that *secularity* certainly isn't the problem. No matter how one interprets the data, the societies that are more secular—most of Europe, for example—also tend to be the least violent and consistently have lower rates of social problems.[5]

And it's no coincidence that the more secular societies are also those in which progressive public policy is strongest. The lesson is clear: If we want progressive public policy, we need to tone down the religious rhetoric in politics and nurture a strong acceptance of personal secularity, in society in general but especially in the political realm.

This does not mean that the progressive agenda is antireligious—only that it is religiously neutral. One of the common cries from the Religious Right is that neutrality itself is somehow antireligious. This is the kind of groundless allegation that a critically thinking public will dismiss quickly.

A common culture war issue provides a good illustration. One need not be a legal scholar to understand that removal of the words "under God" from the Pledge of Allegiance—thereby returning it to its pre-1954 wording— would be an act of religious neutrality, not an act of hostility toward religion. Nevertheless, religious conservatives defending the wording insist that removal of the words would be an *endorsement of atheism*. As I've pointed out in countless debates on the subject, a pro-atheist pledge would not only remove the language favorable to God-belief, but also would add language that actually asserts disbelief (such as "one nation, under no gods . . ."). But no one is suggesting that kind of language, of course.

Similar arguments surface when nonbelievers object to the national motto, "In God We Trust," which was adopted only in 1956. Before that, the Latin phrase *E Pluribus Unum* (meaning "out of many, one"—a reference to the numerous states coming together to form one nation) had been the de facto national motto since the founding era. In the twisted logic of the Religious Right, however, setting aside "In God We Trust" and returning to "E Pluribus Unum" would be a pro-atheist gesture, not an act of neutrality. The Congressional Prayer Caucus even wrote to President Obama in 2010 to chastise him for referring to "E Pluribus Unum" as America's motto and for otherwise not mentioning God in his speeches.[6]

Because these symbolic culture-war issues get so contentious, many progressives prefer to avoid them altogether. Once upon a time, I shared this view, but eventually I came to see that the symbolic issues have more meaning than many realize. Children, standing in classrooms every day for a patriotic exercise that declares the nation to be "under God," learn to see God-belief as synonymous with patriotism. Subconsciously, they are being taught to associate patriotism with God-belief, so therefore nonbelievers become somewhat suspect, even second-class citizens. This bias becomes quickly ingrained in any child who lives in an environment in which he or she does not interact with open religious skeptics—and many children grow up in such environments. And, of course, as time moves forward and fewer people are even aware that "under God" was inserted into the pledge only in 1954, the prejudice becomes harder to rebut.

Such gestures and symbolism define the nation in terms that delight the Religious Right—a fact that too many progressives have chosen to ignore. That's not to suggest that all progressives should make symbolic issues their top priority—I'll be the first to acknowledge that such battles are not for everyone—but it is important that progressives at least understand that these issues are not petty, that they are used by conservatives to mold enduring public perceptions.

A SECULAR EMERGENCE

All progressives—religious and nonreligious—should recognize the significant value of America's secular movement in pushing back against right-wing domination. If America's secular demographic can emerge to become a visible and respected part of society, the political clout of religious conservatives (and therefore their allies as well) is instantly weakened. Put another way, America simply cannot effectively fight back against the Religious Right if its atheists and other seculars—an incredibly valuable segment of the population—remain in hiding politically.

Currently, with the flawed general consensus that America is highly religious, the Religious Right naturally enjoys a certain stature. Not everyone belongs to the Christian Right, of course, and many are actually put off by it, but all are expected to accept that its voice carries great weight and must be taken seriously. After all, America is a very religious country, right? But if a significant part of the population stands up to challenge such assumptions—pointing out that millions of Americans lead ethical, productive lives without any religion or theistic belief—the voice of reason necessarily gets louder.

This is not to suggest that only secular Americans can claim the banner of reason. Many religious Americans manage to apply reason to issues of public policy and other aspects of life, even as they devoutly hold to personal faith. However, even these religious Americans should understand that the emergence of seculars as a respected demographic in American society would be a game-changing development. With seculars visibly participating in policy discussions, the political center of gravity would naturally move away from the anti-egalitarianism and anti-intellectualism that has defined policy for over three decades.

That doesn't mean that all seculars are progressive or left leaning— only that the overall impact of a secular emergence would be a progressive shift. Even though seculars can be found across the political spectrum, as a group they tend to lean progressive (as we saw from the voting patterns referenced earlier, where seculars were among the most reliably strong demographics for Democratic candidates). If politicians and the media actually began paying attention to seculars as a demographic—openly talking about their concerns and rights—who knows how much the right-wing agenda might suffer? Sure, the nonreligious demographic includes some neocons, libertarians, and run-of-the-mill conservatives, but the fuller participation of seculars in the political process would necessarily redefine the landscape in a way that provides more fertile ground for progressive, reason-based policy.

With seculars at the table, America suddenly becomes even more pluralistic—not just a society of various religious faiths but a society of religious *and* nonreligious people—so injecting religious preferences into any debate becomes less acceptable. This not only helps push back against the Right; it encourages more reason-based, fact-based discussion.

Since the emergence of seculars would move policy in a progressive direction, it should be an important part of the overall progressive strategy. This means that those Americans who are personally secular should be open about it to their families, friends, neighbors, coworkers, and others. Currently, many Americans have little regard for traditional theology, yet they still identify as "Catholic" or "Protestant" when asked for religious identity. We need to rethink the consequences of such identification. This isn't a call for religious Americans to drop their religion, but only for those Americans who really aren't religious to recognize the importance of being honest and open about it.

There is increasing recognition, especially among progressives, that false religious identification can be harmful on a social and political level. When nonreligious Americans identify as religious—out of family pressure, habit, or just plain laziness—they reinforce the fence of piety that empowers conservatives. Awareness of this problem is no doubt part of the reason that the number of "Nones"—those who refuse to identify with any religious affiliation—has doubled since the 1990s, to one in five Americans and one-third of those under 30 (both all-time highs).[7] As religiosity is increasingly associated with right-wing politics, more are questioning their religious affiliation.

Religious progressives have a job here as well, since they can promote progressive policy by encouraging an acceptance of open seculars. No longer should Americans cringe when they hear the word "atheist," as if anyone openly claiming that label must be "militant" or "angry." So many religious people I've met will tell me privately that they "have nothing against atheists," only to add: "I just wish they'd keep it to themselves!" Implied in this statement is the suggestion that open atheism is somehow offensive, akin to obnoxious Christian proselytizing. This shouldn't be the case, however, since casual identification as a nonbeliever should be no different from casual identification as a Catholic or an Episcopalian. In fact, most atheists have been "keeping it to themselves" for too long, and the country has been taken over by wing nuts in the meantime. It's time for atheists and other seculars to claim their rightful place in American society, and all who wish for progressive policy should encourage the trend.

Just as the success of America's gay rights movement has relied on reasonable people within the straight population accepting gays and lesbians as part of the diverse tapestry of the nation, so do seculars rely on their natural allies. Without suggesting that atheist prejudice necessarily compares to gay-lesbian prejudice, the game-changing effect that more widespread open secularity would have on American culture—particularly political culture—is undeniable. As with gay rights, there will inevitably be those who oppose the acceptance of seculars—mainly social conservatives and the Religious Right (oddly enough, the same crowd that opposes gay rights)—but this only shows that seculars are perceived as a threat by these right-wingers. We can also expect some resistance from any sector that benefits from the utilization of overt God-and-country patriotism, such as the military and corporate media.

By comparing the concept of open personal secularity with coming out as gay, we need not suggest that the experience of being personally secular is akin to being gay. Certainly, one's sexual orientation affects one's life much differently than does one's personal religious outlook, and the typical atheist doesn't face the same prejudices and difficulties in daily life as someone who is openly gay or lesbian. From a political standpoint, however, the ability of widespread open secularity to push back against the Religious Right is invaluable.

Sometimes resistance to the idea of promoting open personal secularity comes not from conservatives, or even religious liberals, but from individuals who are in fact secular themselves. These closeted seculars are essentially afraid to challenge Christian privilege—or, worse, they feel that open identification as a nonbeliever is socially unacceptable. They often will try to dodge the issue, saying they feel that everyone should "just be quiet about religion." They'll claim they aren't personally afraid to openly identify, only that they think it's undignified to do so. "Religion should just stay out of the equation," they'll say. Oddly, however, these same people are often the ones who will urge atheists not to object to nativity scenes and Ten Commandment displays on public property and other blatantly religious public gestures. It seems that they feel religion should stay out of daily life, but then they passively accept the imposition of public religious symbolism.

Although they won't always admit it, those who don't wish to make waves by asserting secular rights and secular identity often are motivated by fear: fear of openly identifying with a vilified demographic and fear of challenging the majority. This is evident from the semantic gymnastics some will use to avoid the label "atheist." Many religious skeptics explain their refusal to identify as atheist to me by saying something like "I don't believe in God, but I refuse to identify with a negative. I will not identify with what I *don't* believe." Strangely, however, these same people will gladly identify as "nonsmokers" and "antiwar"—both negatives. It quickly becomes clear that there is no principled opposition to identifying with a negative, only an aversion to identifying with the unpopular "atheist" label.

I certainly understand that some may refuse to identify openly as atheist, and I think it's wrong to criticize such individuals. There are many reasons—family, business, job—why some people may feel they need to avoid the atheist label, and few of us are in a position to judge. The problem is not the avoidance of the label but the dishonest reasons for doing so. Besides, if one is personally secular, there are plenty of alternative identifiers that are seen as more socially acceptable: secular, agnostic, humanist, freethinker, skeptic, nonreligious, or, my favorite, *post-theological*. The important thing is that this group is big, growing, and can change the landscape in America as it expands and gains visibility.

In fact, seculars have organized significantly in the last decade, and the movement shows little sign of slowing down. Groups such as the American Humanist Association (AHA), for example, have seen explosive growth and have increasingly become engaged in social and political activism. The few secular groups that existed a decade ago were more like social clubs and mostly intellectual in character. The AHA had a constituency of about 5,000 members at that time, most of whom had little interaction with the group. Today, the AHA's social media following is in the hundreds of thousands and climbing, and these individuals are interacting with the organization sometimes several times a day, receiving relevant news, e-mail alerts, and notifications. If an important church-state decision comes down, if new legislation affecting nonbelievers is proposed, or if a high-ranking politician says something of interest, members and followers will know about it right away.

In 2014, several secular groups joined together to launch the Openly Secular initiative, a serious effort to examine public attitudes about secularism and promote efforts to improve perceptions. With some of the first in-depth polling done on the subject, Openly Secular discovered that the public perceives personal secularity with mixed feelings. Most acknowledge that there is prejudice against the demographic, especially in the area of politics, but still feel that any discrimination falls short of being a civil rights issue akin to race, gender, or sexual orientation. Most seculars probably would agree with that assessment, though several gay atheists have told me that announcing their atheism to their families was just as difficult as coming out as gay, so individual circumstances and experiences no doubt vary greatly. Armed with this new data and conducting more research, Openly Secular hopes to advance the effort of educating the public on the value of the secular demographic.[8]

Much of the activity of Openly Secular and other groups will be happening online, and it's impossible to fully explain the modern secular movement without mentioning the importance of the Internet. Although online activity has affected everyone in the last couple of decades, the Internet and social media have made all the difference to the secular movement, providing the necessary infrastructure through which the movement has reached millions. By making it possible for atheists, agnostics, humanists, and freethinkers to find each other, form local groups, and make connections around the country and around the world, the Internet has empowered seculars by connecting them. Facebook, Meetup, and similar Web sites have allowed a once-isolated demographic to develop a sense of identity and sometimes community, and now almost every metropolitan area has an atheist, humanist, or freethought group of some kind, if not several.

New groups have formed on the national level as well, often reflecting a strong drive to normalize seculars within policy-making circles. The Secular Coalition for America (SCA), the first Washington lobbying group for the secular demographic, was formed shortly after George W. Bush took office, giving seculars a visible presence on Capitol Hill. Besides lobbying, the SCA releases periodic Congressional Scorecards to grade legislators on how well they are voting on issues of interest to secular constituents and otherwise keeps the secular movement engaged politically.

In 2013, the movement went one step further, launching a political action committee, the Freethought Equality Fund, to fund political candidates who support secular humanist positions. Years ago it would have been inconceivable that candidates would even be willing to take "atheist money" this way, but the movement has made steady progress in breaking down such barriers of prejudice.

WINNING THE FIGHT

The secular movement can be seen as one aspect of an overall strategy to advance progressive policy. In the last chapter I noted the importance of strategy, arguing that progressives have for too long focused on their particular areas of interest while largely ignoring the big picture. Long-term success on all progressive issues will be much more likely if we can reshape the policy-making landscape in favor of rational, progressive policy in general. As such, let's recap the five key strategies that will hasten such an outcome:

1. FOCUS ON CORPORATE POWER. Whether one's main interest within the progressive movement is women's rights, poverty, peace, civil rights, the environment, or something else, there must be a determination to make the issue of corporate power a key priority. Directly or indirectly, the power of corporate interests hinders the success

of human-centered policy, so progressives must work together to raise public consciousness about the issue and take the political steps needed to solve the problem.

2. CAMPAIGN FINANCE REFORM. To restore democracy, remove the corrupting influence of institutional interests, and ensure long-term success for human-centered policy, meaningful campaign finance reform is needed. Unlimited funding, often from undisclosed sources, has changed the nature of American electoral politics. There must be a recognition that long-term progressive success is contingent on the restoration of real democracy that can't be sold to the highest bidder.

3. CONSTITUTIONAL AMENDMENT. Recognizing the need to control corporate power and restore real democracy is a good start, but it's also essential to understand that neither of these issues will be won without a constitutional amendment. The Supreme Court has ruled not only that corporations are persons with constitutional rights similar to those of real humans, but that money is a form of free speech in politics. Thus, passing laws on these issues will do nothing, because such laws will only be overturned by the courts. If we want change, we need a constitutional amendment to fix these legal impediments.

4. RAISE THE LEVEL OF DISCOURSE. Widespread anti-intellectualism has dragged down the quality of public discourse in America, and progressives must lead the way in calling it out. We need to encourage—or, better yet, *demand*—rational, fact-based policy discussion and lambaste politicians who proudly reject science. There's plenty of room for vigorous debate on issues, but America needs a broad trend that is sharply critical of any elected official who relies on fear, pandering, and willful ignorance. For a politician to contend that evolution is a hoax, or that the earth is only a few thousand years old, must be considered nothing less than shameful.

5. SECULAR EMERGENCE. From a demographic standpoint, nothing will push back against the right-wing agenda more effectively than the emergence of America's nonreligious population. When seculars are being taken seriously as an important part of the population deserving recognition and respect, even standing for elected office, we can be sure that America has embarked on a road toward progressive,

human-centered policy. This is why all progressives, religious and nonreligious, should welcome this trend.

The common thread that binds these strategic points is a renewed appreciation of reason. The triumph of human-centered public policy is entirely dependent on the triumph of reason as a cultural phenomenon. If the Right maintains its grip on American public policy, it will do so by continuing to use its favorite tool: anti-intellectualism, in all its varieties. Progressives, knowing this, must strategize accordingly, by focusing their sharpest attention on the key areas that can produce long-term success: controlling corporate power, cleaning up the electoral process, renewing appreciation of critical thinking, and ensuring that religious fundamentalism does not exert undue influence in politics.

I understand that many progressives would not consider the five points just cited to be their top priorities—they'd rather focus on other issues, not corporate personhood or constitutional amendments. And that's fine, because nobody is suggesting that we let up in our efforts to promote any aspect of the progressive agenda. But we have to recognize that these strategic issues lay the groundwork for true success in everything else. With corporate power under control, health care can be discussed without the undue influence of insurance companies and pharmaceutical companies, defense budgets can be discussed with less corrupting influence from corporate interests that want to feed at the trough of military spending, industry influence in all areas of policy making can be limited, and money flowing into political campaigns can be regulated and scrutinized. Simply put, the long-term security of those of us on Main Street can take priority over the short-term profits of Wall Street.

This is not class warfare, nor is it socialism. This is a plan to take back America from the institutional interests that have hijacked it. Earlier in the book I mentioned that the trajectory taken by the country was not inevitable, that our current realities are the result of institutions and developments that would have been unimaginable to the framers. Surely, even if we leave aside the astounding technological advances, we must recognize that the political, economic, and social changes that have occurred in America over the last two-plus centuries have resulted in a society that would be unrecognizable to the founding generation. It shouldn't be surprising that some of those developments have been less than admirable, but the real mistake would be to ignore them. We have allowed institutions—large, publicly traded, multinational corporations—to develop, and we've let those institutions seize control of the system. We've also allowed anti-intellectualism to dominate the public sphere in a way that is harmful to society in general and public policy in particular. Recognizing these developments, we can now take practical steps to fix them.

These strategies are a pragmatic attempt to restore reason and sanity to public policy, not an ideological war cry. Given what's happened to the country over the last three-plus decades, such a common-sense approach is long overdue. It's time to reclaim America.

ACKNOWLEDGMENTS

GRATEFUL THANKS TO MY WIFE, KATY NIOSE, FOR ALL THAT SHE'S done to assist with this project. As an all-around advisor and best friend, she provided invaluable support. Thanks also to my editor, Emily Carleton, and the other professionals at Palgrave Macmillan who helped navigate this book from idea to reality. I'm also grateful to my agent, Laura Gross, and to others who provided valuable assistance, particularly Roy Speckhardt and Lou Franco. Finally, special thanks to all of the activist communities and individuals with whom I've worked in recent years—progressives, humanists, secular students, and others—all sharing a common concern about the direction of American society and public policy.

NOTES

INTRODUCTION: THE POLITICS OF ANTIREASON

1. Elise Viebeck, "Republican Says Evolution, Big Bang Theory 'Lies Straight from the Pit of Hell,'" *The Hill*, October 6, 2012, http://thehill.com/blogs/blog-briefing-room/news/260641-house-republican-says-evolution-big-bang-theory-lies-straight-from-the-pit-of-hell.
2. When referring to "right" and "left" in politics, styles vary on capitalization. I've followed the rule of capitalizing when referring to an entity or a bloc, but the terms will not be capitalized when used as adjectives or when referring to a general conservative or liberal direction.
3. See, for example, Kevin Drum, "Why Screwing Unions Screws the Entire Middle Class," *Mother Jones* (March/April 2011), http://www.motherjones.com/politics/2011/02/income-inequality-labor-union-decline.
4. See, for example, Allen Clifton, "The Truth about Republican Racism and the 'Southern Strategy,'" ForwardProgressives.com, June 4, 2013, http://www.forward progressives.com/the-truth-about-republican-racism-and-the-southern-strategy/.
5. References to Reagan and the conservative movement renewing a demoralized nation after the 1960s and 1970s are widespread. See, for example, Ed Rollins, "Ronald Reagan Restored Faith in America," CNN.com, February 2, 2011, http://www.cnn.com/2011/OPINION/02/02/rollins.reagan/; and Gil Troy, "The Age of Reagan," Gilder Lehrman Institute of American History, http://www.gilderlehrman.org/history-by-era/essays/age-reagan.
6. See, for example, Liz Sidoti, "GOP Contenders Embrace Reagan Legacy," *USA Today*, May 4, 2007, http://usatoday30.usatoday.com/news/politics/2007-05-04-1521577326_x.htm.

CHAPTER 1: CORRUPT BLESSINGS

1. David Domke and Kevin Coe, "Happy 35th, 'God Bless America,'" *Time*, April 29, 2008, http://www.time.com/time/nation/article/0,8599,1735972,00.html.
2. "Kate Smith," *Flyers History*, http://www.flyershistory.com/cgi-bin/kate.cgi.
3. Palin's gaffes and jaw-dropping quotes are legendary. A compilation of them can be found at http://politicalhumor.about.com/od/sarahpalin/a/palinisms.htm.
4. Elise Viebeck, "Republican Says Evolution, Big Bang Theory 'Lies Straight from the Pit of Hell,'" *The Hill*, October 6, 2012, http://thehill.com/blogs/blog-briefing

-room/news/260641-house-republican-says-evolution-big-bang-theory-lies-straight -from-the-pit-of-hell.

5. Candace Chellew-Hodge, "GOP Congressman Uses Bible to Justify Punishing Poor," *Salon*, May 28, 2013, http://www.salon.com/2013/05/28/tennessee_republi can_uses_bible_as_weapon_against_poor_partner/.

6. Brian Tashman, "Religious Right Groups Laud Paul Ryan, Highlight Anti-Choice and Anti-Gay Voting Record," *Right Wing Watch*, August 13, 2012, http://www .rightwingwatch.org/content/religious-right-groups-laud-paul-ryan-highlight-anti -choice-and-anti-gay-voting-record.

7. Ibid.

8. Ibid.

9. Views on interracial marriage are one indicator of changing American attitudes on race. Whereas 4 percent of Americans approved of black-white marriages in 1958, the figure had climbed to 87 percent by 2013. See Frank Newport, "In U.S., 87% Approve of Black-White Marriage, vs. 4% in 1958," *Gallup Politics*, July 25, 2013, http://www.gallup.com/poll/163697/approve-marriage-blacks-whites.aspx.

10. Most dictionaries list "freethinker" and "freethinking" as compound words, but not so for the term "freethought." Instead, the technically correct style of that last term is as two words, "free thought." In modern usage, however, "freethought" is commonly seen as a compound word, even if technically incorrect. Out of personal preference for that modern style, I use it throughout this volume.

11. "'Nones' on the Rise," Pew Research, Religion and Public Life Project, October 9, 2012, http://www.pewforum.org/2012/10/09/nones-on-the-rise/. The percentage of Americans who identify as religiously unaffiliated has grown steadily since 1990, to one in five. For those under 30, the figure is now one in three. See also "American Religious Identification Survey (ARIS 2008)," Trinity College, http://commons .trincoll.edu/aris/publications/2008-2/aris-2008-summary-report/.

CHAPTER 2: REAL-WORLD CHANGE

1. Kasie Hunt, "Rick Perry Prayer Rally Speech Decries US Condition," *Politico*, August 6, 2011, http://www.politico.com/news/stories/0811/60799.html; Ewen Mac-Askill, "Rick Perry's Call to Prayer Draws Crowd of 30,000," *Guardian*, August 7, 2011, http://www.theguardian.com/world/2011/aug/07/rick-perrys-call-to-prayer.

2. MacAskill, "Rick Perry's Call to Prayer."

3. Amy Gardner and Philip Rucker, "Rick Perry Stumbles Badly in Republican Presidential Debate," *Washington Post*, November 9, 2011, http://www.washingtonpost .com/politics/republican-presidential-candidates-focus-on-economy/2011/11/09 /gIQA5Lsp6M_story.html.

4. Ibid.

5. See, for example, "How the Faithful Voted," Pew Research, November 10, 2008, http://www.pewforum.org/2008/11/05/how-the-faithful-voted/; and Frank Newport, "Church Attendance and Party Identification," Gallup.com, March 18, 2005, http://www.gallup.com/poll/16381/church-attendance-party-identification.aspx.

6. Stephanie Condon, "Poll: One in Four Americans Think Obama Was Not Born in US," *CBS News*, April 21, 2011, http://www.cbsnews.com/news/poll-one-in-four -americans-think-obama-was-not-born-in-us/.

7. "Little Voter Discomfort with Romney's Mormon Religion," Pew Research Religion and Public Life Project, July 26, 2012, http://www.pewforum.org/2012/07 /26/2012-romney-mormonism-obamas-religion/.

8. Kate Pickert, "Keep Your Gov't Hands Off My Medicare," *Time,* October 21, 2010, http://swampland.time.com/2010/10/21/keep-your-govt-hands-off-my-medicare-cont/.

9. Wolf Blitzer interview with Michele Bachmann, CNN, September 27, 2013.

10. Michael Hirsh, "'Government Sachs' Is Back," *Daily Beast,* March 4, 2009.

11. "Obama White House 'Full of Wall Street Executives'?" *The Wire,* March 1, 2012, http://www.factcheck.org/2012/02/obama-white-house-full-of-wall-street-executives/.

12. Greg Palast, "Larry Summers: Goldman Sacked," *Reader Supported News,* September 18, 2013, http://readersupportednews.org/opinion2/277-75/19459-larry-summers-goldman-sacked.

13. "Cato 2012," IRS Form 990 Revenues Reported, http://www.eri-nonprofit-salaries.com/index.cfm?FuseAction=NPO.Form990&EIN=237432162; "American Enterprise Institute revenues reported for fiscal year ending June 2012," Charity Navigator, http://www.charitynavigator.org/index.cfm?bay=search.summary&orgid=3252#.Ux2fMz9dV8E.

14. Hadas Gold, "John Elway: My Beliefs Align with GOP," *Politico,* February 2, 2014, http://www.politico.com/blogs/politico-live/2014/02/john-elway-my-beliefs-align-with-gop-182520.html; David Edwards, "John Elway to Fox News: I'm a Republican Because 'I Don't Believe in Safety Nets,'" *The Raw Story,* February 2, 2014, http://www.rawstory.com/rs/2014/02/02/john-elway-to-fox-news-im-republican-because-i-dont-believe-in-safety-nets/.

15. "History of Federal Income Bottom and Top Tax Brackets," National Taxpayers Union, http://www.ntu.org/tax-basics/history-of-federal-individual-1.html#_edn10.

16. Wolf Blitzer, "Grover Norquist on tax reform and debt negotiations," CNN interview, *The Situation Room with Wolf Blitzer,* July 13, 2011, http://cnnpressroom.blogs.cnn.com/2011/07/13/grover-norquist-on-tax-reform-and-debt-negotiations/.

CHAPTER 3: OF PEOPLE AND HUMANS

1. "Tea Party State of the Union 2013 Rebuttal: Rand Paul Response," *Politico,* February 12, 2013, http://www.politico.com/story/2013/02/tea-party-rebuttal-text-of-rand-paul-response-87557.html; Senator Rand Paul, "Response: State of the Union 2014," RandPaul2016, January 28, 2014, http://www.randpaul2016.com/2014/01/senator-rand-paul-response-state-union-2014/.

2. Paul, "Response: State of the Union 2014."

3. Emma Brown, James Hohmannn, and Perry Bacon Jr., "Tens of Thousands Protest Obama Initiatives at Capitol," *Washington Post,* September 13, 2009, http://www.washingtonpost.com/wp-dyn/content/article/2009/09/12/AR2009091200971.html.

4. Ibid.

5. Heidi Przbyla, "Tea Party Advocates Who Scorn Socialism Want a Government Job," *Bloomberg,* March 25, 2010, http://www.bloomberg.com/apps/news?pid=newsarchive&sid=aLBZwxqgYgwI.

6. For summary and details of Tea Party politicians' positions, see Theda Skocpol and Vanessa Williams, "The Tea Party and the Remaking of Republican Conservatism," OnTheIssues.com, http://www.ontheissues.org/Remaking_Conservatism.htm.

7. "The Tea Party and Religion," Pew Research, Religion & Public Life Project, February 23, 2011, http://www.pewforum.org/2011/02/23/tea-party-and-religion/.

8. Kevin Fobbs, "Keeping God in Pledge of Allegiance Faces New Legal Attack on America's Soul," Tea Party Command Center Blogger Spot, October 7, 2013,

http://teapartyorg.ning.com/profiles/blogs/keeping-god-in-pledge-of-allegiance
-faces-new-legal-attack-on.

9. See "Standing with Walker in Wisconsin," Tea Party Express, http://www.teaparty
express.org/3639/standing-with-walker-in-wisconsin.

10. Patrick Marley and Lee Berquist, "Abortion, Birth Control Are Wedge Issues in
Governor's Race," (Milwaukee) *Journal Sentinal,* October 2, 2010, http://www.js
online.com/news/statepolitics/104221094.html; Napp Nazworth, "Interview: Gov.
Scott Walker Talks Faith, Compromise and Helping the Poor," *Christian Post,* November 22, 2013, http://www.christianpost.com/news/interview-gov-scott-walker
-talks-faith-compromise-and-helping-the-poor-109271/.

11. Associated Press, "Wisconsin Governor Scott Walker Signs Abortion Bill Requiring Ultrasound," *Politico,* July 5, 2013, http://www.politico.com/story/2013/07
/wisconsin-governor-signs-abortion-bill-requiring-ultrasound-93762.html.

12. "Tea Party State of the Union 2013 Rebuttal."

13. Scott Horton, "James Madison, Corporations, and the National Security State,"
Address to University of Alabama Law School, April 14, 2011, http://harpers.org
/wp-content/uploads/madisoncorporationsnss2.pdf.

14. Ibid.

15. Joel Bakan, *The Corporation: The Pathological Pursuit of Profit and Power* (New York:
Free Press, 2004), pp. 1–2.

16. The Ford Pinto scandal has been covered widely. For a concise but thorough account, see Mark Dowie, "Pinto Madness," *Mother Jones* (September/October 1977),
http://www.motherjones.com/politics/1977/09/pinto-madness.

17. "General Electric Company," *Morningstar,* October 13, 2013, http://investors
.morningstar.com/ownership/shareholders-major.html?t=GE.

18. "General Electric Company," *Yahoo Finance,* October 13, 2013, http://finance
.yahoo.com/q/mh?s=ge+Major+Holders.

19. "State Street Corporation Institutional Ownership," NASDAQ, http://www
.nasdaq.com/symbol/stt/institutional-holdings.

20. Milton Friedman, "The Social Responsibility of Business Is to Increase Its Profits,"
New York Times Magazine, September 13, 1970, http://www.colorado.edu/student
groups/libertarians/issues/friedman-soc-resp-business.html.

21. Suzanne Vranica, "Ad Spending Expected to Pick Up Pace," *Wall Street Journal* online, December 8, 2013, http://online.wsj.com/news/articles/SB100014240527023
03330204579246003193822532.

22. Dustin Volz and Sophie Novack, "Why CVS Is Ready to Lose Billions and Stop
Selling Cigarettes," *National Journal,* February 5, 2014, http://www.nationaljournal
.com/health-care/why-cvs-is-ready-to-lose-billions-and-stop-selling-cigarettes-2014
0205.

23. Ibid.

24. "CVS Caremark Corporation," *Yahoo Finance,* March 12, 2014, http://finance
.yahoo.com/q/mh?s=CVS+Major+Holders.

CHAPTER 4: THE BOOMER BUST

1. Edward M. Kennedy, "Faith, Truth and Tolerance in America," transcript of speech
at Liberty Baptist College, October 3, 1983, http://www.americanrhetoric.com
/speeches/tedkennedytruth&tolerance.htm.

2. Bill Clinton, "All of Us See Through the Glass Darkly," transcript of sermon at
Riverside Church in New York City, August 29, 2004, http://www.beliefnet.com
/News/Politics/2004/09/All-Of-Us-See-Through-The-Glass-Darkly.aspx?p=1.

3. Bruce Buursma, "Lear Group May Ask FCC for Air Time to Counter Robertson Attack," *Chicago Tribune,* September 6, 1986, http://articles.chicagotribune .com/1986-09-06/news/8603060545_1_norman-lear-anthony-podesta-atheist.

4. Ibid.

5. Dan Gilgoff, "Norman Lear May Not Be Jerry Falwell or Pat Robertson, but He Has a Spiritual Side," *USA Today,* February 12, 2009, http://www.usnews.com /news/blogs/god-and-country/2009/02/12/norman-lear-may-not-be-jerry-falwell -or-pat-robertson-but-he-has-a-spiritual-side.

6. People for the American Way advertisement, http://m.youtube.com/watch?v=_qU 6vyydz40&desktop_uri=%2Fwatch%3Fv%3D_qU6vyydz40.

7. Mary Wisniewski, "Illinois Cannot Make Pharmacists Give 'Morning After' Pill: Court," Reuters US Edition, September 21, 2012, http://www.reuters.com /article/2012/09/21/us-usa-illinois-contraception-idUSBRE88K1D120120921; Howard Fischer, "Arizona Senate: Business Owners Can Cite Religion to Refuse Service to Gays," *Arizona Daily Star,* February 19, 2014, http://azstarnet.com/news /local/govt-and-politics/arizona-senate-business-owners-can-cite-religion-to-refuse -service/article_d77c1aa4-99b9-11e3-bd22-0019bb2963f4.html.

8. *Burwell v. Hobby Lobby Stores,* 573 U.S. (2014).

9. Jim Shea, "Boomer Yin & Yang," *Hartford Courant,* October 1, 2008, http:// articles.courant.com/2008-10-01/news/boom1001.art_1_leading-edge-boomers -terrible-twos-baby-boomers.

10. The camel-through-the-needle lesson must have been an important one to early Christians, as it appears in three of the four Gospels: Matthew 19:23–26, Mark 10:24–27, and Luke 18:24–27.

11. See Sara Diamond, "On the Road to Political Power and Theocracy," Political Research Associates, http://www.publiceye.org/eyes/sd_theo.html.

12. See Randall Balmer, "The Real Origins of the Religious Right," *Politico,* May 27, 2014, http://www.politico.com/magazine/story/2014/05/religious-right-real-origins -107133.html#.U7XlF41dV9s; Amanda Marcotte, "It Wasn't Abortion That Formed the Religious Right. It Was Support for Segregation," *Slate,* May 29, 2014, http:// www.slate.com/blogs/xx_factor/2014/05/29/the_religious_right_formed_aro und_support_for_segregation_not_against_abortion.html.

13. Paul Krugman, *The Conscience of a Liberal* (New York: Norton, 2009), pp. 179–180

14. Ibid., p. 197.

CHAPTER 5: NO CORPORATIONS IN FOXHOLES

1. Quoted in Luke Johnson, "Mitt Romney: Defense Won't Be Cut to Balance Budget," *Huffington Post,* September 10, 2012, http://www.huffingtonpost.com/2012/09/10 /mitt-romney-defense-budget_n_1870226.html.

2. John Avlon, "Mitt Romney's Military Budget Hypocrisy," *The Daily Beast,* October 11, 2012, http://www.thedailybeast.com/articles/2012/10/11/mitt-romney-s -military-budget-hypocrisy.html.

3. Maeve Reston, "Romney Invokes God, Slams Obama on Proposed Military Budget Cuts," *Los Angeles Times,* September 8, 2012, http://articles.latimes.com/2012 /sep/08/news/la-pn-romney-invokes-god-20120908.

4. Gilbert Cruz, "A Brief History of the Flag Lapel Pin," *Time,* July 3, 2008, http:// content.time.com/time/nation/article/0,8599,1820023,00.html.

5. Jack Shafer, "Newsweek Throws the Spitter," *Slate,* January 30, 2007, http://www .slate.com/articles/news_and_politics/press_box/2007/01/newsweek_throws_the _spitter.html.

6. Ibid.

7. Dwight D. Eisenhower, *Mandate for Change, 1953–56: The White House Years, A Personal Account* (Garden City, NY: Doubleday, 1963), p. 372.

8. George C. Herring, *America's Longest War: The United States and Vietnam: 1950–1975* (New York: McGraw-Hill, 1986), p. 55.

9. Keith Olbermann, "Lessons from the Vietnam War," MSNBC.com, November 20, 2006, http://www.nbcnews.com/id/15821138/ns/msnbc-countdown_with_keith_olbermann/t/olbermann-lessons-vietnam-war/#.U6Yvpo1dU00.

10. Ibid.

11. The entire speech can be found at Dwight D. Eisenhower, "Military-Industrial Complex Speech," 1961, http://coursesa.matrix.msu.edu/~hst306/documents/indust.html.

12. Kyle Kim, "Here Are the Top 10 American Corporations Profiting from Egypt's Military," *Global Post,* August 16, 2016, http://www.globalpost.com/dispatch/news/regions/americas/united-states/130816/top-10-american-corporations-egypt-military-us-aid.

13. Steve Coll, *Private Empire: ExxonMobil and American Power* (New York: Penguin, 2012), p. 71.

14. Ibid., pp. 81–83.

CHAPTER 6: "OUR SON OF A BITCH"

1. Richard Cavendish, "General Somoza takes over Nicaragua," *History Today* 61, no. 6 (2011), http://www.historytoday.com/richard-cavendish/general-somoza-takes-over-nicaragua.

2. Joyce Battle, ed., "Shaking Hands with Saddam Hussein: The U.S. Tilts toward Iraq, 1980–1984," National Security Archive Electronic Briefing Book No. 82, February 25, 2003, http://www2.gwu.edu/~nsarchiv/NSAEBB/NSAEBB82/.

3. Shane Harris and Matthew M. Aid, "Exclusive: CIA Files Prove America Helped Saddam as He Gassed Iran," *Foreign Policy,* August 26, 2013, http://www.foreignpolicy.com/articles/2013/08/25/secret_cia_files_prove_america_helped_saddam_as_he_gassed_iran.

4. "Nicaragua," Human Rights Watch, http://www.hrw.org/legacy/reports/1989/WR89/Nicaragu.htm.

5. Catholic Institute for International Relations, *Right to Survive: Human Rights in Nicaragua* (N.p.: Catholic Institute for International Relations, 1987), p. 35.

6. "Ronald Reagan," *Democracy Now!,* http://www.democracynow.org/features/remembering_ronal_regan.

7. Robert Parry, "History of Guatemala's 'Death Squads,'" Consortiumnews.com, January 11, 2005, http://www.consortiumnews.com/2005/011005.html.

8. Louis B. Zimmer, *The Vietnam War Debate: Hans J. Morgenthau and the Attempt to Halt the Drift into Disaster* (Lanham, MD: Lexington Books, 2011), p. 86; Margaret Flowers and Kevin Zeese, "Armed Drones Becoming the Norm? At the Crossroads of Robotic Warfare," *Truthout,* November 13, 2013, http://truth-out.org/opinion/item/20008.

9. "Center for the National Interest Leadership," Center for the National Interest, http://cftni.org/index0ad5.html?action=showpage&page=Center-for-The-National-Interest-leadership.

10. Diana Ayton-Shenker, "The Challenge of Human Rights and Cultural Diversity," United Nations Background Note (March 1995), http://www.un.org/rights/dpi1627e.htm; Amitai Etzioni, "Cross-Cultural Judgments: The Next Steps," *Journal of Social Philosophy* 28, no. 3 (Winter 1997): pp. 5–15.

11. For an good discussion of the unintended consequences of American foreign policy, see: Chalmers Johnson, *Blowback: The Costs and Consequences of American Empire,* 2nd ed. (New York: Henry Holt, 2004).

12. Pacifist arguments can be found. See, for example, Howard Zinn, *A People's History of the United States* (New York: HarperCollins, 1980), "Chapter 16: A People's War." In this work Zinn, though an eager combatant against fascism at the start of the Second World War, explains his subsequent disillusionment with all militarism. See also Ted Grimsrud, "How Should a Pacifist View World War II?," Thinkingpacifism.com, January 21, 2011, http://thinkingpacifism.net/2011/01/21 /how-should-a-pacifist-view-world-war-ii/.

13. Charles Higham, *Trading with the Enemy: An Expose of the Nazi-American Money Plot 1933-1949* (New York: Delacorte Press, 1983); Ken Silverstein, "Ford and the Fuhrer," in John Cunningham Wood and Michael C. Wood, eds., *Henry Ford: Critical Evaluations in Business Management,* Vol. 1, (London: Routledge, 2003; first published in *The Nation,* November 16, 2000).

14. Betsy Schiffman, "IBM Gets an Ugly History Lesson," *Forbes,* February 12, 2001, http://www.forbes.com/2001/02/12/0212global.html.

15. ExxonMobil's revenues of over $354 billion would rank it thirtieth in the world if it were a nation, according to Vincent Trivett, "25 US Mega Corporations: Where They Rank If They Were Countries," *Business Insider,* June 27, 2011, http://www .businessinsider.com/25-corporations-bigger-tan-countries-2011-6?op=1.

16. Steve Coll, *Private Empire: ExxonMobil and American Power* (New York: Penguin, 2012), p. 622.

17. Ibid., p. 621.

18. Dave Zirin, "The Pinstripe Patriot Act," *The Nation,* May 4, 2009, http://www .thenation.com/article/pinstripe-patriot-act; Jesse Sanchez, "Settlement Reached in Fan Lawsuit," mlb.com, June 8, 2009, http://mlb.mlb.com/news/article.jsp?ymd =20090708&content_id=5755246&vkey=news_mlb&fext=.jsp&c_id=mlb.

19. John Perkins, *Confessions of an Economic Hit Man* (New York: Plume, 2004).

20. Peter Singer, "The Drowning Child," *New Internationalist,* no. 289 (April 1997), http://newint.org/features/1997/04/05/drowning/.

21. "CAFTA-DR," Office of the United States Trade Representative, press release, http://www.ustr.gov/trade-agreements/free-trade-agreements/cafta-dr-dominican -republic-central-america-fta.

22. "Gap, Walmart Holdout in Bangladesh Safety Agreement Following Safety Disaster," RT.com, May 16, 2013, http://rt.com/usa/gap-walmart-bangladesh-safety-agr eement-340/.

23. Perkins, *Confessions of an Economic Hit Man,* pp. 166–167, 183.

24. The contributions figure is from IRS form 990s from 2009 to 2011 at "Discover SIL," sil.org, www.sil.org/about/discover.

CHAPTER 7: FAIR TO ALL

1. Transcript of "The Polio Crusade," *The American Experience,* PBS, http://www.pbs .org/wgbh/americanexperience/features/transcript/polio-transcript/.

2. George Johnson, "Once Again, a Man with a Mission," *New York Times Magazine,* November 25, 1990, http://www.nytimes.com/1990/11/25/magazine/once-again -a-man-with-a-mission.html.

3. Roy Zwahlen, "The Real Reason Why Salk Refused to Patent the Polio Vaccine," *BIOtechNOW,* January 27, 2012, http://www.biotech-now.org/public-policy/paten tly-biotech/2012/01/the-real-reason-why-salk-refused-to-patent-the-polio-vaccine -a-myth-in-the-making#.

4. "How Much Money Did Jonas Salk Potentially Forfeit by Not Patenting the Polio Vaccine?" *Forbes,* August 9, 2012, http://www.forbes.com/sites/quora/2012/08/09 /how-much-money-did-jonas-salk-potentially-forfeit-by-not-patenting-the-polio -vaccine/.

5. Jason DeParle, "Harder for Americans to Rise from Lower Rungs," *New York Times,* January 4, 2012, http://www.nytimes.com/2012/01/05/us/harder-for-americans-to -rise-from-lower-rungs.html?pagewanted=all&_r=0.

6. Ibid.

7. Paul Krugman, "America's Unlevel Field," *New York Times,* January 8, 2012, http:// www.nytimes.com/2012/01/09/opinion/krugman-americas-unlevel-field.html.

8. Joshua Wright, "Temp Employment Is Dominating Job Growth in the Largest Cities," Economic Modeling Specialists International (EMSI), June 21, 2013, http:// www.economicmodeling.com/2013/06/21/temp-employment-is-dominating-job -growth-in-the-largest-cities-is-that-a-good-thing/.

9. John Quiggin, "Wall Street Isn't Worth It," *The Jacobin,* November 14, 2013, https://www.jacobinmag.com/2013/11/wall-street-isnt-worth-it/.

10. Investment Company Institute, *2013 Investment Company Fact Book* (Washington, DC: Investment Company Institute, 2013), http://www.ici.org/pdf/2013_factbook .pdf.

11. Quiggin, "Wall Street Isn't Worth It."

12. John A. Byrne, "The Highest (and Lowest) Paid MBAs, *CNN Money-Fortune,* January 28, 2014, http://fortune.com/2014/01/28/the-highest-and-lowest-paid-mbas/.

13. "Medical Student Education: Debt, Costs, and Loan Repayment Fact Card," Association of American Medical Colleges, October 2013, https://www.aamc.org /download/152968/data; Skeptical Scalpel, MD, "Think about Medical School Tuition Debt Before Becoming a Doctor," KevinMD.com, April 7, 2011, http://www .kevinmd.com/blog/2011/04/medical-school-tuition-debt-doctor.html; "Medical School Debt," American Medical Student Association, http://www.amsa.org/AMSA /Homepage/About/Committees/StudentLife/StudentDebt.aspx.

14. Lawrence Mishel and Natalie Sabadish, "CEO Pay in 2012 Was Extraordinarily High Relative to Typical Workers and Other High Earners," Economic Policy Institute, June 26, 2013, http://www.epi.org/publication/ceo-pay-2012-extraordinarily -high/.

15. Elliot Blair Smith and Phil Kuntz, "CEO Pay 1,795-to-1 Multiple of Wages Skirts U.S. Law," *Bloomberg,* April 30, 2013, http://www.bloomberg.com/news/2013-04 -30/ceo-pay-1-795-to-1-multiple-of-workers-skirts-law-as-sec-delays.html.

16. Joann S. Lublin and Dana Mattioli, "Penney CEO Out, Old Boss Back In," *Wall Street Journal,* April 8, 2013, http://online.wsj.com/news/articles/SB100014241278 87324504704578411031708241800.

17. "Just the Facts: CEOs and the Rest of Us," *The Globalist,* November 21, 2013, http://www.theglobalist.com/just-facts-ceos-rest-us/.

18. Warren E. Buffett, "Stop Coddling the Super-Rich," *New York Times,* August 14, 2011, http://www.nytimes.com/2011/08/15/opinion/stop-coddling-the-super-rich .html?_r=0.

19. United for a Fair Economy Web site, faireconomy.org.

20. Milos Forman, "Obama the Socialist? Not Even Close," *New York Times,* July 10, 2012, http://www.nytimes.com/2012/07/11/opinion/obama-the-socialist-not-even -close.html.

21. Peter Ferrara, "Is President Obama Really a Socialist? Let's Analyze Obamanomics," *Forbes,* December 20, 2012, http://www.forbes.com/sites/peterferrara/2012/12/20 /is-president-obama-really-a-socialist-lets-analyze-obamanomics/.

22. Pat Garofalo, "GOP Can't Handle Truth: Taxes Are Lower Under Obama than Reagan," *Truthout,* June 1, 2011, http://thinkprogress.org/economy/2011/06/01/233 526/taxes-lower-reagan/.

23. "Tax Me Baby One More Time!" *The Daily Beast,* April 22, 2011, http://www .thedailybeast.com/articles/2011/04/22/mark-zuckerberg-bill-gates-warren-buffett -billionaires-who-favor-tax-hikes.html.

24. Laura Meckler, "McCain Suggests Obama Tax Plan Is Socialist," *Wall Street Journal,* October 19, 2008, http://online.wsj.com/news/articles/SB122435566048047731.

25. FrontPage Magazine Web site, frontpagemag.com

26. Ellen, "Limbaugh and Hannity: The Liberal Media Is in Cahoots with Obama's Divisive, Totalitarian and Socialist Agenda," NewsHounds.com, January 31, 2013, http://www.newshounds.us/limbaugh_and_hannity_the_liberal_media_is_in _cahoots_with_obama_s_divisive_totalitarian_and_socialist_agenda_01312013.

27. Angie Drobnic Holan, "Palin 'Death Panel' Claim Sets Truth-O-Meter Ablaze," Politi fact.com, August 10, 2009, http://www.politifact.com/truth-o-meter/article/2009 /aug/10/palin-death-panel-remark-sets-truth-o-meter-fire/.

28. Ibid.

CHAPTER 8: NEW TRADITIONS

1. George Wallace, 1963 Inaugural Address, http://web.utk.edu/~mfitzge1/docs/374 /wallace_seg63.pdf.

2. Knights of the Ku Klux Klan, www.kkk.com.

3. David Opperman, "Slavery: Its Morality, History, and Implications for Race Relations in America, Part 1," *Faith & Heritage,* April 30, 2012, http://faithandher itage.com/2012/04/slavery-its-morality-history-and-implications-for-race-relations -in-america-part-1/.

4. Frances A. Althaus, "Female Circumcision: Rite of Passage or Violation of Rights?" *International Family Planning Perspectives* 23, no. 3 (September 1997), Special Report of the Guttmacher Institute, http://www.guttmacher.org/pubs/journals/2313097.html.

5. Deuteronomy 22:28–29: "If a man happens to meet a virgin who is not pledged to be married and rapes her and they are discovered, he shall pay her father fifty shekels of silver. He must marry the young woman, for he has violated her. He can never divorce her as long as he lives."

6. "About Heritage," The Heritage Foundation, www.heritage.org/about.

7. The Heritage Foundation Web site contains numerous articles highly critical of government efforts to regulate corporate power. See, for example, James L. Gattuso and Diane Katz, "Red Tape Rising: Regulation in Obama's First Term," May 1, 2013, http://www.heritage.org/research/reports/2013/05/red-tape-rising-regulation -in-obamas-first-term.

8. For details see: "Heritage Foundation," *Right Wing Watch,* http://www.rightwing watch.org/content/heritage-foundation.

9. Elliot Blair Smith and Phil Kuntz, "CEO Pay 1,795-to-1 Multiple of Wages Skirts U.S. Law," *Bloomberg News,* April 30, 2013, http://www.bloomberg.com /news/2013-04-30/ceo-pay-1-795-to-1-multiple-of-workers-skirts-law-as-sec -delays.html.

10. Bryce Covert, "Wealthiest Americans Take Home Biggest Share of Income Ever Recorded," *ThinkProgress,* September 11, 2013, http://thinkprogress.org/economy /2013/09/11/2602151/record-income-inequality/.

11. Eric W. Dolan, "Fox Business Host Stuart Varney Lectures Pope Francis about Capitalism and Religion," *The Raw Story,* November 27, 2013, http://www.raw

story.com/rs/2013/11/27/fox-business-host-stuart-varney-lectures-pope-francis
-about-capitalism/.

12. Cathleen Falsani, "The Worst Ideas of the Decade: The Prosperity Gospel," *Washington Post,* December 2009, http://www.washingtonpost.com/wp-srv/special/opinions/outlook/worst-ideas/prosperity-gospel.html.

13. Quoted in Daniel Gross, "Pope Francis Declares Consumers and Capitalists Need to Help the Poor," *The Daily Beast,* November 26, 2013, http://www.thedailybeast.com/articles/2013/11/26/pope-francis-declares-consumers-and-capitalists-need-to-help-the-poor.html.

14. Jonathan Capehart, "Palin Pounces on Chris Christie and the Pope," *Washington Post,* November 13, 2013, http://www.washingtonpost.com/blogs/post-partisan/wp/2013/11/13/palin-pounces-on-chris-christie-and-the-pope/.

15. Gross, "Pope Francis Declares Consumers and Capitalists Need to Help the Poor."

16. Kathy Shaidle, "Rush Limbaugh Scorches Pope Francis," *WND,* November 27, 2013, http://www.wnd.com/2013/11/rush-limbaugh-scorches-pope-francis/?cat_orig=faith.

17. Richard Middleton, *Colonial America* (Oxford: Blackwell, 2003), pp. 95–100, 145, 158, 159, 349n.

18. "Number of Americans Without Religious Affiliation on the Rise," ABC News, citing Pew data, October 9, 2012, http://abcnewsradioonline.com/politics-news/tag/pew-national-survey.

19. Nathan Miller, *Theodore Roosevelt: A Life* (New York: Quill, 1992), p. 362.

20. On Vardaman's racism, see "Biography: James K. Vardaman," *American Experience,* http://www.pbs.org/wgbh/americanexperience/features/biography/flood-vardaman/.

21. Miller, *Theodore Roosevelt,* p. 363.

22. *Plessy v. Ferguson,* 163 U.S. 537 (1896).

23. Booker T. Washington, "Letter to the Editor," *Montgomery Advertiser,* April 30, 1885; Cary D. Wintz, ed., *African American Political Thought, 1890–1930: Washington, Du Bois, Garvey and Randolph* (Armonk, NY: M. E. Sharpe, 1996), p. 21.

24. *Plessy* dissent, 163 U.S. at 552–564.

25. Deena Bess Sherman, "Anti-trust Legislation Is One of Sherman Family Legacies," *Chicago Sun-Times,* April 5, 2012, http://beaconnews.suntimes.com/news/sherman/11693517-418/anti-trust-legislation-is-one-of-sherman-family-legacies.html#.U5MLaPmwJcQ.

26. Eric Arnesen, *Encyclopedia of US Labor and Working-Class History, vol. 1* (New York: Taylor and Francis, 2007), p. 173. The Supreme Court case is *Loewe v. Lawler,* 208 U.S. 274 (1908).

27. Dave Jamieson, "Union Membership Rate for U.S. Workers Tumbles to New Low," *Huffington Post,* January 23, 2013, http://www.huffingtonpost.com/2013/01/23/union-membership-rate_n_2535063.html.

28. *Lochner v. New York,* 198 U.S. 405 (1905).

29. *Coppage v. Kansas,* 236 U.S. 1 (1915).

30. *Muller v. Oregon,* 208 U.S. 412 (1908).

31. *Hammer v. Dagenhart,* 247 U.S. 251 (1918).

CHAPTER 9: SAME OLD DEAL

1. All FDR quotes in this section are from Franklin D. Roosevelt, 1944 State of the Union Address, http://www.fdrlibrary.marist.edu/archives/address_text.html.

2. "Obama Right that Roosevelt Was Called a Socialist and a Communist," *Politifact*, September 22, 2009, http://www.politifact.com/truth-o-meter/statements/2009/sep/22/barack-obama/obama-roosevelt-socialist-communist/.

3. David Gibson, "Rick Santorum on the Catholic Cafeteria," *Commonweal*, March 30, 2012, https://www.commonwealmagazine.org/blog/rick-santorum-catholic-cafeteria.

4. Anne Godlasky, "Sanford: 'There Are Moral Absolutes,'" Faith and Reason, *USA Today*, June 24, 2009, http://content.usatoday.com/communities/religion/post/2009/06/68462529/1#.U6bX_Y1dU00.

5. Alan Dershowitz, *Rights from Wrongs: A Secular Theory of the Origins of Rights* (New York: Basic Books, 2004), pp. 78–79.

6. Steven Pinker, *The Better Angels of Our Nature: Why Violence Has Declined* (New York: Viking, 2011), pp. 47–56.

7. Nick Spinetto, "Veterinarians Stunned by Generosity for Injured Dog," WMUR-TV, December 20, 2013, http://www.wmur.com/news/nh-news/veterinarians-stunned-by-generosity-for-injured-dog/23582280#!VQzv6.

8. Marta Zaraska, "Lab-Grown Beef Taste Test: 'Almost' Like a Burger," *Washington Post*, August 5, 2013, http://www.washingtonpost.com/national/health-science/lab-grown-beef-taste-test-almost-like-a-burger/2013/08/05/921a5996-fdf4-11e2-96a8-d3b921c0924a_story.html.

9. Dawkins introduced the meme concept in his 1976 book, *The Selfish Gene* (New York: Oxford University Press).

10. Michael Werner, *Regaining Balance: The Evolution of the UUA* (Hamden, CT: Religious Humanism Press, 2013), p. 55.

11. David A. Noebel, *Communism, Hypnotism and the Beatles* (Tulsa, OK: Christian Crusade Publication, 1965), http://conelrad.com/books/spine.php?id=354_0_1_0_C.

CHAPTER 10: A HIGHER COMMON DENOMINATOR

1. Sheldon Drobny, "Eisenhower's Wisdom," *Huffington Post*, July 14, 2007, http://www.huffingtonpost.com/sheldon-drobny/eisenhowers-wisdom_b_56225.html.

2. Richard Hofstadter, *Anti-intellectualism in American Life* (London: Jonathan Cape, 1964, UK edition), p. 393.

3. Ibid., p. 130.

4. Ibid., p. 129.

5. *Kitzmiller v. Dover Area School District*, 400 F. Supp. 2d 707.

6. The Wedge Document can be found at http://www.antievolution.org/features/wedge.html.

7. Per Charity Navigator, 2011 Discovery Institute revenues were just over $5.6 million. See "Discovery Institute," Charity Navigator, http://www.charitynavigator.org/index.cfm?bay=search.summary&orgid=9757.

8. Per Charity Navigator, 2011 Answers in Genesis revenues were just over $19.9 million. See "Answers in Genesis," Charity Navigator, http://www.charitynavigator.org/index.cfm?bay=search.summary&orgid=5214#.Uq3vN9JDt8E.

9. P. Z. Myers, "The Creation 'Museum,'" *Pharyngula*, Science blogs, August 10, 2009, http://scienceblogs.com/pharyngula/2009/08/10/the-creation-museum-1/; Stephanie Pappas, "Creation Museum Creates Discomfort for Some Visitors," *Live Science*, August 18, 2010, http://www.livescience.com/8501-creation-museum-creates-discomfort-visitors.html.

10. "Creationist Organizations in the United States of America," Creation Ministries International, http://creation.com/creationist-organizations-in-the-usa.

11. Hofstadter, *Anti-Intellectualism in American Life*, p. 47.

12. Ibid., pp. 188–189.

13. Quoted in ibid., p. 268.

14. Ibid., p. 280.

15. Al Gore, *The Assault on Reason* (New York: Penguin, 2007), p. 55.

16. Ibid.

17. Ibid., p. 62.

18. Susan Jacoby, *The Age of American Unreason* (New York: Pantheon, 2008), p. 191.

19. Ibid., p. 315.

20. Hofstadter, *Anti-intellectualism in American Life*, p. 159, quoting John William Ward, *Andrew Jackson: Symbol for an Age* (New York: Oxford University Press, 1955).

21. Alexander de Tocqueville, *Democracy in America*, vol. 1 (London: Longmans, Green, and Co., 1889), p. 51.

22. Ibid., p. 50.

CHAPTER 11: IMPOSSIBLE VIGILANCE

1. The Monticello Web site contains comprehensive information about quotes attributed, and misattributed, to Jefferson. See: http://www.monticello.org/site/jefferson/eternal-vigilance-price-liberty-quotation.

2. Ibid.; Library of Congress, compiler, *Respectfully Quoted: A Dictionary of Quotations. The Essential Reference Guide for Writers and Speechmakers* (Mineola, NY: Dover, 2010), p. 200.

3. "About ALEC," American Legislative Exchange Council, http://www.alec.org/about-alec/history/.

4. Brendan Greeley, "ALEC's Secrets Revealed; Corporations Flee," *Bloomberg Businessweek*, May 3, 2012, http://www.businessweek.com/articles/2012-05-03/alecs-secrets-revealed-corporations-flee; Lisa Graves, "CMD's Special Report on ALEC's Funding and Spending," Center for Media and Democracy's PR Watch, July 13, 2011, http://prwatch.org/news/2011/07/10887/cmd-special-report-alecs-funding-and-spending.

5. Graves, "CMD's Special Report."

6. ALEC's 2012 IRS Form 990, American Legislative Exchange Council, http://alec.org/docs/ALEC_2012_Public_disclosure_990.pdf.

7. Graves, "CMD's Special Report."

8. Chris Taylor, "I Caught a Glimpse of ALEC Nation," *The Progressive*, August 9, 2013, http://www.progressive.org/news/2013/08/183297/i-caught-glimpse-alec-nation.

9. Ellyn Fortino, "Report: Hundreds of ALEC Bills Introduced This Year Promote a Corporate Agenda," *Progress Illinois*, August 8, 2012, http://www.progressillinois.com/posts/content/2013/08/08/report-hundreds-alec-bills-introduced-year-promote-corporate-agenda.

10. Lisa Graves, "ALEC Exposed: The Koch Connection," *The Nation*, August 1–8, 2011 (online July 12, 2011), http://www.thenation.com/article/161973/alec-exposed-koch-connection.

11. "Chamber of Commerce: 'Profile for 2014 Election Cycle,'" OpenSecrets.org, https://www.opensecrets.org/orgs/summary.php?id=D000019798.

12. In the series *Cosmos: A Spacetime Odyssey* Neil deGrasse Tyson does an excellent job covering the oil industry's efforts to suppress scientific research on the dangers of lead. Neil deGrasse Tyson, *Cosmos: A Spacetime Odyssey*, season 1, episode 7, Cosmos Studios and Fuzzy Door Productions, 2014.

13. Steve Coll, *Private Empire: ExxonMobil and American Power* (New York: Penguin, 2012), p. 135.

14. Industries don't always oppose regulation. As one pharmaceutical executive pointed out to me, despite complaints about government oversight, companies see regulatory compliance as creating a barrier to entry for potential competitors. Thus, once they have adapted to a regulatory environment, corporations use it to their advantage to discourage start-up competitors.

15. Zachary Roth, "Fighting Corruption Polls of the Charts," MSNBC.com, December 3, 2013, http://www.msnbc.com/msnbc/fighting-corruption-polls-the-charts.

16. Jon Walker, "Majority of Americans Would Support Radical Campaign Finance Reform," Firedoglake.com, June 24, 2013, http://elections.firedoglake.com/2013/06/24/majority-of-americans-would-support-radical-campaign-financing-reform/.

17. *Buckley v. Valeo,* 424 U.S. 1 (1976).

18. *McCutcheon v. Federal Election Commission,* SC Docket 12-536, 572 U.S. __ (2014).

19. "The Money Behind the Elections," Center for Responsive Politics, https://www.opensecrets.org/bigpicture/.

20. "Election Stats," Center for Responsive Politics, https://www.opensecrets.org/bigpicture/elec_stats.php?cycle=2012.

21. Less well known than *Citizens United* is the case of *SpeechNow.org v. FEC,* a 2010 DC Circuit Court decision that ruled contribution limits to issue-oriented PACs are unconstitutional.

22. "Super PACS," Center for Responsive Politics, http://www.opensecrets.org/pacs/superpacs.php?cycle=2012.

23. Quoted in Eric W. Dolan, "Sen. Sanders Files Amendment to End Corporate Personhood," *The Raw Story,* December 8, 2011, http://www.rawstory.com/rs/2011/12/08/sen-sanders-files-amendment-to-end-corporate-personhood/.

24. Ibid.

25. Quoted in "The Progressive Mourns Paul Wellstone: A Eulogy by Matthew Rothschild," *The Progressive,* October 10, 2002, http://www.progressive.org/node/1439.

26. Move to Amend press release, "Democracy Activists Challenge Parties to Take a Stand on Corporate Personhood," September 7, 2012, https://movetoamend.org/press-release/democracy-activists-challenge-parties-take-stand-corporate-personhood.

27. Ibid.; Matea Gold, "Breaking Vow, Democrats Used Corporate Cash to Pay for Convention," *Los Angeles Times,* October 18, 2012, http://articles.latimes.com/2012/oct/18/nation/la-na-convention-money-20121019.

28. Shahien Nasiripour, "Tim Geithner Opposes Nominating Elizabeth Warren to Lead New Consumer Agency," *Huffington Post,* July 15, 2010, http://www.huffingtonpost.com/2010/07/15/tim-geithner-opposes-nomi_n_647691.html.

29. Jeff Connaughton, "Regulatory Rockstar: Elizabeth Warren Is Using Her Senate Seat to Grill Those Who Let the Big Banks Off the Hook," *New Republic,* April 18, 2013, http://www.newrepublic.com/article/112947/elizabeth-warren-senate-banking-committee-rockstar.

30. Jon Cowan and Jim Kessler, "Economic Populism Is a Dead End for Democrats," *Wall Street Journal,* December 2, 2013, http://online.wsj.com/news/articles/SB10001424052702304337404579213923151169790.

CHAPTER 12: SARAH PALIN'S MASSACHUSETTS

1. The video of this interview can be found online at CBS News and YouTube. The excerpt used is quoted from Steve Benen, "Palin's Unique Spin on the Bailout,"

Political Animal, *Washington Monthly,* September 25, 2008, http://www.washing
tonmonthly.com/archives/individual/2008_09/014881.php.

2. George Lakoff, *Don't Think of an Elephant!* (White River Junction, VT: Chelsea
Green, 2004).

3. "Banking on Bondage: Private Prisons and Mass Incarceration," ACLU, November 2,
2011, https://www.aclu.org/prisoners-rights/banking-bondage-private-prisons-and
-mass-incarceration.

4. Alan Greenblatt, "What Makes ALEC Smart?" *Governing* (October 2003), http://
www.governing.com/topics/politics/What-Makes-Alec-Smart.html.

5. Andy Krall, "This Is How Private Prison Companies Make Millions Even When
Crime Rates Fall," *Mother Jones,* September 19, 2013, http://www.motherjones
.com/mojo/2013/09/private-prisons-occupancy-quota-cca-crime.

6. Ibid.

7. Yahoo Finance shows CXW stock closing on October 3, 2011, at a price of $17.51,
and on October 1, 2013, at $37.00. "Corrections Corporation of America (CXW)—
NYSE," YahooFinance.com, http://finance.yahoo.com/q?s=CXW.

8. "Prison Brief: Highest to Lowest," International Centre for Prison Studies, Kings
College London School of Law, March 2010, http://www.prisonstudies.org
/highest-to-lowest.

9. This story was reported widely in the press. See, for example, Ian Urbina, "Despite
Red Flags about Judges, a Kickback Scheme Flourished," *New York Times,* March
27, 2009, http://www.nytimes.com/2009/03/28/us/28judges.html?pagewanted=all;
and Stephanie Chen, "Pennsylvania Rocked by 'Jailing Kids for Cash' Scandal,"
CNN.com, February 24, 2009, http://www.cnn.com/2009/CRIME/02/23/penn
sylvania.corrupt.judges/.

10. Urbina, "Despite Red Flags about Judges."

11. Rachel Weiner, "Rick Perry Repeats Social Security Is 'Ponzi Scheme' Statement," *Washington Post,* September 7, 2011, http://www.washingtonpost.com
/blogs/the-fix/post/rick-perry-and-mitt-romney-come-out-swinging-in-reagan
-debate/2011/09/07/gIQAhygcAK_blog.html; Brad Plumer, "Ryan Supported Social
Security Privatization in 2005. What Was that Again?" Wonkblog, *Washington Post,* October 12, 2012, http://www.washingtonpost.com/blogs/wonkblog/wp/2012/10/12
/ryan-supported-social-security-privatization-in-2005-what-was-that-again/.

12. "Social Security," U.S. Congressman Paul Ryan, http://paulryan.house.gov/issues
/issue/?IssueID=12227#.UwiyBuNdV8E.

13. Eric Wuestewald, "The Long, Expensive History of Defense Rip-offs," *Mother
Jones,* December 18, 2013, http://www.motherjones.com/politics/2013/12/defense
-military-waste-cost-timeline.

CHAPTER 13: TAKING CONTROL

1. Frank Newport, "Americans Favor Jobs Plan Proposals, Including Taxing Rich,"
Gallup.com, September 20, 2011, http://www.gallup.com/poll/149567/americans
-favor-jobs-plan-proposals-including-taxing-rich.aspx; Paul Steinhauser, "Trio of
Polls: Support for Raising Taxes on Wealthy," *CNN Politics,* December 6, 2012,
http://politicalticker.blogs.cnn.com/2012/12/06/trio-of-polls-support-for-raising
-taxes-on-wealthy/; Eric Linton, "Two-Thirds of Americans Back Universal Health
Care: Poll," *International Business Times,* March 28, 2012, http://www.ibtimes.com
/two-thirds-americans-back-universal-health-care-poll-431376.

2. Jim Lardner, "Americans Agree on Regulating Wall Street," *U.S. News & World
Report,* September 16, 2013, http://www.usnews.com/opinion/blogs/economic-int

elligence/2013/09/16/poll-shows-americans-want-more-wall-street-regulation-five
-years-after-the-financial-crisis.

3. A concise and informative overview of the evolution of corporate power can be
    found in Naomi Lamoreaux and William Novak, "Getting the History Right,"
    Slate, March 24, 2014, http://www.slate.com/articles/news_and_politics/jurisprud
    ence/2014/03/hobby_lobby_and_corporate_personhood_here_s_the_real_history
    _of_corporate.html.

4. 2013 S.J. Res. 11, H.J. Res. 34.

5. The various constitutional amendment proposals are outlined at "Other Amend-
    ments," Move to Amend, https://movetoamend.org/other-amendments.

6. Paul R. La Monica, "You're Fired. Stock Rises. Wall Street Loves Layoffs," *CNN
    Money,* October 1, 2013, http://buzz.money.cnn.com/2013/10/01/layoffs-stocks/.

7. Ibid.

8. Quoted in Joe Miller, "Move Over, GDP: How Should You Measure a Country's
    Value?," *BBC News,* April 2, 2014, http://www.bbc.com/news/business-26682206.

9. "Definition of 'Recession,'" *Investopedia,* www.investopedia.com/terms/r/recession
    .asp.

10. "GDP and GPI," McGregor Consulting Group, http://www.consultmcgregor.com
    /documents/resources/GDP_and_GPI.pdf.

11. "The Index of Social Health," Institute for Innovation in Social Policy, http://iisp
    .vassar.edu/ish.html.

12. I'm leaving the debate over free will out of this discussion. There are determinists,
    such as Daniel Dennett and Sam Harris, who believe that free will is essentially an
    illusion, but we need not resolve such philosophical questions here in order to ac-
    knowledge the range of options, or at least apparent options, available to people in
    modern society.

13. These statistics are from Editor, "Endangered Species Population Numbers," *All
    About Wildlife,* November 2, 2009, http://www.allaboutwildlife.com/endangered
    -species/endangered-species-population-numbers/3596.

14. Quoted in Graham Townsley, "The Adaptable Human," *Nova,* PBS, October 26,
    2009, http://www.pbs.org/wgbh/nova/evolution/adaptable-human.html.

CHAPTER 14: REASON FOR WINNING

1. Michael Lipka, "What Surveys Say about Worship Attendance—and Why Some
    Stay at Home," Pew Research Center FactTank, September 13, 2013, http://www
    .pewresearch.org/fact-tank/2013/09/13/what-surveys-say-about-worship-atten
    dance-and-why-some-stay-home/; Heidi Glenn, "Losing Our Religion: The Growth
    of the 'Nones,'" *Morning Edition,* NPR, January 13, 2013, http://www.npr.org/blogs
    /thetwo-way/2013/01/14/169164840/losing-our-religion-the-growth-of-the-nones.

2. Barry A. Kosmin and Ariela Keysa, "American Religious Identification Survey
    (ARIS 2008) Summary Report," Institute for the Study of Secularism in Society
    and Culture, March 2009, p. 10, http://www.scribd.com/doc/17136871/American
    -Religious-Identification-Survey-ARIS-2008-Summary-Report.

3. Kimberly Winston, "Study: Atheists Distrusted as Much as Rapists," *USA Today,*
    December 10, 2011, http://usatoday30.usatoday.com/news/religion/story/2011-12
    -10/religion-atheism/51777612/1.

4. I discuss the correlation between religion and negative social outcomes at length in
    chapter 2 of *Nonbeliever Nation: The Rise of Secular Americans* (New York: Palgrave
    Macmillan, 2012). For an even more detailed discussion of the subject, see also
    Phil Zuckerman, "Atheism, Secularity, and Well-Being: How the Findings of Social

Science Counter Negative Stereotypes and Assumptions," *Sociology Compass* 3, no. 6 (2009): 949–971, http://www.pitzer.edu/academics/faculty/zuckerman/Zuckerman _on_Atheism.pdf.

5. See ibid.; and Gregory S. Paul, "Cross-National Correlations of Quantifiable Societal Health with Popular Religiosity and Secularism in the Prosperous Democracies," *Journal of Religion and Society* 7 (2005), http://moses.creighton.edu /JRS/2005/2005-11.pdf.

6. Letter from the Congressional Prayer Caucus to President Barack Obama, December 6, 2010, http://forbes.house.gov/uploadedfiles/national_motto_letter_to_presi dent.pdf.

7. "'Nones' on the Rise," Pew Research, Religion & Public Life, October 9, 2012, http://www.pewforum.org/2012/10/09/nones-on-the-rise/.

8. Openly Secular Web site, http://openlysecular.org/.

SELECTED BIBLIOGRAPHY

Ali, Ayaan Hirsi. *Infidel.* New York: Free Press, 2007.

Andrews, Seth. *Deconverted: A Journey from Religion to Reason.* Parker, CO: Outskirts Press, 2013.

Bakan, Joel. *Childhood Under Siege: How Big Business Targets Children.* New York: Free Press, 2011.

———. *The Corporation: The Pathological Pursuit of Profit and Power.* New York: Free Press, 2004.

Black, Edwin. *IBM and the Holocaust: The Strategic Alliance Between Nazi Germany and America's Most Powerful Corporation.* Washington, DC: Dialog Press, 2001.

Boston, Rob. *Taking Liberties: Why Religious Freedom Doesn't Give You the Right to Tell Other People What to Do.* Amherst, NY: Prometheus. 2014.

———. *Why The Religious Right Is Wrong about the Separation of Church and State.* Amherst, NY: Prometheus, 1994.

Breyer, Stephen. *Active Liberty: Interpreting Our Democratic Constitution.* New York: Knopf, 2005.

Carroll, James. *House of War: The Pentagon and the Disastrous Rise of American Power.* New York: Houghton Mifflin Harcourt, 2006.

Chomsky, Noam. *The Chomsky Reader.* New York: Pantheon, 1987.

———. *Profit over People: Neoliberalism and Global Order.* New York: Seven Stories Press, 1999.

Christina, Greta. *Coming Out Atheist.* Charlottesville, VA: Pitchstone, 2014.

Coll, Steve. *Private Empire: ExxonMobil and American Power.* New York: Penguin Press, 2012.

Coon, Carl. *One Planet, One People.* Amherst, NY: Prometheus, 2004.

Darwin, Charles. *The Origin of Species by Means of Natural Selection.* 6th ed. London: John Murray, 1876.

Dawkins, Richard. *The Blind Watchmaker: Why the Evidence of Evolution Reveals a Universe Without Design.* New York: Norton, 1986.

———. *The Selfish Gene.* New York: Oxford University Press, 1996.

Dennett, Daniel. *Breaking the Spell: Religion as a Natural Phenomenon.* New York: Viking, 2006.

———. *Darwin's Dangerous Idea.* New York: Simon and Schuster, 1995.

Dershowitz, Alan. *Rights from Wrongs: A Secular Theory of the Origins of Rights.* New York: Basic Books, 2005.

Diamond, Jared. *Guns, Germs and Steel.* New York: W. W. Norton, 1997.

Ehrenreich, Barbara. *Nickeled and Dimed: On. (Not) Getting by in America.* New York: Metropolitan, 2001.

Ellis, Joseph. *Founding Brothers: The Revolutionary Generation.* New York: Knopf, 2001.

Epstein, Greg. *Good Without God: What a Billion Nonreligious People Do Believe.* New York: HarperCollins, 2009.

Faircloth, Sean. *Attack of the Theocrats.* Charlottesville, VA: Pitchstone, 2012.

Frank, Thomas. *What's the Matter with Kansas? How Conservatives Won the Heart of America.* New York: Metropolitan Books, 2004.

Franklin, H. Bruce. *War Stars: The Superweapon and the American Imagination.* Amherst, MA: University of Massachusetts Press, 2008.

Friedman, Thomas. *Hot, Flat, and Crowded: Why We Need a Green Revolution—and How It Can Renew America.* New York: Picador, 2009.

———. *The World Is Flat: A Brief History of the Twenty-First Century.* New York: Farrar, Straus and Giroux, 2005.

Galbraith, John Kenneth. *The Affluent Society.* New York: Houghton Mifflin, 1958.

Gaylor, Annie Laurie. *Woe to the Women: The Bible, Female Sexuality and the Law.* Madison, WI: Freedom from Religion Foundation, 2004.

Goldstein, Rebecca. *36 Arguments for the Existence of God: A Work of Fiction.* New York: Pantheon, 2010.

Gore, Al. *The Assault on Reason.* New York: Penguin, 2007.

Greeley, Roger E. *The Best of Robert Ingersoll: Selections from His Writings and Speeches.* Amherst, NY: Prometheus, 1988.

Hamilton, Marci. *God vs. the Gavel: Religion and the Rule of Law.* New York: Cambridge University Press, 2005.

Harrington, Michael. *Socialism: Past and Future.* New York: Arcade, 1989.

Hartmann, Thom. *Unequal Protection: The Rise of Corporate Dominance and the Theft of Human Rights.* San Francisco: Berrett-Koehler, 2010.

Hedges, Chris. *Death of the Liberal Class.* New York: Nation Books, 2010.

Hitchens, Christopher. *Letters to a Young Contrarian.* New York: Basic Books, 2001.

Hofstadter, Richard. *The American Political Tradition.* New York: Vintage, 1948.

———. *Anti-intellectualism in American Society.* New York: Vintage, 1963.

Irons, Peter. *A People's History of the Supreme Court.* New York: Penguin, 1999.

Jacoby, Susan. *The Age of American Unreason.* New York: Pantheon, 2008.

———. *Freethinkers: A History of American Secularism.* New York: Metropolitan, 2004.

Jefferson, Thomas. *Writings.* New York: Library of America, 1984.

Johnson, Chalmers. *Blowback: The Costs and Consequences of American Empire,* 2nd ed. New York: Henry Holt, 2004.

Kamenka, Eugene, ed. *The Portable Marx.* New York: Viking Penguin, 1983.

Kaminer, Wendy. *Sleeping with Extra-Terrestrials: The Rise of Irrationalism and Perils of Piety.* New York: Vintage, 2000.

Keynes, John Maynard. *The General Theory of Employment, Interest and Money.* Amherst, NY: Prometheus, 1997.

Korten, David. *When Corporations Rule the World.* Bloomfield, CT: Kumarian, 2011.

Krugman, Paul. *The Conscience of a Liberal.* New York: Norton, 2007.

Kuttner, Robert. *The Squandering of America: How the Failure of Our Politics Undermines Our Prosperity.* New York: Knopf, 2007.

Lamont, Corliss. *The Philosophy of Humanism,* 8th ed. Washington, DC: Humanist Press, 1997.

Lembcke, Jerry. *The Spitting Image: Myth, Memory and the Legacy of Vietnam.* New York: New York University Press, 1998.

Lippmann, Walter. *A Preface to Morals.* New Brunswick, NJ: Transaction, 1982.

———. *Public Opinion.* Filiquarian Publishing LLC, 1921. http://wps.pearsoncustom.com/wps/media/objects/2429/2487430/pdfs/lippmann.pdf.

Mehta, Hemant. *The Young Atheist's Survival Guide.* Patheos Press, 2012.

Miller, Nathan. *Theodore Roosevelt: A Life.* New York: Quill, 1992.

Myers, P. Z. *The Happy Atheist.* New York: Pantheon, 2013.

Nader, Ralph. *Cutting Corporate Welfare.* New York: Seven Stories, 2000.

———. *The Seventeen Traditions.* New York: Harper, 2007.

Navasky, Victor. *A Matter of Opinion.* New York: Farrar, Straus and Giroux, 2005.

Niose, David. *Nonbeliever Nation: The Rise of Secular Americans.* New York: Palgrave Macmillan, 2012.

Obama, Barack. *Dreams from My Father: A Story of Race and Inheritance.* New York: Three Rivers Press, 1995.

Orwell, George. *The Orwell Reader: Fiction, Essays, and Reportage.* New York: Harcourt, Brace & Co., 1984.

Paine, Thomas. *Collected Writings.* Edited by Eric Foner. New York: Library of America, 1995.

Perkins, John. *Confessions of an Economic Hit Man.* New York: Plume, 2004.

Phillips, Kevin. *American Theocracy.* New York: Viking, 2006.

Pinker, Steven. *The Better Angels of Our Nature: Why Violence Has Declined.* New York: Viking, 2011.

———. *The Blank Slate: The Modern Denial of Human Nature.* New York: Penguin, 2002.

Popper, Karl. *The Open Society and Its Enemies.* Princeton, NJ: Princeton University Press, 2013.

Reich, Robert. *Supercapitalism: The Transformation of Business, Democracy, and Everyday Life.* New York: Knopf Borzoi, 2007.

Silverman, Herb. *Candidate Without a Prayer.* Charlottesville, VA: Pitchstone, 2012.

Smith, Adam. *(An Inquiry into the Nature and Causes of the) Wealth of Nations.* Amherst, NY: Prometheus, 1991.

Stanton, Elizabeth Cady. *The Woman's Bible.* Amherst, NY: Prometheus, 1999.

Steinem, Gloria. *Outrageous Acts and Everyday Rebellions.* New York: Henry Holt, 1987.

Stewart, Katherine. *The Good News Club: The Christian Right's Stealth Assault on America's Children.* New York: Public Affairs, 2012.

Tocqueville, Alexis de. *Democracy in America.* 2 vols. London: Longmans, Green, and Co., 1889.

Werleman, C. J. *Crucifying America: The Unholy Alliance Between the Christian Right and Wall Street.* Great Britain: Dangerous Little Books, 2013.

Werner, Michael. *Regaining Balance: The Evolution of the UUA.* Washington, DC: Humanist Press, 2013.

Zinn, Howard. *A People's History of the United States.* New York: Harper & Row, 1980.

INDEX